IT'S
ALL
GOD

Also by Walter Starcke

THE DOUBLE THREAD

THE GOSPEL OF RELATIVITY

THE ULTIMATE REVOLUTION

HOMESICK FOR HEAVEN

IT'S ALL GOD STUDY-GUIDE

THE THIRD APPEARANCE

JOEL GOLDSMITH AND I

GUADALUPE PRESS

BOERNE, TEXAS

Copyright © 1998 by Walter H. Starcke
second printing 2006
The Guadalupe Press
P.O. Box 865, Boerne, Texas 78006

LIBRARY OF CONGRESS
CATALOG CARD NUMBER:
98-92525

STARCKE, WALTER H.
IT'S ALL GOD
BY WALTER STARCKE
P. CM.
1. SPIRITUAL   2. MYSTICISM   3. NEW AGE
I. TITLE
ISBN 0-929845-06-4

*Book & Cover Design by
Kathwyn Eron Howell*

IT'S ALL GOD

The Flowers and the Fertilizer

Walter Starcke

GUADALUPE PRESS

ACKNOWLEDGMENTS

God has appeared in my life in so many extraordinary ways, including those individuals who have long since left the earth plane but continue to be a present presence such as my mother who inspired my search, as John van Druten, who encouraged my determination to leave no stone unturned and in the process introduced me to two illumined masters, Joel S. Goldsmith and Swami Prabhavananda, each of whom pointed me in different, although parallel and complementary directions.

I also want to express my appreciation for Teilhard de Chardin, Carl Jung, and many others who shared their vision through the printed word, and presently for Dr. Tadashi Akaishi who was responsible for Harper and Row's publishing my first three books and who has edited all that followed, including this one.

For Kathwyn Eron Howell, my partner for the past twenty years whose support and ability to let me know if my words have said what I meant for them to say, my heart-felt gratitude. Finally, without the wisdom, love, support, and agreement I have received from my extended spiritual family, this book would never have been written.

CONFESSIONAL

I have been helplessly driven all my life by what has simplistically turned out to be an inability to accept either/or. On one side there has been an insatiable appetite to experience and merge with what is universally conceived of as God. On the other hand, though Lord knows I have tried, I have been unable in the process to ignore, reject, or dishonor my personal presence as a materialized human being. The carrot that has constantly dangled before my eyes is the possibility that I can arrive at and live with the full compatible and simultaneous realization that my two selves are one and the same.

Though I am willing to take both credit and blame for what you will be reading, I have not written this book. You are writing it as you read it. No one else is now, ever has, or ever will read the book you are holding in your hand. That would be impossible because you are reading it through the lens of your own concepts and no one else entertains exactly the same amalgamation or mixture of perceptions you do nor has anyone your particular inner guidance waiting to help you define your life and actions.

For better or worse and not by accident, your consciousness has drawn this book to you as your way of hopefully adding some additional pieces that will help you complete the puzzle of your existence. That will happen either by the reinforcement that comes from your agreement with what is being said or it will arrive by the stimulation you receive from your disagreement that becomes a springboard propelling you into arriving at your own truths.

At best, this book is our co-creation. I have embodied in it a lifetime of concepts and intuitions that have unlocked many mysteries and enhanced my earthly existence in extraordinary ways, both spiritually and materially. Similarly, you are now and always have been your only teacher. From time to time you have drawn to you those guides that you have thought were your teachers, but you would not have been able to hear them and absorb what they had to say unless there was that within you which identified and then recognized the truth.

Though each of you will read these words differently, there is one common denominator: This is not a book. It is a tool, a vehicle. Its purpose is to catalyze an experience for you, not just to sharpen your intellect or encourage your ego to believe that more knowledge means more power. It can potentially carry those of you who have committed yourselves to discovering how to intuit its underlying message into a mysterious journey, into a different place than you were when you entered its space.

> *My prayer is that a miracle will somehow take place and that you will not listen to the words I am saying but rather to the language of spirit and freedom I am trying to offer you—and myself.*

CONTENTS

INTRODUCTION & FOUNDATION

*B*efore committing myself to writing this book, I often asked why, in the light of the many erudite and profound books being published daily, was it necessary for me to write this one. I have no desire to invent a new philosophy or religion or to refute any that presently exist. I feel that everyone is attending the right church, studying the right teaching, and learning the lessons they are ready to learn in the process of discovering what works for them in their present state of consciousness. Everyone is being led by an invisible hand.

However, apart from following internal orders, every time I have asked myself why I have had the urge to write this book, three purposes have come to mind. First, I want to tell everyone that it is never too late. Profound concepts that I personally responded to and have entered into my diaries as long as fifty years ago have just now, in my late seventies, shifted gear from mind into conscious experience. Truths that I longed to be able to implement in my life have finally become livable for me.

I am almost the person now I have always wanted to be—not quite, thank God, but much closer than I was just a few years ago. If I had totally succeeded, there would be no reason to continue being enrolled in this often-confusing university we call the human experience except, perhaps, to share myself. The personal episodes which have brought me to this point have shown me, without a doubt, that at last it is possible for the man of earth aspect of my being and my man of God potential to finally communicate with each other and truly function as one. I have discovered how to consciously access freedoms that I could only have speculated about in the past—and finally know what it means to glimpse ascension consciousness. There hasn't been any thing or any experience that I, or any of us, have gone through that has been accidental or wasted; all have been necessary to bring each of us individually to this moment of time and to this stage of our spiritual growth. What's more, at this precise instant we are receiving unparalleled help from other dimensions that can now accelerate our evolution if we have developed the capacity to open ourselves and are sensitive to them.

The second reason I am writing this book is because, though there are a number of writings which clearly explain the "what"—what is taking place and what needs to be done—there are few that successfully balance the preliminary "what" with the complementary and necessary "how."

The third, and perhaps most important reason that I am writing this book, is to create a bridge that has for me (and may for you) revealed a meaningful continuity between our existing culture, our current stage of evolution, and our inherited spiritual roots. Who we are today is not happenstance. Until we understand and are reconciled with how we got where we are, our futures are hit and miss. Who and where we are have to do with the power of myth and our need to reinterpret the primary myth upon which our Western culture has been formulated and based, the Judeo-Christian myth.

Finally, as my intention is to share my thoughts in hopes that they will fuel yours, I have no intention of posing as an academic, I am not an ordained minister, and have no Ph.D. to hide behind. I hope that you will read this book more as a written conversation than as any kind of final word. Because the "what" has to precede the "how," the first section of this writing will concentrate on my interpretation of what I surmise has taken place in the past and what it has led to in the present. This part is less personal and more factual. The later sections of the book are the more personal "how to" parts: How to use the tools we have been given through the ages in order to find the multidimensional and cohesive level of fulfillment that makes it possible for us to see that it is all God.

The Myth

*I*t would be a mistake to claim that in referring to our Judeo-Christian tradition as a myth, I in any way reduce it to the level of fantasy. Its substance is grounded on actual experiences from which, in time, the central meanings or consciousness has been extracted. All of the world's major religious myths began because some individual had a transcendental experience. Myths close the gap between fact and fiction precisely because they are not just made up stories divorced from reality. We refer to them as myths because in isolating the central meanings, they become symbolic examples of how "the Word" is made flesh. Contrary to common belief, myths have a literal basis in fact whereas allegories are defined as invented stories in which people, things, and events have a singularly symbolic meaning. Myths, like poetry, are attempts to reveal universal and profound truths via as few personalized words as possible. Our Scripture is, therefore, our mythological poetry.

Until those of us who are products of our Western culture review and are reconciled to the Judeo-Christian crucible, which has consciously or subliminally conditioned our present way of life, we won't discover a meaningful approach to the future. We do not have to accept the interpretations of Scripture we have heard all of our lives; however, I do not believe we can consciously understand how we arrived where we are and become completely free unless we pry open the inner meanings of our traditional myth to see how they have consciously or subconsciously affected us. All those who were conditioned in families that attended church or synagogue regularly and were from infancy inculcated with Scriptural implants may have something to overcome. We all may be burdened with a subconscious that is still crammed full of Biblical distortions, sitting there waiting to be freed from stifling old theology—and ourselves along with them.

Throughout history, interpretations of the Judeo-Christian myth have been filtered by social circumstance and elaborately contorted by institutions in order to fit the viewpoint of a particular sect, or they have been manipulated to benefit an imposed power structure. It is no wonder that many Westerners have rejected our traditional myth in favor of foreign myths because, being unfamiliar, foreign myths seem less overloaded with contorted interpretations that have diluted the truths of our myth.

I happen to believe that many if not all of the stories in the Old Testament and the significant experiences of the man we call Jesus Christ were not purely fiction. In essence, our Judeo/ Christian principles—secrets if you will—have the power to transform lives, whether the incidents in the Bible that led to them were literally true or not. It is not my mission to confirm or refute the validity of the Scripture. I do, however, want to show how we can work with them as they currently exist, and find our own spiritually inspired answers that have the power to erase past limitations and animate our lives. What's more, after over fifty years of studying Scriptures, I am more dazzled than ever. I feel not only that we have barely touched the edge of the mystery they contain, but also that we are just now—finally—*beginning to evolve into the consciousness they were intended to create.*

I lump the Old and the New Testaments together and call them the Judeo-Christian myth because there is, or should be, a kind of symbiotic understanding between Jews and Christians that every idea in the New Testament is tucked away somewhere in the Old Testament if one can discern its evolution. To me, it is as though Jesus was a divine mechanic who chose various concepts from the Old Testament and knew how to assemble the parts in a way that created a vehicle that would work for him and his followers.

Underlining the inclusive nature of the twenty-first century, I want to express my appreciation for the oriental masters in India and Japan with whom I was led to study in my early years. I am grateful not only for their turning me on to the invaluable inspiration of meditation and for the wisdom they imparted, but also for an extra special bonus they gave me. Through their generosity, I was able to see what each of the world's most widely accepted spiritual myths have contributed to the world, and, more importantly, being exposed to those other myths made it possible for me to discover what is unique in the Christian myth. By viewing life from different religious perspectives, I was able to see my own Christian roots from a fresh and illuminating viewpoint, freed of dogma, sect, exclusiveness or the misconceptions of my early conditioning. I was then able to see how we are just now only on the edge of the grandeur and the depth of what was revealed through the Master, Jesus the Christ.

My Personal Parable— The Double Thread

*J*esus knew what he was doing when he camouflaged his wisdom via parables. Parables are built around identifiable human traits that experientially trick spiritual implications out of words. The Christian teaching would not have withstood time if Jesus had not hid his abstract truths in personalized allegories to which human beings could relate, stories which masked underlying truths so that only those who had the eyes to see or the ears to hear could mine the mystery.

In the past, most authors have resisted sharing their personal parables, fearing that if they revealed their imperfections, failures, and even successes, what they had to say would be considered superficial. Today, however, in order to be authentic, authors, both psychological and spiritual, must have the willingness and capacity to be totally honest. That means they must share their humanity, their human parable, as well as their knowledge and divinity. Today we are beginning to sense that we are all actually extensions of one being. That is why it is necessary for us to love each other enough to refuse the withholding of any nuance from each other, our shadows, as well as our brilliance. As such, both the concepts I include in this writing and the personal experiences I profile make up my individual parable.

If I had to choose a label that would summarize my lifetime parable, it would be the title of my first and foundation book, *The Double Thread*. I borrowed that phrase from Pierre Teilhard de Chardin's prayer, "Lay hold on me fully both by the within and the without of myself. Grant that I may never break this double thread."1

I won't take time now to fully detail the breakthrough I experienced at the age of thirty-one in a meditation atop Haleakala, the giant extinct crater on Maui, which led to this double thread concept, because I have elaborated on it at length in my book, *Homesick For Heaven*. However, that experience opened the Bible to me for the first time and dangled a spiritual carrot before my eyes, which I have constantly pursued until this very day. At that time, I was astounded to discover that if there is one paramount secret in the Christian Scripture. It is hidden in a divine paradox, the significance of which has remained unrecognized and unappreciated until now. By offering us two commandments instead of just one, Jesus was telling us that at this third-dimensional level of time and space, it is necessary to accept, work with, and even love an "apparent" duality in order for us to achieve a transcendent non-duality. In doing so, he reduced the Ten Commandments of the Old Testament to two, which were like unto each other when understood and lived. By reconciling this seeming dualism, he said "*On these two commandments hang all the law and the prophets.*"2 This reconciliation is the key to the solution of all of life's problems and the modus operandi by which we come to realize that it is all God.

In modern language Jesus' two commandments, the commandment to love God and the commandment to love one's neighbor as one's self, translate into our need to love both "cause" and "effect," to love the creator and the creation. Cause is subjective and invisible. Effects are objective and visible expressions, the results of cause. Jesus added that when the two commandments, the subjective first commandment and the objective second commandment, are both perfectly loved, they are like unto each other, one and the same.

To oversimplify, what we feel and experience is subjective. The qualities of love, patience, and compassion are subjective. When expressed, they become objectified. One's perception is subjective, but when it turns into a concept, it is an object. As a guideline, the subjective is something that is experienced rather than thought. The objective is something that is externalized rather than felt.

When I had my breakthrough in Hawaii, I saw that if I subjectively felt "It's all God" without expressing that love objectively by my acts, I would end up creating the very duality I claimed did not exist. In reverse, if I took action that was not based on the Spirit of Love I would be doing the same thing. I realized that if I could love God, the subjective nature of life, and neighbor and self, the objective world, all in the same way and to the same degree I could honestly say, "It's all God." In other words, the turning point came for me when I realized that I was not a man of God or a man of earth, but both. Though those two "me's" did not seem to be the same, my lifelong quest has been to find out how to make the two "me's" communicate and work as one.

Until I found out how to reconcile the two strands of my nature—the subjective spiritual, and the objective physical—I had always felt that I was out of place and that something was wrong with me. When I listened to the spiritual concepts that came from the mouths of masters, something in me hungrily responded in agreement. In the background there was that personal side of me that doubted I could ever fully live up to what I heard, and, frankly, I hadn't seen any two-legged breathing creatures who lived it absolutely either. On one hand, I was more comfortable in a fundamentally hedonistic society that did not place me under a microscope of a spiritually judgmental morality. On the other hand, at those times when spiritual content was lacking, I felt the magic of life was missing because the divine center within me or others was not being revealed and experienced. Everywhere I went, I felt something was lacking in me until I had my vision of the double thread.

The term, "double thread," is my shorthand for saying that nothing is either/or, nothing is either subjective or objective, nothing only visible or only invisible, nothing just occidental or just oriental, nothing just masculine or just feminine, nothing just spiritual or just material. When I saw how cause becomes visible as effect, I realized that my life was one thread made up of two strands. The opening line of Joel Goldsmith's *Infinite Way* puts it most succinctly:

> *There is not a spiritual universe and a material world, but rather that what appears as our world is the word made flesh, Spirit made visible, or Consciousness expressed as idea.*[3]

Unfortunately, language limits me to saying only one thing at a time; so I ask that each statement I make be held in suspension until its complement is added. If I seem to be loading the gun in favor of one conclusion over another, it is unintentional. I have most likely done so because less commonly accepted viewpoints often need a greater amount of in-depth explanation than traditional opinions. To create balance, subtleties need greater emphasis than the obvious. Above all, look into the spaces between the ideas and listen for the Spirit.

Truth is within ourselves; it takes no rise
From outward things, whate'er you may believe.
There is an inmost centre in us all,
Where truth abides in fulness; and around,
Wall upon wall, the gross flesh hems it in,
This perfect, clear perception-which is truth.
A baffling and perverting carnal mesh
Binds it, and makes all error: and, to KNOW.
Rather consists in opening out away
Whence the imprisoned splendor may escape,
Than in effecting entry for a light
Supposed to be without.

Robert Browning, Paracelsus

Part One
The What

THE WAY TO THE PRESENT

$\mathcal{C}$hapter 1

THE TWO "CHRISTIANITIES"

For it is written, I will destroy the wisdom of the wise, and will bring to nothing the understanding of the prudent. where is the wise? Where is the scribe? Where is the disputer of this world? hath not God made foolish the wisdom of this world?
I Corinthians 1:19,20

$\mathcal{T}$he most spiritually motivated and dedicated advocate of the teachings of the Master Jesus Christ I have ever known refused to call himself a Christian. That was because he felt that the majority of the people who called themselves Christians and most of the churches that claimed to be Christian neither understood nor followed the truths inherent in the life and words of Jesus the Christ.

By judging what is popularly called Christianity, my friend stumbled over his own criticism. In implying that his interpretation was the right one and that the viewpoint taught in most churches was wrong, he indulged in the same judgmental attitude for which he often faulted orthodoxy. Both my friend and those who support traditional Christian churches diminish the Christian message if and when they become exclusive in their approaches. All of us have at times been confused in our personal relationships because we have firmly believed that at one time or another someone we were talking to was disagreeing with us, when in fact we were saying the same thing from a different angle or frame of reference. In analyzing a situation, one of us was judging it from a left brain or masculine state of consciousness that approaches things in a logical or objective fashion, while the other one of us was coming from the right brain, the more feminine, feeling, intuitive or subjective consciousness. Though we would swear it wasn't so, both of us were in complete agreement, but because each of us was talking from a different level of awareness, we thought we were being contradicted and opposed. The same condition has been present throughout history in what I call "the two Christianities." For the words and life of Jesus to be fully understood and appreciated, they need to be interpreted and followed from both of two fundamentally different, but equally important, viewpoints.

In order to lay the foundation for what we can do to end this split in ourselves as well as in our spiritual landscape, I want to take time to go back to the beginning of our Christian myth. First of all, the earliest Christians were not Christians. They were Jews. As such, many of them were attracted to the subjective teachings of the Kabbalah and Jewish mysticism that was prevalent at that time, and others followed the more objective approach we usually associate with Orthodox Judaism. Around 70 AD, Jerusalem fell to the Romans and with it the destruction of the temple resulting in a loss of a national Jewish identity. As Jews became more and more out of favor in the Roman empire, even the Jewish followers of the teachings of Jesus began to separate themselves from traditional Judaism until Christianity emerged into something other than just another version of Judaism.

For the first three hundred-plus years of the Christian movement, both the mystical and the objective approach to Christianity co-existed harmoniously side by side without the necessity of anyone's having to take sides in one camp or the other. Eventually, there were those on each side who took their particular point of view to its exclusive extreme and thus alienated those who, having different temperaments, were unable to identify with each other's approaches. Then, as now, there are two ways to arrive at a truth. One can see a form and then deduct the consciousness that has brought it about—the objective approach—or one can discern a state of consciousness and then deduce what form will result from it—the subjective approach. Those who look at things from a materialistic standpoint are objective; whereas those whose approach to life is intuitive, who think in terms of cause rather than effect, ordinarily see things more subjectively. Both are valid states of consciousness though all of us tend to tune in to one much more than to the other.

On one hand, from the beginning there were those who approached the Judeo-Christian myth objectively, arriving at the substance of their beliefs by identifying with the confrontations or personal experiences that Jesus and other personalities of the Old and New Testaments went through. This objective personal approach tended to take the Bible literally, often overlooking what the stories were meant to symbolize in terms of their subjective messages. Those early objectively motivated Christians were naturally drawn to the first three Gospels that detailed the life and experiences of the historical Jesus, the physical Jesus, the suffering on the cross Jesus, rather than to his subjective mysticism which was paramount in the fourth Gospel, The Gospel of John.

On the other hand, the other major faction of the early Christian Church was predominantly subjective in its approach to life and its vision of reality. They were attracted to Jesus' mysticism rather than to his personal story, somewhat ignoring his human trials and suffering. At best they tried to define what Jesus' experiences symbolized subjectively. They internalized his message and tended to look for answers from the God within themselves rather than from a God outside. They sought guidance from intuition rather than from moral law or the authority of a designated leadership. To them, the subjective mystical experience was more pertinent than the attainment of objectified logic.

The difference between the two systems lies in the dissimilar way they dealt with the same basic facts. It would be a mistake to decide which way was "best," because each approach was working from a completely different level of consciousness with a different end in mind. Through the years the conflict between the two approaches has mistakenly continued to be dealt with as a competition. Then, as now, all individuals included within themselves the capacity to arrive at a conclusion via both an objective viewpoint and a subjective one. For wholeness, both are necessary and no one should be judged for taking one approach or the other because each person is naturally drawn to and able to understand life more succinctly via one than the other.

Without falling into the either/or trap, I want to make it clear that I am not advocating either the objective or the subjective viewpoint because they are equally relevant and equally important. Each has virtues and each, when followed exclusively, has faults.

The Traditionalists & The Gnostics

To broadly characterize those who followed the two basic approaches, I will call one group the Traditionalists and the other the Mystics or Gnostics. The Traditionalists were those whose approach was fundamentally objective. They ended up organizing and institutionalizing the Church and they established traditions that have existed in most organized churches until the present. The Traditionalists' approach to the Christian message has been fabricated in terms of its historical and objective foundation or fundamentals. Traditionally, organization perpetuated itself by appointing leaders, priests, bishops, or ministers who called the shots. On the other hand, the Mystics, or Gnostics, took a more impersonal subjective approach. Rather than looking to organization or leaders for guidance, they tended to look within themselves individually and accepted no other authority than that of the Spirit.

Webster's Third New International Dictionary tells us that the word "Gnostic" comes from a Greek word meaning "knowing," and that Gnosticism was "A system of mystical, religious, intuitive, and philosophical doctrines, combining Christianity with Greek and Oriental philosophies propagated by early Christian sects." As a Judaic teaching, Gnosticism was a mystical approach to the

Kabbalah and the Torah that predated Jesus and eventually lost favor in Orthodox Judaism just as it did in Orthodox Christianity. The Gnostics taught that there was a difference between knowing and believing. Believing, they said, was mental but knowing was experiential. Therefore, the word, "agnostic," came to be understood as one who did not know and had not experienced belief.

After several hundred years of successful co-habitation, a crucial break between the Traditionalists and the Gnostics was instituted at the Council of Nicaea. By that time, the Christian movement had become so prevalent throughout the Roman Empire that the emperor, Constantine, either had to lick them or join them. In calling together all the bishops of the many Christian sects for a council at Nicaea, Constantine had a clever and necessary administrative purpose in mind.

Naturally, in order to govern a couple of million people, Constantine had to solidify and accredit his authority. In order to do so, he had to cripple or get rid of dissidents. How could a social government that of necessity had to organize great numbers of people control those who did not recognize its authority as supreme? Unfortunately for their cause, those who followed the Gnostic approach took Jesus' words and actions to mean that the ultimate authority was within them, and believed that their ability to internalize God's instructions precluded any other authority. So the Roman emperor told the bishops that he would make the Christian religion the official religion of the whole Roman Empire if they would establish a single all-powerful organization. In order to do so, they had to codify, legalize, and thereby objectify the message.

Because the bishops recognized the obvious social virtues of such a proposal and also because of the enticement of the power it offered them, the bishops were won over. In doing so, they disregarded what it would do to a considerable percentage of the Christian family who had followed a more subjective Gnostic or mystical approach to their spiritual life. At that moment, an alliance between the Church and State was born which, by the end of the century, would squelch diversity, demand conformity, and perpetuate a belief system which did not allow freedom of thought or action. The bishops began the process of organizing and objectifying Christianity by arbitrarily editing the many existing Gospels down to four. These four became the acceptable books of the Bible and, as far as possible, the Church started to obliterate any writings and disband any faction that had anything to do with Christianity's Hermetic or Gnostic roots.

Both Christianities had their virtues, but when either side in pursuing those virtues became exclusive of the other, they sacrificed important elements of their initial wholeness. In the end, along with their virtues both sides denigrated the importance of the individual. For instance, in a crowded world where the poor need to be fed and the masses educated, organization and social concern is obviously a good and necessary thing. Without organization, anarchy and ineffectiveness can dominate. Fundamentally, Christian teachings outline the exigency of helping one's fellow beings in objective and concrete ways. *"What man is there of you, whom if his son ask (for) bread, will he give him a stone?"*[1]

The Traditionalists built hospitals and schools, but, though admirably concerned for the needs of fellow man, they tended to overlook the sacredness of each individual by sacrificing him or her for the good of the organization. The government, leaders, and laws took precedence over the importance of an individual soul.

On the other hand, the Gnostics emphasized the mystical message in such Scripture as *"The hour cometh when ye shall neither in this mountain, nor yet at Jerusalem, worship the Father... But the hour cometh, and now is, when the true worshippers shall worship the Father in spirit and in truth,"*[2] and tended to reject all formal organization. They taught that every individual should only worship at the temple within their own being. In its extreme, Gnosticism ignored fellow man through a kind of spiritual narcissism. Those Gnostics who took their beliefs to an exclusive extreme became so self-centered on their own inner search as to ignore the material needs of their fellowman just as some metaphysically-related groups that claim to be spiritually motivated do today. To those Gnostic groups, the word "bread" as it appeared in the Scripture, "...*If his son ask* (for) *bread will he give him a stone?*"3 was interpreted to mean "spiritual food" and stomachs went empty.

The paradox is that both the extreme Traditionalists or fundamentalists and the extreme Gnostics or mystics ended up in the same place. Both denied the importance of the individual. The Traditionalists did it by subordinating the individual to the organization, by telling him what he had to think and do, and by denouncing those who looked within themselves for God. The Gnostics did it by denying human existence through advocating transcendence over one's humanity by a kind of spiritual self-centeredness that did not take into account responsibility for others and thus ignored the material needs of their fellow human beings.

The Difference

The Traditionalists believed that one had to receive one's knowledge from teachers and experiences outside of one's self via the Church and its leaders. The Gnostics believed that the intuitive powers of Self-knowledge, with a capital S, were the way to liberation.

The Traditionalists believed that the teacher was supreme. The Gnostics, quoting Jesus' statement, "...*the works that I do shall he do also; and greater works than these shall he do,*"4 believed the student should go beyond the teacher. The Traditionalists were drawn to a God that was "other than" their own being, outside of themselves, transcendent; an Old Testament objectified sense of God. They thought of God as a Supreme Being. By calling God "Father," Jesus inadvertently encouraged the objective approach because it is impossible to think of Father without relating it to one's own father or fathers in general. The Gnostics, on the other hand, believed that God was imminent, "present within," not a being but a Spirit—"The" Spirit. Their approach was subjective in that they believed that the Christ was the state of consciousness or experience that Jesus exemplified and that Jesus as a man was not as important as his consciousness, perhaps throwing the baby away with the bath water.

Without an objectified concept of God, when the Gnostics couldn't feel God within, they were in a boat without a paddle; whereas the Traditionalists, by objectifying God as something outside of themselves, were unable to find it within themselves.

As for Jesus, the Traditionalists believed that Jesus, the man, was all-important and that he was a person to whom followers could offer themselves. The Gnostics believed that when Jesus was anointed, he became the Christ and that Christ consciousness was not only all important, but was a presence to which one could personally experience and offer one's self.

The Traditionalists, again identifying objectively, believed that Jesus' resurrection was a unique experience that happened to him alone. The Gnostics believed that resurrection was a present experience for all. To them, resurrection stood for the moment of enlightenment at which time they would be born again.

The Traditionalists, seeing Jesus objectively as a person, believed that the Second Coming would be the moment when Jesus reappeared on earth in the same form he had appeared in when he walked the earth. The Gnostics, who saw Jesus subjectively as a consciousness, believed that the Second Coming would be the moment when the awakening of Christ consciousness takes place in humankind.

The Traditionalists accepted a ruling hierarchy down from the pope, cardinals, bishops, priests, and ultimately ministers, elders, and husbands. The Gnostics' hierarchical authority was a line of succession from those who had personally experienced higher divine levels of consciousness on down from ascended masters, evolved souls, and enlightened beings to those just putting their foot on the path.

The Traditionalists believed they were created by God. The Gnostics believed they created God in themselves by being conscious of the God within. They Traditionalists believed in the existence of the devil as a personalized being. The Gnostics believed there was a Satanic state of consciousness that when entertained was responsible for all the evils the Traditionalists attributed to the devil.

The Traditionalists, thinking objectively in terms of bodies or personalities, naturally saw reincarnation as illogical. The Gnostics believed in reincarnation, but not reincarnation as it is generally thought of. They did not see reincarnation as the resurrection of personality but, being subjective, they saw reincarnation as what we would think of today as a continuity of evolving consciousness.

The Traditionalists believed that Jesus, the man, was literally God. The Gnostics did not believe that Jesus was God in the same way the Traditionalists did. They believed that as all cause and effect are one, everyone and everything is God manifest. In that, they saw Jesus as a divine representation of God. They did not say that Jesus was God so much as that Jesus was God's creation.

Basically the Traditionalists' approach was, and still is, fundamentally objective and whenever we approach life subjectively we show Gnostic tendencies. Because all of us see life both objectively and subjectively, we might better understand ourselves if we recognize which of those two basic approaches we tend to favor. Are we predominantly Traditionalists or are we Gnostics? It need not be a matter of either/or; but if we find which approach predominates, we can consciously try to understand and incorporate the virtues of the other approach in our lives. When we do, we will become whole, an integrated being, and no longer a house divided.

The Lost Teachings

*T*he transformation brought on by the Council of Nicaea changed the conditioning of society in often subtle but profound ways. The Traditionalists honored Jesus as the embodiment of the Christ consciousness, but by the Nicene Creed's calling Jesus the only Son of God, they objectified him and set him apart from the rest of humanity. In opposition, the Gnostics were quick to point out that the Scripture did not intend to make Jesus unique. They claimed that Jesus himself made it clear he believed everyone was equally a creation of God by praying "*That they all may be one; as thou, Father, art in me, and I in thee, that they also may be one in us...And the glory which thou gavest me I have given them; that they may be one, even as we are one: I in them, and thou in me, that they may be made perfect in one.*" 5

Naturally, it did not take long after the Council of Nicaea for the establishments of government and Church with their collective resources and militant power to almost stamp out Gnosticism and its writings. At the Council, many apocryphal and/or Gnostic scriptures were eliminated, which are now being rediscovered through such carbon dated findings as the *Dead Sea Scrolls* and the *Nag Hammadi*. I have always felt that it is a minor miracle that the Gospel of John with its Gnostic leaning mysticism was not also suppressed.

The Gospel of Thomas, which has recently been rediscovered and confirmed by the unearthing of the Nag Hammadi scriptures, was a great loss because it, above all others, tried to close the gap between the objective and subjective approaches. Perhaps it was eliminated because it was so overtly metaphysical by making such statements as: "*The lamp of the body is the mind.*"6 Perhaps Thomas' mysticism was too blatantly subjective to be included when he quoted Jesus as having said, "*He who will drink of my mouth will become as I am. I myself will become him. So that things that are hidden will be revealed to him,*"7 implying that when one is in the Christ consciousness that one would be the Christ, thus doing away with the uniqueness of Jesus. Thomas also said "*When the disciple achieves enlightenment, Jesus will no longer serve as his master because the two will become equal, even identical.*"8

Thomas quoted Jesus as having said, "*The kingdom is inside of you and it is outside of you. When you come to know yourself you will be known and you will realize you are the sons of the living father. If you do not know yourself, you live in poverty and it is you who are the poverty.*"9 Tough stuff, but easily translated into the thrust of much of modern psychotherapy. Subjectively, Thomas was saying that you are whatever state of consciousness you are in. If you are in Christ consciousness, that is you. If you are in the supply state of consciousness, that is you. If you are in the health state of consciousness, that is you. Thomas' Gnostic statements show he believed we are not bodies alone but that we are the consciousness that creates and maintains the body as well. Thomas further alienated the Traditionalists by having Jesus make a statement that smacked of the Hermetic teachings that predate Jesus. He quoted him as saying "*When you make the two one and when you make the inside like the outside and the above like the below and you make the male and the female one and the same then you will enter the kingdom of heaven.*"10 Subjectively, once the male and the female or the above and below are reconciled or integrated in one's consciousness, there is no longer any split, no duality, and the infinite nature of individual being is experienced.

Though Gnosticism was stamped out during the century after the Council of Nicaea, the basic subjective approach and the concept of self-realization kept reappearing over the years. It emerged in the writings of such men as Jacob Boehme, Meister Eckhart, and even William Law.

Listen to some of the absolute statements Eckhart espoused in the thirteenth century: "*I pray God to rid me of God because conditionless being is above God and above distinction.*"11 What he was really saying was, "Rid me of the concept of a God that is out there in the objective world where conditions exist because a conditionless God is all and above distinction." He was saying he wanted to be rid of an objective sense of God because subjectively all is God. Talking purely in term of his oneness with God consciousness, Eckhart wrote:

> *Therein I was myself. Therein I willed myself and knew myself to make this man* (his human objective self) *and in this sense I am my own cause both of my*

nature which is eternal (subjective) *and of my nature which is temporal* (objective) *for this I am born and as to my birth which is eternal I can never die. In my eternal mode of birth I have always been, am now, and shall eternally remain. That which I am in time* (objectively) *will die and come to naught for it is of the day and passes with the day.*[12]

At the end of his life, Eckhart was labeled a heretic, and those who believed in his teachings became victims of the Inquisition in the fifteenth century, at which time anyone who claimed oneness with God was burned at the stake. Eckhart, however, made another statement that encouraged exclusivity and was a rejection of the material world, "Unchangeableness and complete detachment from creatures (objects) sets me nearest to God."[13] By implying that creatures are bad, that it would be better not to be a human, he may have been creating the very duality he opposed. If it is all God, so is the human body. He went on to add, "Detachment is the best of all because it cleanses the soul, clarifies the mind, kindles the heart, wakens the spirit. He who would be serene and pure needs but one thing, detachment."[14] Yet when detachment becomes a rejection of caring and responsibility for fellow man, it results in a denial of "this world," and faith without works is meaningless.

As I said earlier, for the first three hundred plus years the Traditionalists' personal concepts that honored the material side of life were combined with the purely subjective mystical or Gnostic approach. However, in the end, like a road that divides, eventually the two destinations became extreme and far apart, almost completely losing sight of each other. Fanatical Gnostics indeed so ignored the historical Jesus as to deny his presence at all, and many Traditionalists ended up in idolatry, superstitiously worshipping statues representing, among other things, a bloody body hanging from a cross.

Nevertheless, because nothing in consciousness can ever be lost, the basic Gnostic approach has reappeared in the last hundred or so years with both its virtues and its faults in what is loosely called the metaphysical movement or New Thought. Ralph Waldo Emerson, whom many believe was the father of the metaphysical movement in America, had Gnostic-like beliefs. He was excommunicated from his own church for criticizing the doctrine that placed God above and outside of man by stating, *"That which shows God out of me makes me a wart and a wen."*

Gnostic concepts permeated Christian Science and the writings of Mary Baker Eddy and are included in Ernest Holmes' Religious Science, in Charles and Myrtle Fillmore's Unity, in the *A Course in Miracles*, and throughout Joel Goldsmith's *Infinite Way* writings. Because many but not all of those who are considered part of the New Age movement have been attracted to Gnostic mysticism, those very old ideas were labeled "new."

Modern-day Transpersonal Psychology which combines the mental and the spiritual includes a degree of Gnostic consciousness as do a number of those writing for Noetic Science publications. But the most extraordinary and unexpected area for Gnostic principles to appear has been and is in the discoveries of quantum physics.

Quantum Physics

*W*hen practitioners of Quantum Mechanics departed from logic by dissolving our ordinary understanding of time and space, they had come up with the scientific equivalent of mystical concepts that were very Gnostic. By proving the existence of realms beyond material existence, as we have known it, the gap began to be closed between objective fact and subjective fiction, between matter and spirit. When Max Born, Werner Heisenberg, Neils Bohr, and others proved scientifically that by observing something "here," you could affect something "there," they opened a panorama of infinite possibility, which led to the splitting of the atom, the ultimate object. What they were really bringing to light was the age-old alchemist's secret: *Consciousness transmutes form.* More importantly, they also included the removal of spiritual healing, or mind over matter from the realm of superstition and made it acceptable as a scientific fact.

When Quantum Mechanics came up with the belief that something had to be observed in order to be present, they showed us in Gnostic fashion how our observations create our reality. They even dignified Carl Jung's concept of synchronicity and authenticated it as a rationale for simultaneous happenings ordinarily attributed to God.

Quantum Mechanics has further stupefied reason by outlining an entirely new understanding of the myth of time and the truth of eternality, mathematically proving that thought or observation can even change the past. Besides getting rid of the illusory division between space and time, wave and particle, energy and matter, spiritual and material, they are doing away with the basic dualism of subject versus object, thereby transcending all dualism and showing us that when we combine the two Christianities we will create a richer and more meaningful Christianity.

The Purpose of Paul

*I*n order to understand how our two Christianities came to differ and what needs to be done to reunite them, it is important to also understand what part Paul of Tarsus has played. Paul was a mixed bag, but we should be thankful for Paul, because if it had not been for him, Christianity would have ended up being no more than a footnote in the annals of Jewish sectarianism. Paul became our bridge to today. Without his dedication, charismatic influence, and proselytizing inclination, it is doubtful that Christianity would have included Gentiles and have been spread throughout the world. The most important reason to identify with Paul, however, is because Paul started where most of us have begun, and therefore he had to overcome many of the same problems that we have. Despite his obvious shortcomings—his sense of self-importance, that he was the ultimate authority, and his contradictory judgments—Paul eventually broke through, experienced the mystical level, and showed us that what he did with all his human baggage we can do as well.

In *The Last Temptation of Christ*, Greek author, Nikos Kazantzakis, proposes a fantasy that was doubtless fictional but which was his way of pointing out the reason there was a difference between Paul's and Jesus' Christianity. He begins by claiming that Jesus survived the cross rather than that he was resurrected. Schonfield made a similar claim in his book, *The Passover Plot*, and Basilides, a Gnostic/Christian teaching in Alexandria in the second century, taught a variation of the same hypothesis. Kazantzakis proposes that after surviving the cross Jesus went on to live with Mary and Martha.

Whether true or false, Kazantzakis went on to propose another addition to his fantasy that is a possible explanation why we have two Christianities today. He proposed that a number of years after Jesus had left the public scene, he was in disagreement with the way his message was being taught by Paul and sent out the word that he wanted to talk to him to set the records straight. When Paul paid him a visit, Jesus admonished him saying that he wasn't completely accurate in his teachings. Paul, knowing that for all practical purposes Jesus was dead and could not once more come out in public, told him to take it or leave it because his, Paul's, version was the one that was going to become Christianity. Kazantzakis's story is doubtless pure conjecture, but in terms of the Christian message it is exactly what has happened, and for two thousand years Christianity has mainly reflected Paul's interpretation.

There is no doubt that Paul's teaching was colored by his personal sense of self and smacked of egotism. A. N. Wilson, in his book titled *Paul*, details Paul's background and points out that Paul claimed his authority not from what he learned in personal contact with those who were actually present with Jesus, but rather he based his authority from what he received on his own out of either his imagination or his personal sense of divine intuition.

Using *The New Revised Standard Bible* to make his point, Wilson quotes Paul's own words, *"I want you to know, brothers and sisters, that the gospel that was proclaimed by me is not of human origin; for I did not receive it from a human source, nor was I taught it, but I received it through a revelation of Jesus Christ... I did not confer with any human being, nor did I go up to Jerusalem to those who were already apostles before me."* As you can see, by his own confession, Paul did not confer with any other human beings; therefore one could claim his version was touched with self-pride and was uniquely his own—not dissimilar to mine or anyone else's personal interpretations.

Although Paul was more objective than subjective and his teachings ended up being fodder for a purely objective viewpoint of Jesus' message, he did include some subjective or mystical truths along with his objective viewpoint. If we are alert, we can avoid the pitfalls by being aware of from which side Paul was speaking when we read him and thereby not be influenced by his judgments and excesses.

What we have not realized is that there was a difference between Jesus' mysticism and Paul's often overly objective point of view, an attitude that was eventually responsible for the creation of a sectarian interpretation of who Jesus was and what he taught. However, somewhere along the way he had obviously been initiated into the secrets of consciousness, higher mysticism, and Gnostic thought. At times he doubtless experienced a direct contact with what I would call "Christ consciousness." Nevertheless, Paul could not help but look at things in a different way than Jesus did, the main reason being that Paul, though Jewish, was brought up and conditioned in a Hellenistic society, in a well-to-do family, where logically based Greek was his number one language in his formative years. Paul reasoned in terms of literal and logical Greek thought, whereas Jesus spoke and thought in Aramaic—a feeling, symbolic, and oriental language.

Jesus, as far as we know, was actually an Oriental born and raised in the Middle East, which is part of the Asian continent, and as far as we know he never set foot in Europe or the Occident. However, because of his Greek conditioned mind, Paul metabolized Jesus' words through his literal, reasonable, and proof-oriented Greek intellect. What we have not consciously taken into account is that the original Aramaic dialect that Jesus and his followers spoke was an oriental language that was primarily symbolic in its conception.

The most critical and unrecognized stumbling block we bump into today in trying to accurately interpret the Judeo-Christian myth is our literal Western mind's inability to cope with languages designed for symbolic interpretation. We arrive at a conclusion following a progression from A therefore B therefore C until we have constructed a mental theorem based mainly on intellect rather than feeling or spirit. The Aramaic dialect that Jesus spoke was an oriental language that, like all oriental languages, intended to engender an experience through its symbolism, rather than a language that was to be taken literally. The Oriental mind is more subjective, more ritualistic, more experiential, more feeling, and more inclined to search for the meaning of the consciousness beneath the words than for a literal verbatim interpretation.

Ever since Paul's Christianity predominated, the life and words of Jesus have been interpreted by objectified Greek logic. That is the same imperious attitude that resulted in Jesus eventually being portrayed as a blond blue-eyed European, rather than as a dark oriental who as far as we know never put his foot on the continent of Europe. The problem with our linear Western approach is that if one assumption is even slightly out of line, the final conclusion strays far from its original intention, becoming an erroneous product of the intellect rather than illustrative of what has really been felt or experienced.

In reverse, the Oriental mind may fall short because it can be too ritualistic, experiential, and more inclined to search for the subjective meanings and feelings inherent in words than for the empirical nature of what those words imply. That is why, to the Westerner, the significance an Oriental places on saving face seems out of line with the importance of some seemingly insignificant incident that has taken place. To us the incident is more important than the consciousness it reveals. To the Oriental, one's intent is more significant than the incident. The problem with the Eastern approach is that unless it also aims at an objective result, subjective speculation turns into fantasy, and material well being becomes a secondary and often neglected by-product.

Paul did do something Jesus could not. Because Paul was not Jesus, he could stand outside and be objective about Jesus, could talk of Jesus as a third party just as all of us who examine the Christian myth can and do. That was both the virtue and the fault of Paul's teaching. To the limits of his own vision, Paul did try to reveal the spirit or consciousness of the Christ. However, Paul nevertheless objectified Jesus, created his own version of who Jesus was, and laid the groundwork for the Traditionalists to make Jesus a personality who was unique and separate from the rest of humankind.

Finally, after two thousand years, we have evolved to the point where we are ready to understand and appreciate both the mysticism of the man Jesus who attained a state of consciousness we call "the Christ" and the man himself. Personally, I feel that Jesus and his message was so far ahead of its time that we are only now able to comprehend the full implications of his advent or to touch the edge of it.

Paul versus Jesus

What is the basic difference between Pauline Christianity and Jesus' true message? Though Paul hinted at the "secret teachings" of Gnostics, he may have thought that the masses were not yet able to understand the mystical nature of the message and therefore they needed a more personally identifiable application with specific laws that they could follow. Historically, the objective personal facts outlined in Paul's accounting were accurate enough, but his interpreting Jesus' esoteric message in terms of laws of conduct and moral judgments resulted in the traditional church's personalizing the man Jesus rather than emphasizing his transcendental consciousness and its message.

The most obvious difference between Jesus' and Paul's teachings was the manner in which both of them personally conceived of themselves and their own identity. Paul saw himself objectively as primarily a material human being. Rather than visualizing himself as a divine being with a body, he saw himself as a body with a divine potential. He would make such statements as *"For we know that the law is spiritual: but I am carnal, sold under sin. For which I do I allow not: for that what I would, that do I not; but what I hate, that do I."*[15]

When Jesus talked of himself he might at times refer to his objective self in such statements as *"I of my own self can do nothing,"*[16] but while doing so, he was totally and constantly aware of his true nature as Spirit, *"I and my Father are one,"*[17] or *"He that hath seen me, hath seen the Father,"*[18] his creative cause. He was constantly aware of his divine nature as his ultimate reality and wanted everyone else to see himself or herself in the same way. Predominantly throughout his ministry, Jesus demonstrated that he was an embodied spiritual being. He even took Peter, James, and John up to the mountain and translated himself into light to demonstrate it.[19] Paul may have believed that cause and effect are one, but in explaining that Jesus and God were one and the same, he did it objectively in a way that excluded the rest of humankind. To say that Jesus was God without differentiating between cause and effect fit right into the schema of the Church. In order to maintain its authority, the Church needed to objectify both Jesus and God and set them apart, thus widening the gap between humanity and an all-powerful God that had to be obeyed.

Here, again, both the Gnostic and the Traditionalist approaches are true and valid from their own standpoints. Traditionally, Jesus and God are one and the same because, following the two commandments, cause and effect are like unto each other. *Mystically, until we see Jesus as God, we cannot see ourselves as one with divine cause.* As individuals we have to understand that though being human, we are nonetheless made in the image of God. On the other hand, when we are thinking of ourselves objectively only as material beings, which we do most of the time, we are coming from the effect viewpoint where sin or shortcomings are made possible.

St. Augustine's Follow-Up

*M*ore than a hundred years after Paul, as a follow-up to what was begun at the Council of Nicaea, Saint Augustine fully established the Church's legal approach to Christianity by underlying the objective aspects of Paul's theology. He discounted the possibility of living purely by Grace, or a subjective inner guidance, and brought the Church squarely under the influence of a dogmatic set of laws that were to dictate human conduct from then on. That made it easy for the Church to believe that the ends it wished to achieve justified its methods. Basic human sexuality became the crucible in which human nature was ground into submission.

Despite the fact that Jesus himself did not judge sexual behavior one way or the other, Augustine took Paul's attitude, and perhaps his personal frustrations about his own sexuality, and blew them up into the central doctrines and moral code of the church. He may have taken his cue from the openly licentious and excessive sexual conduct of the Romans at that time, but Augustine did set the course which made a natural and vital part of life a cause for guilt and self-loathing for many ever after. Before Augustine dominated the Church's theology, sexuality was just one among many possible stumbling blocks, but he established laws for sexual conduct and created the concept of original sin. His implication that a female's sexual attractiveness was what tempted mankind became a reason for perpetuating the belief that women were spiritually inferior to men.

Augustine's insistence on the importance of the virginal birth's having taken place without a sexual encounter, a concept the Gnostics did not accept, also contributed to the belief that sexual relations were somehow other than spiritual. He didn't judge sex subjectively in terms of the spirit in which the act was performed, but judged the act objectively as something that was purely physical. He condemned having sex for pleasure and set it aside exclusively for one purely objective purpose, the procreation of the species, which in turn increased the church's membership and power. Because the subjective nature of sexuality was not included, countless numbers throughout the centuries have either consciously or unconsciously felt guilty for enjoying their intimacies.

Once more, remember this is not to say that one approach is right and the other wrong. *Any exclusive approach falls short.* The subjective and the objective viewpoints, when inclusive and properly understood, can simply be different and alternative ways of getting to the same principles. In a crowded world we cannot exist without the objectivity provided by organizations, governments, and institutions; but the time has come when our establishments can and must combine the two Christianities and become the way of life Jesus came to declare is possible.

Chapter 2

CONSCIOUS EVOLUTION

When I was a child, I spoke as a child, I understood as a child, I thought as a child: but when I became a man, I put away childish things.

I Corinthians 13:11-12

I have fed you with milk, and not with meat: for hitherto you were not able to bear it.

I Corinthians 3:2

He said unto them, I have meat to eat that ye know not of.   John 4:32

I have yet many things to say unto you, but you cannot bear them now.

John 16:12

Jesus answered and said unto him, 'What I do thou knowest not now; but thou shall know hereafter.

John 13:7

If ye have heard of the dispensation of the grace of God, which is given me to youward: how that by revelation he made known unto me the mystery; ... whereby when ye read, ye may understand my knowledge in the mystery of Christ, which in other ages was not made known unto the sons of men, as it is now revealed unto his holy apostles and prophets by the Spirit.

Ephesians 3:2,4&5

When the divine process becomes a synonym for God, an evolutionary purpose behind every thought or action becomes evident. Even a brief sortie into the past reveals that every step and every facet of belief that humankind has experienced has been necessary in order to bring us collectively to where we are today. In my researching the evolutionary roots of Christianity, it has been hard for me to keep from getting bogged down in elaborate complexities that have constantly clogged the religious pipeline both within and outside of orthodoxy. Though we have come a long way, simplifying chaos should remain a top priority.

My favorite uncle, Uncle Gilbert, celebrated his twenty-fifth year of sobriety in AA before he died at seventy. Years ago, when I would visit him on his humble river-side farm outside Seguin, Texas, in my youthful zeal I over-enthusiastically expounded on the esoteric mysteries I had been exposed to while visiting both Christian and Oriental monasteries around the world. In a quiet but loving way, Uncle Gilbert brought me down to earth with, "Keep it simple."

I did not realize at the time how profound and Christ-like my uncle's advice was. When Jesus gave us two commandments to replace ten, he was taking us from the complexity of law to the simplicity of Grace. Complexity, like the wave, is made up of infinite possibility. Simplicity, like the individual particles that make up the wave, is needed for an individual to find where he or she is at and what his or her next step should be.

Similar to the dilemma facing a juggler, objectivity demands the ability to assimilate many different aspects or parts at once without losing sight of any. On the other hand, subjectivity is simplicity because it depends on only one cause: The presence of unity within the diversity. In other words, simplicity zeros in on the spirit of a situation rather than on the need to compile a catalogue of facts. However, if we want to move forward into a simpler unified understanding of God and ourselves, we have to take a big step: We have to accept something that the ego rebels against.

The ego doesn't just denounce what I am going to propose as the way to transcend complexity, but also sees this belief threatening everything the ego has accomplished. Egotism's control depends on making one's intellect, rather than one's Spirit, primary, and keeping us constantly analyzing complexity. In order to simplify, we have to stop rationalizing the past. There is only one way to deal with complexity, and that is to realize: *Everything from the past, every teaching and every concept is as of this moment obsolete.*

I didn't say "valueless." We wouldn't be where we are if every bit of our past hadn't taken place. In order to get to the one hundred and second floor of the Empire State Building, we have to pass through every one of the previous one hundred and one other floors, floors that now though obsolete nevertheless gave rise to and support the hundred and second. Alan Watts, in his first and most profound book, *The Wisdom of Insecurity*, made the claim that though we cherish our hard-earned concepts, unless we accept their obsolescence, we are frozen in our innate desire for security.

To approve of obsolescence seems menacing to everything we value and on which we have built our lives. Indeed, it would be if it meant we had to turn our back on our cherished beliefs and those beloved teachers from whom we have received so much in the past. If we were to lose sight of or if we were to devalue the part they played in pushing our evolution forward, we would be denying that it is all God; therefore everything has had its valued place and time. However, the second we have individually experienced the slightest transformation of consciousness, we are a new person and the past becomes obsolete. To hold on to yesterday's truths, yesterday's manna, out of a misguided sense of loyalty after they have served their purpose would deny the divinity of one's own evolution.

Faithful Evolution   ·

*E*volution and its by-product, obsolescence, does not disprove God as many have thought in the past. Rather, it confirms God's omnipotence. To have faith in evolution is to have faith in the process of life. It is that simple. Nothing in life just happens. It evolves. All beliefs are based on the promise of evolution. Every study promises us that we will be in a different place after we have mastered it or else we wouldn't be studying it to begin with. Either we trust the process or we don't, which is to say, either we trust God or we don't. Someone didn't just give you this book you are reading nor did you just pluck it off the shelf. Every incident in your life had to take place in order for you to evolve into this moment. In that, you, I, and everyone else who may read this book have one thing in common—we are all sharing a similar stage of evolution.

In *Christianity and Evolution*, Teilhard de Chardin eloquently made an encouraging case for evolution and for letting go of the past. He wrote,

> *We need to shift our outlook unreservedly into that of a world which is evolving. I believe that the universe is an evolution. I believe that evolution proceeds towards Spirit. I believe that Spirit if fully realized is a form of personality. I believe that the supremely personal is the universal Christ.*

He went on to say,

In the first century of the Church, Christianity made its definitive entry into human thought by boldly identifying the Christ of the gospel with the Alexandrine Logos. The logical continuation of the same tactics and the prelude to the same success must be found in the instinct which is now urging the faithful, after two thousand years, to return to the same policy; but this time it must not be with the ordaining principle of the stable Greek cosmos (logic) *but with the neo-Logos* (metaphysics) *of modern philosophy—the evolutive principle of a universal movement.*[1]

Later Teilhard voiced his fear that evolution would fail to be incorporated in the Church by saying,

So long as the Church neglects, by means of a refashioned Christology, to solve the apparent conflict that henceforth exists between the traditional God of revelation and the 'new' God of evolution, so long, too, will there be an increasing distress not only on the fringe of the believing world but at its core; and pari passu, Christianity's power to attract and convert will grow less.[2]

Oddly enough, the discovery that two-legged beings existed millions of years ago need not upset, threaten, or invalidate the beliefs of those whose literal interpretation of the Bible claims that man was created only five thousand plus years ago. Simply put, that time could possibly just stand for the moment in evolution when souls evolved in our two-legged ancestors, at which time mankind finally became fully human. Thus Adam may symbolize or represent the first man to have evolved a soul.

I have to believe that whatever God is, God has to be the ultimate cause, so whenever I was told about the fall of man as though man had been perfect and fell from his perfection, the Spirit in me rebelled. I couldn't buy the guilt that accompanied that premise. Finally I realized that man didn't fall; he evolved. I saw that the Gospel of John explains it in its opening words. *"In the beginning was the Word* (logos or idea) *and the Word was with God, and the Word was God,"* and that *"the Word was made flesh."*[3] In the beginning, there was the perfect word, signifying the perfect idea or concept of man, but it takes time for the perfect idea to evolve or "man-ifest" the perfect form.

It isn't that man was perfectly formed in mind, body, and spirit, and then fell and is now paying the price. The perfect ideal concept of man came into being eons ago, and it is just taking this long for that concept to be perfectly fleshed out. Evolution is no more or less than the process of *"the Word"* becoming flesh; so we can rejoice and rest in the fact that God or creation is working in our lives to eventually flesh us into our perfect being. If we are dissatisfied with ourselves we should try to push evolution ahead by living as perfectly as possible, but at the same time we must be patient knowing that God, the divine process, isn't finished yet.

When Jesus said, *"Touch me not for I am not yet ascended,"*[4] he was saying, "Don't hold me back, my evolution is not complete yet." I am not saying that everyone is at the same stage in the process or that some of us don't participate in the process. Our collective task today is to fulfill our duty to forward the great work of evolution and help guide it to its completion. Evolution began billions of years ago when the world was nothing but gases. Finally billions of years later those gases solidified as water and earth. Eventually, primitive life forms began to mutate and multiply, all leading up step by step to the high point of evolution thus far as man and woman. Who knows what we will be after the next level of evolution? Evolution has reached a new stage today because for the first time we have intellects, technologies and spiritual powers that are affecting evolution itself. It is important for us to realize and take responsibility for our newly evolved ability to affect collective evolution.

As infinity is never minus anything, within the consciousness of every human being all the stages of creation that have come into being thus far continue to exist as part of us. When we fully evolve, we will have access to a conscious awareness of all of them. If anything, we should be enormously encouraged by our realization of evolution and joyously contemplate it, because evolution not only reveals that God is indeed the only power or process growing us into our own divinity, but it also explains a rational for the presence of evil.

Evolutionary Evil

Theologians have always had a problem reconciling an omnipotent God, a primal cause, with the presence of evil. To say that evil does not exist at the level of *this world* is just as divisive as to call evil good. Somehow we have to reconcile our concept of evil with an eventually utopian state of body and mind. Evolution is the way. Due to the fact that it takes time for *"the Word"* to evolve into its perfect material expression, evil is a kind of secondary cause. It exists as the void that precedes fulfillment. It is a spur, the overcoming of which pushes us into our eventual perfection. When we arrive, evil will cease to exist. Like the dark that is without power in the presence of light, or the shadow that ceases to exist when that which is blocking the light is removed, evil is exposed as a nothingness when the materialized presence of divinity is experienced.

Evil is the signature or trademark for the shadow side, which points to the light—its opposite. Unless light was possible to begin with, we wouldn't recognize evil. The universe is converging into its being, into its "as-ness," and as it moves through the transitory levels of time and space, it leaves a trail, a litter of discarded spent refuse, a smoke trail. This trail, though ugly and wasted, is the necessary casting off of the old and undesirable. To see this smoke of evil as other than part of the process is to deny omnipotence, but to see it as desirable is to also deny omnipresence.

In other words, no one is asking anyone to accept evil as either God's presence or a presence apart from God but rather for us to see evil as the shadow side of the evolutionary process which draws us to an awareness of God. The need to overcome evil is what leads us to God. It's the junk left behind from the burnt energies of love pushing consciousness into becoming conscious. There is no contradiction in omnipotence when we see evil as a symbol of the irresistible forces of cosmogonesis in its thrust to unite all into a single oneness. Fire leaves ashes. Without something to burn there is no fire. The ashes are what are left after the good has been extracted, and thus God is confirmed as truly the only power.

In *God Is A Verb*, Rabbi David A. Cooper shows how Jewish and Christian mysticism is in agreement about evil by claiming:

> *When we reach a transcendental point in which good and evil overlap to the extent that we can perceive how either can transform into the opposite, the intensity of the experience can be so great that we lose our sense of personal identity. If we do so, we can center into a world that is called devekut, constant awareness of God. But the process of understanding the relationship of good and evil is paradoxical and not as easily accomplished as it sounds...Good and evil is not a dichotomy at all, is not a split between opposites, but an enclosed universe of curved time and space."*[5]

We should rejoice that the process with all its ups and downs continues because it means we are still being grown into our Godliness. When it completes itself, there will be no need for continued growth and no refuse, no evil, left. Fear not the human scene because, as Chardin cried, "Son of man (which Jesus called himself), bathe yourself in the ocean of matter; plunge into it where it is deepest and most violent; struggle in its currents and drink of its waters. For it cradled you long ago in your preconscious existence; and it is that ocean that will raise you up to God."[6] The world of good and evil is what fuels the evolution flowering your consciousness.

In the meantime, don't fall for the temptation to run away from life and involvement. See your humanity as the process that is still moving forward, that will strengthen your ability to overcome. That's pretty heavy stuff, I admit, but once the flesh and spirit are reconciled so that we see the divine in all, we will have overcome the last obstacle and we will fly like angels, knowing it is all God.

In terms of our Judeo-Christian myth, it isn't that Jesus was the missing link in evolution; he was "the" link, our present link to the evolution of our own potential. We could say that Jesus represents or symbolizes the first fully evolved, fully conscious man in Western history. His life was a gift. It promises us that we too can evolve into the same perfection that he did through a combination of divine evolution and free will. When Jesus said, "*My Father sent me*,"[7] he could as well have said, "Evolution has sent me and will send you." The evolutionary process sent Jesus into being a fully conscious being.

Each of the Scripture passages I quoted at the beginning of this chapter were intimations of this evolution, were promises that each of us will evolve into being aware that we are not only fully conscious but that we are consciousness itself.

The Evolution of Consciousness

*T*he time has come. Because of evolution we can "*Let this mind be in you, which was also in Christ Jesus*," and now eliminate evil as the secondary cause.[8] No one said it would be easy, but we can accomplish it because it is finally possible to become fully conscious. Carl Jung forecast our spiritual and mental evolution a half century ago when he said, "Man has developed consciousness slowly and laboriously, in a process that took untold ages to reach the civilized state (which is arbitrarily dated from the invention of script in about 4000 BC). And this evolution is far from complete, for large areas of the human mind are still shrouded in darkness."[9] He was right, but, precisely because of creative beings like himself, we have evolved in just the last hundred years to the point where we are at last able to know what it means to be "conscious"—so we have come a long way since Jung objectified consciousness.

The good news is that because of evolution we are now able to digest greater bites of scientific, psychological, and spiritual truths than ever before. In every walk of life, from examples of record-breaking Olympian feats of physical strength and prowess, to medical breakthroughs that tinker with God-like powers of creation, we are able to stretch in ways that were considered completely impossible a scant few years ago. Our spiritual evolution hasn't been excluded from the process, which has speeded everything up. How fast we individually wish to evolve is up to us. We can continue to live in yesterday and see ourselves as limited human beings that still need to be taught and refuse to allow our newly evolved capacities to fully express themselves, or, as Joseph Campbell said, we can follow our bliss and be super beings. By becoming consciously aware of unity in complexity, we can simplify complication and escape from obsolete dualistic teachings. We can trust our own inner process to reveal how things work. We can take the old wine and by filtering out the contradictions inherent in the past, we can simplify truth, put it in new bottles and become intoxicated by life.

Because evolution itself has speeded up, the maturing process, which took hundreds of years in the past, can now fulfill itself in just a few years. It is possible now to mature spiritually in what would have taken lifetimes of effort before. For that matter, just look at our children. Many of them are being born way ahead of where we were when we incarnated. The ease with which they become computer-literate at the age when we were just learning our ABC's should tell us something.

Even thirty years ago many of us could only digest milk, but because we were prepared by great teachers and because evolution has speeded up the process, we are now ready for meat, spiritually speaking. Now we can all become fully conscious beings. But, first, we have to become consciously aware that we have that potential and accept that we do. We have to feel it in our bones, so to speak. The Scripture says that the time would eventually come when we would be ready for meat. That eventuality is now. However, we will never recognize the difference between milk and meat unless we trust (love) ourselves enough to let go of the obsolete past and take responsibility for becoming fully conscious now. Frankly, we have no choice in the matter; we must or we will strangle in our double standards and our contradictions.

Because we were made in the image of God, each of us potentially has the capacity to create, not just procreate, but create new forms. We are here to do a job, to be co-creators with life energy. However, potential talent is not enough. Until we have a conscious awareness of our creative capability and a firm grasp of our craft, our lives become hit-and-miss, success one day and failure the next. To be fully and consistently conscious is to know constantly who you are, what you can do, and why you are here.

When we can see that every experience we have had in the past and every one we are now having—good and bad—has taken place for the purpose of making us conscious beings, we are that much closer to realizing what it means to be made in the image and likeness of God. Though it is debatable whether we can now finally speed up the process , for all practical purposes we should try, because, rest assured, we will continue in whatever particular experience we are in, over and over, until we do discover what it is telling us. After becoming conscious, whatever our particular mistakes have been, they will never happen to us again. Their purpose for being no longer exists.

As we go up the ladder of evolving consciousness, humankind is at present the high point of awakened consciousness. From the first one-cell amoeba, each more sophisticated life form has demonstrated increased consciousness until in human beings consciousness has reached the zenith of this present stage of evolution, at least on this earth plane. The masters, the Jesuses, and Buddhas of this world are outstanding because they represent the most fully conscious beings of whom we know. Jesus' birth is to be honored as the advent of the first fully conscious being in our Western culture, a portent of the future for all of us.

Humans have a Christ-like spiritual healing potential, which stems from the fact that we are the only life form in which consciousness is able to be aware of itself. Though there are many stages of consciousness, from the most primitive to the seemingly almost human beings, we are the only ones who promise to have the capacity to become fully conscious. We are the only ones who think and know we are thinking. The more conscious we are, the more we will automatically produce harmony in place of disease. That is because disease and disharmony signify the absence of developed consciousness. A fully conscious person doesn't have to do or think anything in order to create harmony. Their very presence is harmony. In the presence of illumined consciousness, there is no place for disharmony or ignorance to get a toehold. Our most important job now is to know what consciousness is and how we can become more fully conscious.

Mystical Consciousness

*H*istory is dotted with men and women who have stood out from the crowd because they had attained or evolved to the personal experience we call a mystical or transcendental level of consciousness. It is important to understand that there is no such thing as one's being a little mystical. Either a person has experienced that mystical dimension some call the Fourth Dimension or one has not. Mystics draw others to them because those others have sensed something "special" about them. Their attained transcendental consciousness and its spiritual energy had been the magnet.

The dictionary tells us that mysticism is "the belief that direct knowledge of God, of spiritual truth, of ultimate reality is attainable through intuition, insight, or illumination in a way differing from ordinary sense perception." Anyone who has the capacity to listen to his or her inner voice and speak from Spirit is a mystic. All true mystics have had the same experience—a peek into an underlying reality where their individual self has merged with infinite beingness, an experience that is really beyond words and thoughts. Each has seen, or for a moment has become, the light. The difference between mystics is not what they have personally experienced but what they were given to teach from their experience. Each has taught at the level that people could hear when they were bodily present.

In order for him to be able to say *I AM THAT I AM*, Moses obviously experienced God consciousness. Nonetheless, those who followed him still had to be led out of the wilderness of law; so Moses taught his followers at the level they were able to comprehend at their particular stage of evolution. His followers were not capable of understanding the fullness of his mystical vision at that point. All the great Old Testament prophets had touched the Christ level or they could not have spoken as they had. Isaiah, Elijah, and the others broke through into that higher consciousness, but even though each hinted at the eventual presence of the Christ state of consciousness, each could only take the message the next step beyond the one before, and none could fully voice what they had personally experienced.

Finally, the collective consciousness of the Western world was raised to the point of spiritual evolution where it was possible for the appearance of a Jesus who could voice the Christ level of consciousness, a higher or more evolved level than human beings could comprehend up to that time. For the past two thousand years, that spiritual yeast has been leavening or evolving the collective consciousness to the place where, at last, we can all eat spiritual meat.

Conscious Mind

I have been sandwiching in such words as "becoming conscious beings," "consciousness," and "higher consciousness"; so it is time to stop for a second and make sure we mean the same thing by those words. It is certainly easy to see why there is so much confusion surrounding the words "conscious mind, subconscious mind, superconscious mind, and consciousness." All of these words relate to each other in one way or another, but all have different meanings; all are used objectively one minute and subjectively the next, as nouns one minute and adjectives the next. On top of that, with the advent of psychology and its desire to be accepted as an empirical mental science, words relating to consciousness have taken on a specific, clinical, and limited, if not limiting, meaning. I feel that in order to become fully conscious it is important to establish a current and comprehensive definition of these words, how each relates to us, and the different dimensions of our multi-dimensional presence.

Psychoanalytically, according to *A Comprehensive Dictionary of Psychological and Psychoanalytical Terms,* published in 1958, the word "conscious" is most often used as a noun, "that part of the mind, which is momentarily (temporarily) aware." It goes on to say, "All psychologists use it, relating it to objective observation by various theoretical interpretations." In other words, except for some modern psychologists who now include spiritual awareness in their therapies, many psychologists believe that being conscious is a behavioral matter rather than one which equates consciousness with one's total self or one's degree of spiritual acumen.

Webster's Dictionary points out that the word, "conscious," comes from the Latin word "conscire" meaning "to know," and primarily relates being conscious with being aware. So the conscious mind is the aware mind, and to be fully conscious is to be fully aware. Because only a spiritually enlightened person fully knows what he or she is doing and why, when a person becomes fully conscious that person becomes a spiritual master. To be fully conscious, one has to be aware of the double thread— actively aware of one's divine being in relationship to the earth and at the same time aware of one's self and other beings at their physical, mental, and spiritual levels inclusively. Being fully conscious means having the capacity to be simultaneously aware of physical appearances without losing sight of one's spiritual significance and one's relationship to the whole of life.

SubConscious Mind

*T*he Psychological Dictionary describes the subconscious mind or subconscious as "Not clearly conscious but capable of being made so." It also equates the subconscious with the word, "subliminal." We have often heard that our conscious mind is limited to that one-eighth part of our intelligence that is above the surface, like the top of an iceberg, and that our subconscious mind is the seven-eighths below the surface level of awareness. The subconscious is filled with not only every experience we have had in this life (most which has been forgotten) but also our racial and reincarnation experiences as well.

Science tells us that even our cells are communicating with each other, that a subconscious intelligence is telling our hearts to continuously beat, that a digestive intelligence is processing our food, and that this subliminal intelligence is fulfilling all our countless bodily functions of which we are not remotely aware. As such, our "sub" conscious mind contributes far more to our daily lives and total being than just the fraction of our selves constituting our conscious awareness. Rather than our conscious awareness being one-eighth of our total intelligence, it is more like a fraction of one percent. We are not fully in control of our lives nor can we be totally responsible for our actions unless and until we have a way of bringing our subconscious into conscious awareness when needed, a subject we will get into in the "how to" part of this book.

The possibility of accessing the subconscious mind explains how and why Yogis in India, by bringing their subconscious bodily functions into conscious awareness, can even stop and start their own heartbeats. Thank goodness that all our bodily functions have been relegated to our subconscious minds or we would be so busy growing our bodies, digesting our food, and staying healthy that we wouldn't have time to do anything else. When we become fully conscious, we can bring any part of our subconsciousness into conscious awareness when we need to.

As the storehouse from which almost all of our feelings, judgments, and intuition automatically appear, our subconscious has much more power over our daily activities and is more Godly than our conscious awareness. Our egos do not like to hear this. Egotism wants us to believe that our intellects are in control. It doesn't want to accept the fact that our subconscious Spirit is the bridge between our awareness and Omniscience. Therefore, we should take courage because we now have ways, through intuition, to tune into our superconscious or Divine Mind at will. We can now consciously access all that is in the subconscious.

SuperConscious Mind

*F*inally, there is the superconscious mind. Neither the *Psychological Dictionary* nor the *Webster's Dictionary* includes anything called the superconscious mind. Perhaps if they did, they would find themselves entangled in theology, because in verifying a total collective universal body of knowledge or truth, they would be defining God as the ocean in which our individual icebergs float. They may be right in assuming that no individual person has been able to fully access the totality of the superconscious mind, but they would be wrong in assuming that we cannot at times tap into that total consciousness as Jesus did. Perhaps that is what Paul meant when he said, "*We have the mind of Christ.*"[10]

It is as though, like computers, we have this superconscious, all-inclusive, transcendental intelligence stored in our selves, our hard drives, but we have to have the right software in place and know how to use it in order to access the information we desire. I believe that if we are fully conscious beings we can, through the software of meditation or prayer, go from our limited conscious mind into our subconscious minds, and by clearing the way at that level we can open ourselves to the superconscious mind of God.

Accepting the reality of our connection to superconsciousness is the major step we must take on the road to ascension. If we can fully accept our innate ability to listen to the superconscious mind, we do away with the superstition that we are helpless victims of circumstances, that there is a "will of God" apart from that that is within us. We can free ourselves from any outside influence over us whatsoever. We can realize that heaven is right at our fingertips. All we have to do is to open ourselves up to and let the superconscious flow through our different levels of consciousness into conscious awareness. We enter this world like murky ponds into which clear water begins to flow until the whole pond becomes transparent, at which time we are fully conscious.

Consciousness

*N*ow, to sum it up, I would like to explain the difference between what it means to be conscious and what I mean when I refer to one's consciousness. It is as difficult to define consciousness as it is to explain God. Consciousness is so all-inclusive that its meaning has to be understood experientially rather than intellectually. Instead of saying, "*In the beginning was the Word, and the Word was with God, and the Word was God*"[11] it would be more understandable if the Scripture had said, "In the beginning was Consciousness, and Consciousness was with God, and Consciousness was God."

We may become "conscious" but we are "consciousness." We are consciousness expressing ourselves in or as bodies. Our actions, our presence, our physical being, our total persona is our consciousness appearing in or as who we are. Consciousness is almost impossible to define because it includes all of our total "beingness." Our consciousness is our conscious awareness, our subconscious, and our potential super or divine consciousness all wrapped up in one. When we are fully conscious, we will realize we are our consciousness.

In proclaiming that the latter half of the twentieth century, was the time when the importance of consciousness became evident, Peter Russell, author of *The Global Brain Awakens*, said:

> *Science isn't getting anywhere in trying to understand or explain consciousness. I think the reason for this is that we are still stuck in a paradigm, which has eventually got to crash the paradigm that claims that the material reality that we observe is the fundamental reality. I think the new paradigm, which will emerge, isn't fully here yet. We are heading towards a very different point of view than we had in the past. It is not space, time, matter, and energy that are the fundamental reality; instead, consciousness is the fundamental reality, out of which space, time, matter, and energy emerge.[12]*

Lincoln Barnett in the *Universe and Dr. Einstein* confirms Russell's conclusions by adding, "Gradually philosophers and scientists arrived at the startling conclusion that...the whole objective universe of matter and energy, atoms and stars, does not exist except as a construction of consciousness...Einstein carried this train of logic to its ultimate limits by showing that even space and time are forms of intuition." It is indeed startling to accept that our consciousness—our intuition—is of the same construct that created the universe.

In the *Spectrum of Consciousness*, Ken Wilber authorized our personal quests with his uniquely modern twist of agreement. He wrote, "The only believable, the only scientifically reliable authorities today are those conscientious explorers who have experienced all the various levels of consciousness, including both that of being an ego and that of transcending the ego."[13]

The Scriptures I quoted at the beginning of this chapter were meant to sound encouraging. They imply that there are all kinds of fabulous realizations or states of consciousness that can now, through spiritual evolution, come into being which will lift us into heaven. We can take Jesus' words literally and realize that his consciousness is potentially our consciousness, and then the quality and substance of our lives can become the quality and substance of his. All is consciousness and all of us are at various levels of becoming " fully conscious."

The good news is that every one of us is consciousness; therefore, every one of us will eventually be fully conscious—fully Christed and fully reconciled.

Reconciliation

> *Therefore if any man be in Christ* (Christ consciousness), *he is a new creature: old things are passed away; behold, all things are become new. And all things are of God, who hath reconciled us to himself by Jesus Christ, and hath given to us the ministry of reconciliation; to wit, that God was in Christ, reconciling the world unto himself, not imputing their trespasses unto them; and hath committed unto us the word of reconciliation.*
>
> II Corinthians 5:17-19

> *For he is our peace, who hath made both one, and hath broken down the middle wall of partition... for to make in himself of twain one new man, so making peace; And that he might reconcile both unto God in one body...*
>
> Ephesians 2:14-16

> *First be reconciled to thy brother, and then come and offer thy gift.*   Matthew 5:24

*A*t age twenty-five, after my stint as a naval officer in the Second World War, I became addicted to the search for a meaningful God. I was making my living in the theater in New York, first performing in and then successfully producing Broadway plays, but the rest of my waking hours were spent in passionately reading everything I could find of a mystical nature. I would meditate long hours and run off to visit monasteries and spiritual masters between engagements.

Finally, when I was past thirty, a concerned friend told me, "Walter, you have your feet in two different worlds. You have come to the Y in the road and must now decide which way you are going or you will split yourself in half." In a flash, I saw that my friend was absolutely right and absolutely wrong. I was at the Y in the road, but it was an inverted Y. Instead of splitting apart, the two roads now had to join and become one.

After I had just experienced the double thread concept at the crater in Hawaii, I saw that society in general had been exclusively walking two either/or roads, either approaching life primarily objectively or primarily subjectively. I saw that now the two had to and could come together and become one road, perhaps a super highway. It became obvious that before I opened my mouth I had to walk my talk and personally reconcile the spirit and the flesh, cause and effect, the subjective and the objective, God and man.

(I just this second realized something—an inverted Y is the peace symbol. When the two roads come together and are reconciled, one becomes at peace with one's self and the world.)

Webster's Dictionary tells us that reconciliation comes from the Latin word "conciliare," which means to bring together. The dictionary defines the word as "to make friendly again, to compose a difference" and "to make consistent, compatible; to bring into harmony." If I had to choose a single word that would sum up the consciousness of the entire Christ message and its unique emphasis, it would have to be "reconciliation." Taken as a whole, what's new about the New Testament is its insistence on reconciliation, both in terms of objectively bringing together two or more people or things and, subjectively, the necessity of reconciling our man of earth selves with our man of God selves. Reconciliation replaces "*an eye for an eye and a tooth for a tooth*"[14] with "*that they may be one, even as we are one: I in them, and thou in me, that they may be made perfect in one.*"[15] When reconciled, I am you and you are me, and it's all God.

From beginning to the end, the Christian myth is about the reconciliation of spirit and flesh, of God becoming man, about cause and effect being one and the same. The whole purpose of the Christ message is to tell us that through reconciliation the illusion of duality or the isolation brought about by personal sense or ego ceases to exist as reality. Deepak Chopra often refers to it as getting over "the superstition of materiality."

Through reconciliation, we see everything simultaneously as both consciousness expressing itself in form and the form appearing as consciousness without any division between cause and effect. By stating that "... *all things are of God, who hath reconciled us to himself by Jesus Christ,*"[16] Paul finally came to the conclusion that reconciliation was the true substance of the Christ message. By adding "...*God was in Christ* (consciousness), *reconciling* (bringing together) *the world unto himself* (the infinite One), *not imputing their trespasses unto them; and hath committed unto us the word of reconciliation,*"[17] Paul showed that he finally saw that the way to oneness was not through informing others of their trespasses but rather through reconciling them with the spiritual truth of their being.

The same principle is expressed elsewhere in Scripture in two parts: "*God so loved the world, that he gave his only begotten Son, that whosoever believeth in him* (in what he taught) *should not perish, but have everlasting life.*" And the following verse is the other half: "*For God sent not his Son into the world to condemn the world; but that the world through him might be saved.*"[18] In other words, reconciliation is ultimately how the world will be saved. When you recognize the paradox inherent in reconciliation, you will have discovered the alchemist's secret that can change a life of dross to one of pure gold. Ordinarily, people have believed that to achieve the absolute duality has to be eliminated, but the truth of the matter is that union is found in diversity: To become whole, we must entertain and understand what appears as duality and reconcile it—not resist, exclude, or ignore it.

Jesus didn't give us two commandments as the way to reconcile God and man just to hear himself talk nor to play metaphysical games, nor in doing so did he compromise his absolute belief that God was the only power, the only presence, and the only reality. In other words, he was uncompromisingly subjective and yet he felt the need to love both the subjective (first commandment) and the objective (second commandment) and by doing so reconcile them into universal omnipresence. *Until we can look right out at the world and reconcile the human or material with the spiritual or subjective and see that they are one and the same, we will never know that it is all God.*

Oil and Water

*R*econciliation has failed in the past because it has been thought that to reconcile two things they had to become the same. For centuries mankind has made a futile mistake. They have tried to make human beings spiritual. It cannot and should not be done. Trying to spiritualize humanity is like trying to mix oil and water. You can stir them up, shake them vigorously to the point where they appear to have homogenized, but when you stop forcing them to mix, they settle down and become separate again. Paradoxically, when you stop trying to make either of them other than what they are, you love them for what they are, and in that they are reconciled. When it is realized that both oil and water come from the same source, reconciliation has taken place and we are able to see that it is all God.

Reconciliation is an internal matter. In a way, it has nothing to do with anyone else. It is something that takes place within ourselves. Each one of us has to bring our own lower or outer opinion of what has happened in line with the principles of our Higher or Inner consciousness. We must be objective about what has taken place while at the same time becoming free of judgment before we can find peace at the altar in the center of our own beings. Reconciliation may result in a physical act at a personal level, but, spiritually, reconciliation has to do with what takes place in our own souls. In order for us to become reconciled, we have to bring the spiritual identity of another person into perspective with that person's human conduct. If we get to the point where we are able to release another person from spiritual judgment, that person has been reconciled. When there is a cause for our anger and we can arrive at the place within ourselves where we are able to blame the ignorance that is using the other person, but not the person, we can reconcile the inner being of the person with their mistake. That is called *forgiveness.*

The way we forgive someone who has violated principle is to realize that the person was hypnotized by ignorance. It is then possible for us to love the person who is trapped in his or her ignorance without ignoring the ignorance. In that state of love we can come to the altar and pray the prayer of reconciliation even if we still hold the other person accountable. That is what happened to Jesus on the cross. When he said, *"Forgive them; for they know not what they do,"*[19] he didn't add, "to me," as is most ordinarily thought. He was saying, "Forgive them; for they know not what they do to themselves." He was reconciling their ignorance with the truth of their being.

In other words, to be reconciled may on occasion have something to do with an objective act, but spiritually it means for us to reconcile appearances with their inner reality. It has to do with our being able to be aware of ignorance without losing sight of the divinity of each other's souls. Ascension consciousness is the ultimate reconciliation. When that happens, we are all included in the one body of Christ consciousness, we transcend the intellect, and we become aware that it is all God.

Double Think

*R*econciliation can't really take place for us as human beings until another paradox is resolved—the incongruity of "double thinking." The idea of double thinking was first mentioned way back in the 1930s in Aldus Huxley's book, *Brave New World,* and later elaborated to a greater extent in George Orwell's *Animal Farm.* They proposed a world where we could and did equally think two different and often contradictory ways at the same time. We can't voice two things at the same time but until we manage to be consciously aware of the subjective nature and the objective nature of things simultaneously, we have a problem seeing the dualistic world all-inclusively. As long as we believe that we must constantly and only think beautiful subjective thoughts, we live in a state of denial that rejects rather than includes wholeness. Until we can look right at human conditions and simultaneously be aware of what we see and the fallacy of appearances, we divide rather than reconcile.

What I am saying is that because of where our thinking minds have now evolved, we can potentially double think and entertain several viewpoints at the same time without denigrating or diluting any of them. Because of our newly evolved capacity for simultaneous realization, we can observe the objective level without denying its subjective nature and see both its infinite oneness and its limited form without losing sight of either. It isn't a matter of our thinking 40 percent of one thing and 60 percent of another or of 50/50. We can be 100 percent aware of one aspect of something and at the same time we can we aware of 100% of the other side by holding one understanding suspended in consciousness while we intellectualize the other. Actually, we already do this, but when we begin to do it consciously, when we become conscious beings, we will be consistent and no longer involved in half-truths. By double thinking, we can reconcile appearances, and by closing the gap experience the only true absolute. The absolute, looked at through thought forms appears as phenomenon, but when freed of the superimposition of thought forms, God is all that is—absolute and complete.

The secret, again, is not either/or. We do not either think subjective thoughts that include, nor are we limited to objective thoughts that separate and exclude. Our thoughts are both eminent and transcendent at once. That does not mean that we either refuse to see where we are in the process of our individual evolution toward perfection, nor does it suggest that we must in any way surrender to limitation. By double thinking we can be aware of our need to grow and achieve a pure consciousness without, for a second, believing we are not already subjectively perfect beings. By double thinking we can be realistic about the degree of inflation we are experiencing, while simultaneously realizing that we are perfectly where we should be in the divine process without ignoring our need to work on ourselves.

As you can see, at this point I am itching to get beyond the "what's" to the "how to's," but before we build a house, or a state of consciousness, we have to have a blueprint. We need some knowledge of what the house is to look like and how it works as a living space. Ultimately that space is ascension consciousness.

The Christian myth did not reach its fulfillment until Jesus demonstrated ascension consciousness at the end of his ministry. It is a blueprint drawn by Jesus as the Christ to lead us to a new dimension, but because his vision was ahead of the collective evolution, a veil was placed over it. It takes time for either a child or an idea to grow into its maturity, and until it does, a veil hides it from understanding.   Because ascension consciousness is experiential, it is beyond intellectualization. We can experience flashes of it that we call our spiritual experiences, but we can only hint at it until we evolve into it as Jesus did at his finale. Nevertheless, by accepting that ascension consciousness is possible and is our ultimate aim, we come closer and set up the possibility for ourselves.

Ascension Consciousness
A Divine Gestalt

*B*efore we can lift the veil, we have to arrive at some kind of concept of what is behind the veil. We have spent so many centuries approaching life either objectively or subjectively, dealing with either cause or with effect, that lifting the veil is no easy matter. Behind the veil is a completely different reality, a reality we cannot imagine until we have experienced it.

When we experience ascension consciousness, we find that it is similar to a surprising experiment we discovered in our high school chemistry class. At that time we found that if we took ingredient "a" with its various components and mixed it with ingredient "b" and its different components, together they become ingredient "c" which had no resemblance whatsoever and nothing in common with either "a" or "b." What we ended up with followed "a" and "b," but was a totally different product. Similarly, by reconciling the subjective and the objective—cause and effect—we attain ascension consciousness, which is the fulfillment of Christ consciousness and is a totally different dimension than anything we can either think of or explain in our humanity.

Ascension consciousness is a kind of divine Gestalt where the whole is not only more than the parts, but when they come together they become different from the sum of the parts. Psychologically, according to *Webster's Dictionary*, a Gestalt is "any of the integrated structures or patterns that make up all experiences and have specific properties which can neither be derived from the elements of the whole nor be considered simply as the sum of these elements." That is what takes place when the Christ consciousness is finally attained, when the subjective and the objective are reconciled and become one and a totally new self comes into being. That new self is not a refinement of the old self but is a completely new self. That is what happens when one is truly born again. Because we are all microcosmic replicas of a macrocosmic process, an even more literally mind-blowing explanation of what spiritually happens to us when we attain ascension consciousness was explained by Stephen Hawking. He tells us that the universe is made up of matter and anti-matter, and that where and when matter and anti-matter make contact, they are both blown away in a flash of light to become something completely new.

Actually, arriving at ascension consciousness has been the goal of every religious path, but few have passed through the veil because we have been disciplined to believe that freedom and spiritual fulfillment can be achieved by intensification. We have thought that if we intensified our human effort, that if we tried harder, if we more intensely lived our beliefs and didn't fall short of the mark, which is to say that if we didn't sin, we could reach heaven. We have been aware that others have attained that consciousness, but we haven't discovered any clean-cut discernible pattern for how they got there. Above all, we have not wanted to hear that it is impossible to succeed through dedication and diligence. We know that somehow it is possible to break through to the Spirit and that there is some condition that introduces this transcendental experience, but we do not know what it is.

On this score, Jesus said something that caused many of his followers to turn back and follow him no more. After he had fed the multitude with loaves and fishes, they wanted *"to make him a king."*[20] So, frustrated at the realization that they were not really interested in the spiritual principles he was trying to show them but that they just wanted material bread, he escaped from them and crossed the lake. They soon chased after him. In exasperation Jesus admonished them saying, *"...Ye seek me, not because you saw the miracles* (saw the principles that brought forth the loaves), *but because ye did eat the loaves, and were filled."*[21]

To give Jesus' followers their credit, the Scripture does tell us that they did ask him to try once more to explain what he was about: *"Then said they unto him, What shall we do, that we might work the works of God?"*[22] In making another attempt, Jesus used an old pagan ritual as an example, but he meant it in a subjective or symbolic manner. That was when he said, *"Except ye eat of the flesh of the Son of man and drink of his blood..."*[23] Obviously he wasn't prescribing cannibalism; so subjectively he was saying that unless they filled themselves with his consciousness—that *"the Word"* is made flesh—and let the same spirit that ran through his veins flow through their being and their actions, that they could not enter ascension consciousness.

They still didn't get it; so out of frustration he gave them the truth—the truth that we are no more prepared to accept today than they were then. He said, *"Therefore said I unto you, that no man can come unto me* (unto Christ consciousness), *except it were given unto him of my Father* (by the divine process of creation)." The next verse says that then, *"From that time many of his disciples went back and walked with him no more."*[24] That is to say, that unless one's evolution prepares the way, unless one's consciousness has evolved to the point where it is ready to experience one's divine nature, there is nothing anyone can do by human effort to make it happen.

The paradox is, though we cannot experience illumination until our consciousness has evolved through having an appetite to study and to fill our minds with spiritual concepts, we can help evolution along. To leave no stone unturned in order to arrive at illumination is a prelude to the experience and a sign that Grace is working in our lives, whether we know it or not. The freeing thing about coming to the realization that illumination happens by Grace is that it lets our egos off the hook. We can enjoy putting effort into the search without fearing that we will miss the boat because we haven't figured out some heretofore undiscovered truth. We can realize that at this very moment we wouldn't be reading about ascension consciousness if we hadn't evolved to the point where we were being led to it.

Take heart, today it is possible to conceive of ascension consciousness even before one experiences it and at least have a feel for it. Though thinking about it won't give us the experience, by projecting the concept into consciousness where *"the Word"* becomes flesh and by coupling it with the power of imagination, we can somehow encourage its evolution and at least bring ourselves to the door.

That door opens a way to a conscious awareness that goes beyond having to think in terms of either/or, either subjective or objective, either spiritual or material, either divine or human. When the "and" is taken out of "cause and effect," what remains is a kind of subjective objectification. When we see forms and, through double thinking, are simultaneously aware that the forms are consciousness appearing, we can understand what our spiritual masters have meant when they showed us that they were aware of the material world and also said that it is spiritual—that it is all God.

There is no way that we can understand or conceive of what the masters have experienced until we can transcend believing in good and bad or what the Orientals call the pairs of opposites. Until we can conceive of a world beyond either good or evil, we have nothing to which we can compare ascension consciousness. A true Gestalt is a totally different life and unlike anything we have experienced in the past. We can look at the great saints that have broken through to this divine Gestalt and see beyond their surface actions and accomplishments. When we do, we find that they had all gone beyond differences. They were all in the world personally demonstrating admirable human traits, and yet they were all beyond judging others, all beyond being exclusive in their service to the world, all reconciling the Spirit and the flesh in a transcendent way, and all were full of light.

If we need role models, Jesus in the West and Buddha in the East are classic examples of those who embodied ascension consciousness. That is why we picture them with haloes around their heads and set them apart. Because they lived as they did, their lives have become models for the kind of persons we can become when we experience what is called God consciousness. Though we can only speculate about what it means to experience ascension consciousness, it is important that we put the concept and possibility in our mental computers and allow our subconscious minds to begin the process that will eventually evolve us into the experience. Before we know it, we may even have flashes of ascension awareness as what the *A Course in Miracles* calls the "Holy Instant," or Joel Goldsmith called the "Click."

Plato in his cave analogy said that we see shadows on the wall and think they are reality, but if we were to turn and look straight at the light, at the Holy of Holies, in our present collective state of consciousness, we would burn our eyes out. You might say that Jesus, being the Light, was a new kind of person who could look straight into ascension consciousness and in doing so brought on the crucifixion of the limitations of humanity and his ultimate spiritual transcendence into the full ascension. However, every time we have the most minute breakthrough in meditation or prayer, we are experiencing a degree of ascension awareness and that is enough to transform our lives to that degree. Just as a camera can expose a film in a thousandth of a second, when we experience ascension consciousness, we transcend obsolete concepts and are on our way to being born again into a new way of life, a totally new life, a life where it's all God.

Chapter 3

THE MYSTERIOUS WORD

But the hour cometh, and now is, when the true
worshippers shall worship the Father in spirit and
in truth: for the Father seeketh such to worship him.
God is a Spirit: and they that worship him must
worship him in spirit and in truth.

John 4:23-24

Under the guise of one word, humankind has shed more blood and also healed more illnesses, excused more hate and also bestowed more love, created more confusion and also solved more problems than any other word or combination of words. Every action, major or minor, in every walk of life for us has consciously or unconsciously been affected by our interpretation of and belief in this one word. It has a tremendous archetypal impact that has been conditioned by the energy with which countless souls have empowered it. Until the world's collective consciousness accepts a universal, all-inclusive understanding of what we mean by this word or its equivalent in other languages, the world will continue to tear itself apart. Obviously, that mystery-filled word is "God."

Part of me looks around and knows that it is impossible to find a definition of God or a purpose for the underlying process of life that both believer and nonbeliever can accept. It is both naïve and presumptive of me to even propose such a possibility. However, intuition tells me that we have no choice in the matter. We must begin to try to accept and become aware of an all-inclusive multi-dimensional concept of God that is simultaneously personal and impersonal, simultaneously imminent and transcendent, one that is accepted in both the East and the West.

To confound the problem, from the beginning to the end of our Judeo-Christian myth, we are told we should love God. Not only that but we should love God with our whole being. As human beings, we have every right to feel frustrated by this command. How can we love something we cannot know or understand with our minds? We may identify various qualities we associate with God, but a finite mind cannot encompass infinity; so how can we as finite beings love God? We can't. At least, we can't love God if loving means knowing what God is.

However, there is something we *can do*. We can sense that beyond our most profound concepts of God something exists that transcends anything we can know with our intellects, something that is beyond limitation, something that includes us in all that it is, something we can experience at the inner depths of our beingness. We cannot know what it is, but we can know "that" it is. We can love the fact that whatever God is, God is more profound and all-inclusive than anything we, or anyone else, can conceive of.

In fact, it is a blessing that we cannot know God with our intellect, otherwise our intellect would be greater than God. The way we love God is by a simple and pure acceptance that that something we instinctively feel deep within ourselves called God does exist. We cannot know it with our intellect, but we can experience it with our hearts. If the family of humankind can at least come to an agreement that although we can't completely define God, It does exist, we are halfway home Then we can aim at It and come closer to universally experiencing that Presence than ever before.

Until this chapter, I have been avoiding using the word God as much as possible because our beliefs are so personal and vital to our lives that few of us are comfortable having them tampered with, including those who call themselves "atheists." For that matter, there really aren't any atheists. There are those who do not ⸱ believe in a theistic concept of God, but we all believe that there is "something" that makes life possible. Anyone who will admit that there is a supreme process at work creating the seasons, getting the sun to rise in the morning, and that there is the existence of an incredible intelligence that can take a single cell and transform it into an unbelievably complex body believes in God. It's just a matter of semantics. "Atheists" most likely don't like the word "God," because they have difficulty accepting a finite word to properly describe infinity or they cannot believe that God is a personality made in the image of the human intellect. However, none of us would drive a car or fly in a plane if we didn't trust the process; *so call it what you will, that process is God.*

In dealing with people and with what they mean when they refer to God, there is one sure-fire way we can avoid judging others at those times when we do not agree with their concepts of God. The one common denominator that we must appreciate is that every person's concept of God, including our own, is the highest and most divine image of divinity that any of us can conceive of at that moment. Although other people's concepts may be a far cry from ours, we can honor their intent and realize that being infinite, God can be conceived of in countless, all significant, ways.

A Unity minister in Texas recently told me of an experience she had which changed her whole life. She was on a Caribbean island, and passing a tent revival where the people were joyously praising God, her first reaction was that the God they were calling on was a different one than hers. As she stood there listening and feeling the Spirit of Love that was pouring out of that tent, she was blown away by the realization that their way was just as important to them as hers was to her. Ever since, she has accepted and included everyone's concept of God.

The Nature of God and Error

*W*e may have to start from scratch and agree on the nature of God, and the nature of error, what God is and what God is not, in order to appreciate and accept the many ways and levels at which God is present. When I talk of the nature of error, I am referring to mistaken identity. Error is a lie claiming to be truth. It has no existence apart from that which we give it by believing in it. Ignorance is not truth. It is the absence of truth. Error or ignorance has no power over us apart from that which we give to it by believing in it. Therefore, whenever I talk about the nature of error, I am talking about something that exists only when we confuse it with the nature of truth or God. In order to arrive at a concept of God that we can universally accept, we have to agree on both the nature of the reality of God and the nature of the non-reality of error.

Fortunately, we have a model to emulate—Jesus. To him, *"righteous judgment"*[1] was an awareness of the nature of truth or God, and any belief in an existence or power apart from God was his definition of the nature of error or unrighteous judgment. By talking of God objectively as his Father one minute and subjectively as love the next minute, and by seeing God as greater than himself one minute and simultaneously as his own being the next, he was illustrating the multi-dimensional nature of God. Exploring the multi-dimensional nature of God is similar to polishing the facets of a diamond. It would be a lie to imply that any of the facets are the diamond. Yet, by contemplating as many of the facets as we can, we somehow encourage an experience of the diamond.

For the rest of this chapter, as an example I am offering a few of those facets. None are true—by themselves. But if we can touch on a few and then let them go, in the end we may come closer to an experience that transcends all concepts. Throughout the rest of this book I will be taking the liberty of capitalizing words that I feel signify divinity.

The Two Gods

*A*s far as we know, when humans first inhabited the earth they created Gods to answer every need. They had a sun God and a rain God because obviously the sun and rain were needed in order to grow food and for life to continue, and on and on to take care of every human condition. They also attributed human emotions and personality traits to their Gods. Gods could get angry, be jealous, or benevolent. In a way, that was a good thing; because by giving Gods human traits similar to their own, human beings were subconsciously seeing themselves as being made in the image of the Gods.

Eventually, the Judeo-Christian myth got its start when all the Gods were lumped together and were conceived of as one all-powerful God. Unfortunately, when that one God was turned into the theistic concept of a Supreme Being, humankind could no longer personally identify itself with something so all-inclusive and unlimited. Nevertheless, when God was thought of as omnipotence, the subjective nature of God also came into being. Originally, each of the words the Hebrews used for God (and there are many) carried a perhaps subtly different meaning, like individually different but similar facets of one diamond. But when the Bible was translated into what is now the English language, the ecclesiastical scholars lumped together all the different words representing divinity that were in the original Hebrew and called this sum total "God," whether they were speaking of God subjectively or objectively.

Jesus represented a line of Jewish mystics and mystery schools that integrated the subjective nature of God with an objective concept of God. He had no intent of destroying the Father God image, but rather of broadening it to include the transcendent subjective nature of God that could be experienced in all of us. That is why he would double think and talk of God in both ways. In making a case for the acceptance of Jewish mysticism and a subjective experience of God, Rabbi Cooper says:

*God is not what we think It is. God is not a thing,
a being, a noun. It does not exist, as existence is
defined, for It takes up no space and is not bound
by time. Jewish mystics often refer to It as Ein Sol,
which means Endlessness. Ein Sol should never be
conceptualized in any way. It should not be called
Creator, Almighty, Father, Mother, Infinite, the One,
Brahma, Buddha mind, Allah, Adonoy, Elohim, El,
or Shaddai; and It should never, never be called He.
It is none of these names, and It has no gender.[2]*

If we return to Scripture, we can see how these two
concepts of God—the objective one and the subjective one—
were conceived. The Bible itself starts with the words, "*In the
beginning God...said,*" and though it doesn't say to whom God
was speaking, the very fact that there is a "He" that speaks implies
that God is also personal and to be understood both subjectively
and objectively. God not only speaks but He must have eyes
because He sees as well. "*God said, Let there be light... And God
saw the light.*"[3] It is easy to see how the objective concept of God
as a God apart from man, a God greater than and different from
human beings, has been perpetuated for the past five thousand
years.

The most Gnostic or mystical Gospel, and perhaps the one
that closely resembles how Jesus himself thought of God, is the
Gospel of John. It opens with a more subjective or impersonal
definition of God than the other Gospels, "*In the beginning was
the Word* (the idea or consciousness), *and the Word was with
God and the Word was God.*"[4] By saying God was the Word, God
was impersonalized and identified subjectively as consciousness
rather than as a Supreme Being. Traditionally, "*the Word*" is
interpreted to mean Jesus himself, but it can be construed that it
was saying that the Christ consciousness was with God and was
God and was finally made flesh as Jesus, which is to say that cause
and effect were one.

I am trying to establish by repetition what Jesus meant by
asking us to incorporate the two commandments—one subjective,

one objective—in order to have a true non-duality. *When we can see that God is not either/or, not either a supreme being or a divine principle of life but both at the same time, we can experience a God that is immanently personal to us yet simultaneously transcendentally impersonal.*

Oriental teachings, which are by and large more subjective and impersonal in their approach, have a hard time with what we Westerners generally mean when we talk of God. When I was visiting Tibetan Lama Govinda at his ashram below the towering Himalayas, I inadvertently used the word God and he cautioned me saying, "Find another word. The word God is an Old Testament theistic concept of God, God as a father figure, a being outside of one's self." My answer was that I understood and used the word as an abbreviation for both the personal and the impersonal, for ultimate cause, consciousness, or Spirit as it appears at whatever level or dimension from which I am observing life. I said that I experienced God as both, both visible and invisible, both all and each, both subjective and objective, both as consciousness and as form.

I explained that I felt for me to avoid using the word altogether because so many think of God exclusively one way or the other, either objectively or subjectively, would be for me to leave it dishonored in my subconscious as a concession to ignorance. Precisely because I come from a Judeo-Christian culture and because I relate to the *King James* translation of the Bible that uses the word God, and because I believe it is my heritage to experience the ultimate through my inherited myth, I will continue to use the word God. However, when I say "God," I will envision it in the multiple ways I believe Jesus experienced it, and I will hope that there are others who also see beyond the limitations placed on the word into the all-inclusive nature of consciousness.

Whether we know it or not, as long as we are on earth we all to some degree feel things personally, and whenever we say "God" or refer to God as a "he," we are still conceiving of God personally. If we do not have a personal sense of God to fall back on when we are unable to receive help and comfort from an impersonal subjective sense of God, we are up the creek without a paddle. In reverse, if we are unable to identify with the subjective, impersonal nature of God as love, compassion, peace, or joy, we will have difficulty in finding those qualities in ourselves, and a personal experience of God becomes a remote possibility. All of us benefit from having an appreciation of each other's approaches because at one time or another each of us will be left without hope when our usual belief system shuts down on us for a time.

Panentheism

Whereas we in the West have a predominantly theistic concept of God, a God that is transcendent and apart from us, the religions of the Orient, particularly Zen Buddhism, are much more pantheistic. That is to say, they see God as immanent—in things, in everything for that matter. They see God in nature, in a bird, in a tree, in the sunset. Their problem, if there is one, is that pure pantheism tends to limit God to what you can see and touch.

Though I find that dictionaries vary greatly in their definition of the word, "pantheism," *Webster's New Twentieth Century Dictionary* says that pantheism is "the doctrine or belief that God is not a personality, but that all laws, forces, manifestations, etc. of the self-existing universe are God; the belief that God is in everything and everything is in God." The problem with the purely pantheistic point of view is that it implies that God is no more than the sum of things.

The purely theistic concept of God falls short because it tends to make God other than what is present in the world. A theistic God by its very nature is always transcendent and apart. Up until now, and that includes some modern pantheistic new age and metaphysical approaches, God has been thought of as being either eminent or transcendent. Now we can at last experience a "panentheistic" concept of God.

In the fifteenth century, Eckhart arrived at what he called the panentheistic God. He saw God as an integration of the subjective and objective, simultaneously immanent and transcendent, both personal and impersonal. Paul must have at some time seen God panentheistically in order for him to say "*For of him, and through him, and to him, are all things...*"[53] What statement could be more panentheistic, more simultaneously objective and subjective, one visioning God as greater than, and at the same time the same as, than Jesus' words, "*That they all may be one: as thou, Father, art in me, and I in thee, that they also may be one in us; that the world may believe that thou hast sent me. And the glory which thou gavest me I have given them; that they may be one even as we are one: I in them, and thou in me, that they may be made perfect in one;...*"[6] His consciousness of God was so far ahead of human kind's collective evolution at that time, that no wonder they crucified him!

The Chameleon God

*E*very concept of God that appears in every one of the great religions of the world is included in or at least hinted at in the Judeo-Christian myth. It doesn't take a brilliant scholar to show that somewhere in the Hindu Vedas and Buddhist Sutras appear what we may have thought are exclusively Christian concepts. Each of the world's major religions has different ways of expressing these identical truths. Most often, the differences seem contradictory only because one teaching places a far greater emphasis on one aspect of God than the other does. If we can work through our past conditioning and look beyond the objective appearances to what those appearances symbolize, we can at least find a basis of agreement that frees us to love and understand what we all have in common, as well as what is unique in each.

For instance, the Hindus, who being Oriental, tend to view life symbolically rather than literally, symbolize God's infinity by picturing a figure that is grotesque and repulsive to Western eyes—Mother Kali. She not only stands for the Creative Source, the Mother of All That Is, but she is depicted by what is to us a frightening figure with all kinds of arms sticking out from her body, each holding the material symbols of all the good and bad things we encounter in life. She represents all that is simultaneously divine and human, all the good traits as well as the bad ones that are included in human and divine nature. In our Western theistic religion, where God is a kind of absolute inhuman perfection that is materially inconceivable, it is impossible for us to relate Kali's all-inclusive consciousness to our God.

It may be difficult for those of us in the West who are conditioned to think of God as a father figure, but to be inclusive we must double think. We must begin to see our God as a kind of chameleon God, a God that takes on a different appearance at every level or dimension at which we exist, one that takes on the color of each of those levels as we contemplate them. Only in this way can we reconcile duality and see that God is not only truly omnipotent but that God is all.

Gertrude Stein achieved fame saying, "A rose is a rose is a rose," as though everyone's concept of roses or God was similar, but as Shakespeare said, "A rose by any other name would smell as sweet." If so, the words, God, Brahma, Allah, or Buddha-mind may be different names for the same genesis of flower. Roses may fundamentally all smell the same, but there are thousands of varieties of roses with countless different colors. To some, a dozen red roses means romance; to others who have been hurt by love affairs, the first thing they think of when they hear of roses are the thorns beneath the beauty. To many, God is a punishing authority figure; to others God is too pure to behold iniquity. All viewpoints can be explained without any contradicting the other if our thinking includes both the objective and subjective viewpoints.

If we take the words of the Bible at face value as factual truth, we see only one face of God. However, if we read our Scripture carefully, we will discover a God in Genesis 1 who creates out of

Spirit and says that everything is good including man and woman who are made in His image. In the second chapter of Genesis, however, a God with a different face appears—the Lord God. This God doesn't create out of Spirit but out of material effects. His approach is objective. He creates Adam out of dirt and Eve from a rib. Instead of conceiving of them made in the image of spiritual perfection and two aspects of one being, this Lord God misleads Adam and Eve. Then they are viciously tricked out of their freedom and wholeness by being told not to eat of the Tree of Good and Evil. This God does that because he knows that if they do eat of it, they would then become God and go beyond both good and evil into ascension consciousness. Nevertheless, the God of Genesis 1 and the God of Genesis 2 are not contradictory. The first is the subjective or spiritual way of looking at God; the second is the objective or psychological interpretation of how God works. It takes all kinds of concepts of God to make up the One God or to see God as a chameleon who changes according to what concept is appropriate at the moment. To double think is the only way one finally sees that it is all God.

When we are tricked into thinking that every reference in the Bible is to the One true God, the loving God, we cannot help but be confused when God slaughters whole nations or will punish or condemn us when we are naughty. However, if we see God subjectively as the one creative source or power behind all of life, we end up with a Kali-type God. That is a God who is always appearing as whatever there is in us that is necessary for our evolution, though it appears to be pleasant and loving at one moment, or hurtful and unpleasant at the next.

I say that God is a chameleon God because when we want God to be handed to us as a complete package all tied together with a pretty ribbon, we miss the exciting blessing of eternal discovery and eternal growth. *We are ready for ascension when we become aware that every experience we have in life is for the purpose of birthing our souls. When we include all the faces of God and no longer see God or ourselves as either good or evil, we enter the Kingdom.*

The most important thing in life that we can do in order to enter the Kingdom is *to trust the process*, which is to say to trust our highest comprehension of God, and allow ourselves to embrace an all-inclusive awareness of God. In doing so, we will see how God expresses Itself differently at different dimensions.

The Metaphysical God

*M*ost of us have come from traditionally religious homes and are familiar with the generally accepted objective concept of God that is preached in most churches. Because the Gnostic or predominantly mystical concept of God has just re-surfaced in the last century, I believe that it is necessary at this point for me to spend more time explaining the metaphysical approach than the traditional one. One perhaps oversimplified but effective way often used by metaphysical groups to explain the impersonal nature of God to beginners is to equate the nature of mathematics with the nature of God. They state that mathematics is impersonal. It just is. If we mistakenly believe that two times two is five, we end up going broke. Mathematics didn't punish us. We punished ourselves by violating the truth of mathematics. Mathematics doesn't know anything about it one way or the other. Therefore, mathematics doesn't punish anyone any more than God does. We do it to ourselves.

Mathematics is indeed a universal and omnipotent power in that if we apply mathematics truthfully we can triumph over limitation, build skyscrapers, and split the atom. But, being impersonal, mathematics doesn't know who or when we are in violation of the principles of mathematics. Praying to mathematics or lighting a candle to it in order to influence mathematics or to get mathematics to correct an error would be an absurd waste of time. It would be as ridiculous to believe we had to either please or fear mathematics.

However, if one has faith that mathematics exists as a prime mover or first cause and if one's heartfelt desire is to come in line with the principles of mathematics, one will be blessed with harmony and success. Mathematics doesn't reward people as a parent rewards a child, but because the truth of mathematics does exist, those who are in line with it are rewarded. They are not rewarded because they have faith in mathematics as though it were some concept or thing to have faith in, but because they came subjectively in line with its truth of being. You might say that they became mathematical. Mathematics is the prime mover, but because it expresses itself at many levels, it cannot be pinpointed in any finite way, and yet being the prime mover or first cause, it is felt at the core of each mathematical expression. In this way, mathematics does not make things. It is what makes things make themselves.

To hear people say, "It was God's will," when they find out someone has died is like their saying, "It's mathematics' will," when their books do not balance. *To blame our failures on God's will reveals a refusal to take responsibility for our own lives.*

Another analogy that is often used to explain one's personal relationship to God in an impersonal way is to equate God with the ocean. The ocean is universal and all-inclusive. There is nothing in the ocean that is apart from the ocean. Waves, like angels, are individual expressions of the ocean that return to the source. We, as individuals, are like drops of water in the ocean. Each drop is less than the ocean, but each drop, though unique, has the entire ocean within it. We have no life of our own apart from the ocean and the ocean has no substance apart from the drops that make it up. You might be able to put a drop of water under a microscope and analyze it, but the only way you can conceive of the ocean is to experience it.

Metaphysics also preaches that God is not a power over evil as though evil were an opposing power. God is omnipotence, the *only* power. Objectively it appears to us as though it is a power over evil, but subjectively to believe that God overcomes evil is the same as believing that light gets rid of the dark. Neither light nor dark can exist as concepts without the other. Evil is the dark side of the light just as ignorance is the dark side of the truth. When the light shines, the darkness no longer appears. In the presence of light, there is no apparent darkness. No matter how powerful the dark seems, it has no power to stop the light that comes from either a searchlight or a tiny candle. If you believe that God is a power over evil, you not only create the duality of good and evil, but you place yourself under the power of evil by accepting it as a power apart from God's omnipotence. Evil, like beauty, is in the eye of the beholder. When you behold the truth of God, error disappears, and you become aware that it is all God.

The same principle applies when we think of God subjectively as love. It isn't that love overcomes hate, it is just that in the presence of love hate no longer exists. If you think of how love appears objectively, love is a force that overcomes hate, but resistance has no place in subjective matters. That is what Jesus meant when he said to resist not evil but rather to replace it subjectively with the Spirit of Love and then evil would cease to exist. Subjective concepts, such as love, peace, joy, or divine presence, just are, and at that level there is no such thing as resistance.

By the same token, when we call on God to give us something, it reveals that we are thinking of God objectively rather than subjectively. God has nothing to give because God is already being all that there is. God doesn't give us peace. God is the peace. God doesn't give us supply. God is the supply. There is no lack of supply in the world. The sea has more fish in it than we can ever consume. The jungles produce more fruit than we can eat. The problem isn't in lack of abundance but in a lack of our ability to avail ourselves of this abundance we call God. Subjectively, have God, and you have peace, supply, joy, and all the heavenly riches.

God does not hide Itself so that we will have to look for It. We hide ourselves from It by ignorance, by ignoring Its omnipresence. God is not a withholding God, but neither is It a giving God. God is Love and It neither rewards nor punishes. Sin is punished by the sin. God doesn't do it. If you touch a hot stove, you will get burned, but don't blame the stove, blame the ignorance. Teilhard de Chardin put it beautifully when he said, "God, I am quite certain, does not hide himself so that we shall have to look for him any more than he allows us to suffer in order to increase our merit. On the contrary, reaching out to the creation which is making its way up to him, he works with all his strength to beautify and illuminate it."[7]

If God waited for us to light the right candles, say the correct prayers, to discover the right method of meditating, or for us to be deserving, It would be a cruel God. If It condemned whole segments of the world's population because they didn't know of or offer themselves to a particular avatar, It would be a monster. No. God is forever being life, being love, and being infinite intelligence. *"God is light, and in him is no darkness at all."*[8]

We are one with God as the wave is one with the ocean; therefore, we can never be apart from God; we can never be lost; we can never be alone. Wherever we are, God is. *God is our individual being. Our oneness with God is our oneness with all spiritual being.* Every blessing is an expression of God's presence in or as our lives. The sun that shines on us, the rain that brings on life, the stars in the sky, the intelligence of the universe, the source of all that is, is God. All of this is God's gift to us. His Grace is our sufficiency in all things. The divine Love and Wisdom that provides for our needs is God being itself. God is our consciousness by which we co-create with life.

God is appearing as Its own being, as your being and my being, as glory, as harmony, as joy, as understanding. God is the strength that allows us to mount up as the eagle, and then his infinite understanding becomes our understanding. His infinite love becomes our love. God's blessings flow into his own self as the Son, our presence on earth. As Sons of God we are receiving the blessings of our own God consciousness. In union with God is our peace, joy, power, dominion, and every blessing.

There is no God to love and there is no God to do anything apart from what you do for your fellow man. You are only serving God when you serve your fellow man. There is no God apart from man because God has manifest himself as man on earth, God incarnated as us. *There is only one infinite being, one person, since God is One and God is infinite. There is only one life appearing infinitely.* When we realize that God is One, we never fear because we, too, are that One. There is an invisible thread tying us together. That thread is the Christ consciousness that God is. God is within us because God is our consciousness and we need not look to anything outside of ourselves for God except to see the God in and as all that is.

Omnipresence, Omniscience, Omnipotence

This brings us to three words to contemplate—three words I have personally found to be the most comprehensive way for me to subjectively experience the impersonal and universal nature of God—Omnipresence, Omniscience, and Omnipotence. The most common mistake that a well-meaning spiritual student will make in trying to think of God subjectively is to refer to God as being omnipresent, omniscient, or omnipotent. By the addition of the "t" at the end of those words, God is objectified and made into something apart from ourselves. There has to be a thing or a being in order for it to be omnipresent, omniscient, or omnipotent. Take away the "t" and add a "ce" and the whole meaning changes. God is Omnipresence. God is Omnipotence. God is Omniscience itself. The words become plural, infinite, all-inclusive, and impersonal.

Omniscience exists, but the minute one thinks of God as being intelligent or all knowing, one has objectified God as something outside of one's own self, some thing that is intelligent and all knowing, a supreme being. For God to be intelligent there would have to be duality—God and someone or something for God to be intelligent about. On the other hand, an infinite intelligence does exist and that all-inclusive intelligence is God.

Omnipresence is "everywhereness." That means there is no place God is not present because "beingness" is everywhere being. If Omnipresence is one's concept of God, then to pray for God to be somewhere where God is not already being would be a denial of God. When you think of God as Omnipresence, everywhereness, then you no longer have to call on God to come to you because you realize that God is already where you are.

As for God being Omnipotence, the moment we as human beings think of power we are once more thinking objectively because we are thinking of power as something that is a power over some other thing, and that means there is some other power for God to be over. When a sense of good and evil enters our thinking, the idea of Omnipotence insults our intelligence. Only when we think of God as first cause from which everything else has evolved can we begin to understand God as a single energy or cause. If you want to conceive of God as Omnipotence, think for a moment of Omnipotence in terms of energy, just unconditioned energy. Energy is everywhere in all things. Scientists tell us that everything is made up of atoms, which are bundles of energy. Even thinking is an expression of energy. Undefined energy just is. It can be expressed in infinite ways. This unconditioned energy is not a power over anything and yet it is the cause of everything. By realizing that this prime cause, this one and only source of life and action, is God, then you can surrender your self to this first cause and presence. Our trust in Omnipotence makes it possible for all of us to believe that eventually there is nothing to keep us from experiencing all that God is, and thus be liberated from believing that we are finite and excluded from anything we wish to experience.

For the first time in history we do not have to speculate about our own oneness with God in terms of such an abstract concept as Omnipresence, Omniscience, and Omnipotence. We no longer have to wrestle with the idea of how we as finite bodies can be all of these three words. Science has made it possible for us to personalize them. As for Omnipresence, our bodies can be sitting in our breakfast room watching television and simultaneously be in the snow atop mount Everest or watching a tiger in the jungles of Africa, or singing along with the choirs of the world at the opening of the Olympics. In terms of Omniscience, we can punch up our computers, tune into the internet, and have access to every bit of knowledge that has ever been recorded. And, having discovered the power of consciousness, we realize our potential oneness with Omnipotence.

By talking about God in such an abstract way, I am not eliminating personal feelings for God. When we feel God's omnipotence in or as our lives, a personal feeling for God becomes understandable. When we feel God's omnipresence during a walk in the woods, God is very personal. When we receive inner guidance, we are tuned into Omniscience. Through these three words for God we can simultaneously feel our oneness with God personally and be aware of God impersonally as our own infinity.

The Ultimate God

Now the Lord is that Spirit: and where the Spirit of the Lord is, there is liberty.

II Corinthians 3:17

But as it is written, Eye hath not seen, nor ear heard, neither have entered into the heart of man, the things which God hath prepared for them that love him. But God hath revealed them unto us by his Spirit: for the Spirit searcheth all things, yea, the deep things of God. For what man knoweth the things of a man, save the spirit of man which is in him? even so the things of God knoweth no man (with his mind), *but the Spirit of God. Now we have received, not the spirit of the world, but the spirit which is of God; that we might know the things that are freely given to us of God. Which things also we speak not in the words which man's wisdom teacheth, but which the Holy Ghost teacheth; comparing spiritual things with spiritual. But the natural man receiveth not the things of the Spirit of God: for they are foolishness unto him: neither can he know them, because they are spiritually discerned. But he that is spiritual judgeth all things, yet he himself is judged of no man.*

I Corinthians 2:9-12

...ye are not in the flesh but in the Spirit, if so be that the Spirit of God dwell in you. Now if any man have not the Spirit of Christ, he is none of his. And if Christ be in you...the Spirit is life because of righteousness. But if the Spirit of him that raised up Jesus from the dead dwell in you, he that raised up Christ from the dead shall also quicken your mortal bodies by his Spirit that dwelleth in you.

Romans 8:9-11

...the hour cometh, and now is, when the true worshippers shall worship the Father in spirit and in truth: for the Father seeketh such to worship him. God is a Spirit: and they that worship him must worship him in spirit and in truth.

John 4:23-24

It is the spirit that quickeneth; the words that I speak unto you, they are spirit, and they are life.

John 6:63

...I will pray the Father, and he shall give you another Comforter, that he may abide with you for ever; Even the Spirit of truth; whom the world cannot receive, because it seeth him not, neither knoweth him: but ye know him for he dwelleth with you, and shall be in you.

John 14:16-17

Howbeit when he, the Spirit of truth, is come, he will guide you into all truth: for he shall not speak of himself; but whatsoever he shall hear, that shall he speak, and he will shew you things to come.

John 16:13

$\mathcal{I}$n quoting the preceding Scriptures, I have been trying to sneak up on the one single word that is the essence of God consciousness—Spirit. My problem is that this word represents a different sense than any of the senses most people live by. Just as you cannot fully explain color to a blind person who has never seen in terms of how color feels, smells, or sounds, spiritual sense can only be experienced on its own terms. God is literally Spirit. Perhaps it would be more accurate to say, "Spirit is God," because, as the Scriptures quoted at the beginning of this section state, Spirit defines the quality of our lives

The main reason it is so difficult to define Spirit is because the definition is so simple. In fact, the spiritual life is so simple that it can be put into a few words and, if understood, we no longer need to go to church or read any more books, this one included. It is this: *When the Spirit in which you do something is more important to you than the results you wish to achieve, you are spiritual. When the results are more important to you than how you go about getting them, you are material.* It is that simple.

Every action carries a quality of Spirit: if of love it is Godly, if of self-seeking it is the anti-Christ, anti-love. It sounds simple, but few choose to follow Spirit consistently because it leaves us without any place to hide. There is nothing outside of us that justifies the Spirit we project. We can't blame our partner, the government, or any other circumstance. At any moment we can put logic and its justifications aside and choose the quality of Spirit we wish to express. We can look at everything around us and view it in terms of the quality of Spirit that is being expressed.

For instance, one Sunday morning I turned on my TV set and listened to two ministers who speak to countless hundreds of thousands around the world every Sunday giving sermons back to back. The funny thing is that they were both using the same Scripture, but the first minister was using it in a way that was full of hate, judgment, and guilt-making innuendoes. The second minister, though substantiating his comments with the same Scripture, was loving, positive, encouraging, and not judgmental.

In other words, the first minister was expressing the spirit of hate, the other of Love.

The world will never find peace and harmony, despite all our treaties and negotiations, until the Spirit of Love permeates the proceedings and transcends our differences, until how we relate to each other is more important than desired results. But, now, as Jesus said to the woman at the well, "...*the hour cometh, and now is, when the true worshippers shall worship the Father in spirit and in truth: for the father seeketh such to worship him. God is a Spirit, and they that worship him must worship him in spirit and in truth.*"[9] The only way to worship the Spirit is to be in the Spirit. Jesus' words about God as Spirit were not recorded for many years after he left the earth plane; so I can't help but wonder if he was accurately quoted when he said "*God is a Spirit*,"[10] or if he actually said, "God is Spirit," "a" would be an objective interpretation, but beholding God "as" Spirit is subjective.

We are aware of God's presence when and where the Spirit that is the essence of God is present. It is often quoted that God is Love. If that is so, then the reverse is also true; the Spirit of Love *is* God, and whenever that Spirit is present God is present. An unknown God off in the heavens is hard to call upon at those times when one needs God, but the Spirit, like a light switch, is always right at hand ready to be switched on, nearer than hands and feet, closer than breathing. What else can be closer than breathing and within us than Spirit? All we have to do is, as the poet Browning said, "Open out a way for the imprisoned splendor to escape." Spirit is energy, the only energy. When we turn it on, our Spirit energizes our lives.

Tricky Spirit

*N*ow it gets tricky. As long as we judge life in terms of good and bad, we have to perform some pretty fancy mental footwork when we try to make what we see with our eyes conform to a belief that God or Spirit is always loving Omnipotence, the only power. God or Spirit is indeed the only power, because Spirit is the only cause, but just as the dark only exists in the absence of light, Spirit can appear to be destructive or creative depending on how we judge appearances. In order to understand God as the Spirit of Love, we have to transcend time and space in which the illusion of separation takes place. We have to believe that there is a Divine plan at work that is beyond human intellectual understanding. No matter how appearances seem to be, Love is the only Spirit or Presence.

This again is where double thinking is required. It is insulting to our intellect to see man's inhumanity to man or the unequal circumstances many are born into and say there is no evil power. At the level of appearances, evil does exist and needs to be dealt with or defeated. However, when the nature of error is realized as a no-thing-ness claiming to be a power, as ignorance imposing itself on the process, we can simultaneously realize there is another level at which God, or Spirit, is the first and only cause. When that level is experienced, the hypnotism of duality is broken and appearances appear to be healed in seemingly miraculous ways; or by inner guidance we are shown how to turn on the light and transform appearances.

Personally, I remember the exact moment when this metaphysical or mystical truth broke into my consciousness. I had been studying with the mystic, Joel Goldsmith, for some years when one day I finally confronted him. I said, "Joel, if you tell me that sin, sickness, poverty, and such are not powers at some spiritual level, all right, but to me as a human being they are powers." He answered, "Precisely, and if you want to stay a human being under those laws, help yourself, but you don't have to." At that moment I saw that it was up to me. If I allow my spirit to be negative and destructive, that is the law I am creating for myself, but it doesn't have to be. I do not have to be a victim of either ignorance or the spirit of negativity. I can wake up. It is my choice.

The difference between the Spirit of Love and of error was clearly stated by St. John:

Beloved, believe not every spirit, but try the spirits
whether they are of God: because many false
prophets are gone out into the world. Hereby know
ye the Spirit (written in the Bible with a capital S)
of God: Every spirit that confesseth that Jesus Christ
(cause appearing as effect) *is come in the flesh is of*
God: and every spirit (written with a small s) *that*
confesseth not that Jesus Christ is come in the flesh
(that human beings can be Spiritual) *is not of God:*
and this is that spirit of antichrist (that rejects the
anointing), *whereof ye have heard that it should*
come; and even now already is in the world… We
are of God: he that knoweth God (knoweth the
Spirit) *heareth us; he that is not of God* (cannot
love) *heareth not us. Hereby know we the spirit of*
truth, and the spirit of error. Beloved, let us love one
another: for love is of God and every one that loveth
is born of God; and knoweth God. He that loveth
not knoweth not God: for God is love."[11]

How much clearer can it be said? In that Scripture, John
said that knowing the Spirit of Love alone is not enough. He
introduced the nature of error and said that we must also know
the spirit of error in order to speak the language of Spirit.

The Language of Spirit

*T*here is another language besides the language that uses
words. It is the language of Spirit—God's language. This
language is not intellectual. Only those who have recognized
Spirit can hear this language. Only those who can take their
eyes off the material or objective world for a moment and feel or
listen to the Spirit that is present in appearances can consciously
understand with their Spirit. Saints are those who listen to the
language of Spirit and speak it fluently by their love. In Revelation,

John says, *"I was in the Spirit on the Lord's day, and heard behind me a great voice."*[12] In other words, when the Spirit was on John, it spoke to him in powerful ways that he could hear.

In Revelation it says, *"...the Spirit saith to the churches,"*[13] implying that the Spirit speaks to all the different levels of consciousness we entertain. In another place it says *"...a door was opened in heaven* (higher consciousness): *and the first voice ...said, 'come up hither, and I will shew thee things which must be hereafter. And immediately I was in the spirit..."*[14] A door in consciousness was opened and the language of Spirit told John to come up into the Spirit of Love and be shown what the results would be, and immediately he was in the Spirit.

In reverse, we are shown what happens when we try to cheat on Spirit. *"Be not deceived; God* (Spirit) *is not mocked: for whatsoever a man soweth* (in Spirit), that *shall he also reap. For he that soweth to his flesh* (in a carnal spirit) *shall of the flesh reap corruption; but he that swoeth to the Spirit* (again, written in the Scripture with a capital S) *shall of the Spirit* (Spirit of Love) *reap life everlasting."*[15]

The action of Spirit is automatic, just as 2x2 is automatic. Violate the spirit of mathematics by saying that 2x2 is 5 and you will reap dishonest results. Again, Spirit isn't punishing you. You have punished yourself by placing yourself under the influence of a negative spirit. Innocent or not, you punish yourself. God doesn't do it. You do. God, Spirit, is not mocked. Whatever spirit you project will mold your life. You do it to and for yourself.

We have all read how Moses put a veil on the truth, but until now we haven't understood what that veil was, even though the Scripture says it in black and white:

> *Their minds were blinded: for until this day remaineth the same vail untaken away in the reading of the old testament; which vail is done away in Christ,* (when spirit is anointed). *Nevertheless when it shall turn to the Lord, the vail shall be taken away. Now the Lord is that Spirit: and where the Spirit of the Lord is, there is liberty. But we all,*

with open face beholding as in a glass (a mirror)
the glory of the Lord, are changed into the same
image from glory to glory, even as by the Spirit of
the Lord.[16]

When we learn the secret that everything is Spirit and that
we can live in the Spirit of Love and speak the language of Love,
the veil is removed and we see God, but not before. Still to this
day most people live primarily objectively by the Old Testament,
but the message of the Christ tells us we can live in a spiritual
universe, one He referred to as *"My Kingdom."*[17] We can interpret
the material scene in terms of what it spiritually symbolizes in the
language of Spirit, and when we do, *"My Kingdom"* is revealed.

To reinforce this truth, once more read I Corinthians 2:11:
For what man knoweth the things of a man, save
the spirit of man which is in him? even so the
things of God knoweth no man, but the Spirit of
God. Now we have received, not the spirit of the
world but the spirit which is of God; that we might
know the things that are freely given to us of God
(of Spirit). *Which things also we speak, not in the*
words which man's wisdom teacheth, but which the
Holy Ghost teacheth; comparing spiritual things
with spiritual.

Without our having to condemn our humanity as so many do
when they misinterpret this passage, in the context of Spirit we
can understand the next verse, I Corinthians 2:14:
But the natural man (the one who hasn't learned
to listen to the language of Spirit) *receiveth not*
the things of the Spirit of God (of love): *for they are*
foolishness unto him: neither can he know them,
because they are spiritually discerned (understood
in the language of Spirit). *But he that is spiritual,*
(who listens to Spirit) *judgeth all things* (according
to Spirit,) *yet he himself is judged of no man*

(because man who doesn't understand Spirit has no way to spiritually judge). *For who hath known the mind of the Lord* (of Spirit), *that he may instruct him? But we have the mind of Christ"* (the mind that hears in the language of Spirit).

John says it all in a few words, *"...when he, the Spirit of truth, is come, he* (Spirit) *will guide you into all truth,"*[18] and *"But the hour cometh, and now is, when the true worshippers shall worship the Father in spirit and in truth...God is a Spirit: and they that worship him must worship him in spirit and in truth."*[19]

The Spiritual Universe

*W*hat would you think if I were to tell you that right now you already live in a Spiritual universe? It is true. You do, but not in the way we ordinarily conceive it to be. No wonder we can't make that belief effective in our lives. We look at the material universe, the objective viewpoint, and try to convince ourselves that it is Spiritual. When we think of the universe, we naturally think of all that makes up the world and planets in the universe. There's nothing wrong in that except that such thoughts are half-truths, not multi-dimensional. Something is present. Things do exist, but they are not what we think they are when we believe that their substance is material. From a material point of view, the universe is not spiritual. When we begin to automatically become aware that everything we see symbolizes the consciousness or Spirit that created it, that maintains and sustains it, we take the first step towards the realization that we live in a Spiritual universe. Things exist as formed Spirit. They have no existence apart from that Spirit. Understanding is a two-way street. *We can see a form and from that we can become aware of the Spirit that it represents or we can be aware of a quality of Spirit and know what form will result from that Spirit.* The quality of the symbol is the quality of Spirit that it represents and vice versa. Appearances are representative of their cause. In reality, all true cause is Spiritual; so in reality the whole universe having been created out of Spirit is Spiritual.

Now, that is fine as far as it goes, but it doesn't help us to live our lives unless we are able to divorce ourselves from the belief in good and bad. You see, Spirit just is. It is the substance of all form. By the same token, Spirit is God and God is the only power; so all appearances are God appearing, but as long as we judge appearances as either good or bad, we have missed the point and we are contradicting our belief system. Spirit just is. God just is. Consciousness just is. The universe is a reflection of Spirit—both what we believe to be good and what we believe to be bad. By its nature, everything is consciousness or Spirit formed. God is consciousness, and when we come to that awareness we begin to take control of the universe, because we begin to realize that we create our universe out of the quality of Spirit we entertain in our consciousness.

If the universe were material, we would forfeit dominion because as physical beings we would be limited. However, if we realize that because we are one with a Spiritual universe, we have the power of Spirit within and we can direct that Spirit to manifest in whatever way we wish, unrestricted by physical limitation. Just as we can direct our hand to pick up an object, we can direct our Spirit to form appearances in the image of whatever quality of Spirit we choose to express. The paradox is that as long as we look through the lens of good and bad, we cannot always express the Spirit of Love because Spirit is unconditional and the belief in good and bad places conditions on it. Yet if we are aware of the Spirit of Love, of fulfillment, of the laws of completion and attraction, by our expressing this Spirit the forms we create conform to it—all because we live in a Spiritual universe that is not limited by appearances.

"My Kingdom", the Kingdom of Spirit, is very real, very tangible, and very much right here, right now. We have but to step out of the thinking mind into the walk of Spirit where every step we take is taken in the awareness of the spiritual implications of our moves, of that belief, of that approach, of that God. It has

nothing whatsoever to do with being a good or a bad person. It has nothing to do with being moral or ethical. In fact, thinking in terms of law rather than Spirit is what has kept us from seeing that we are in a Spiritual universe right now.

This takes us to the final words of Mary Baker Eddy's Scientific Statement of Being, "*Spirit is God and man is His image and likeness. Therefore man is not material; he is spiritual.*" We are not human beings. We are humanized Spirit. We walk by Spirit. We act by Spirit. We move by Love. Because Spirit or consciousness is God, when we begin to understand that we, too, are Spirit, we begin to realize what it means when we hear that we are made in the image of God.

When we can look at every situation that comes along and judge righteous judgment, which means to judge it in terms of its Spirit, we can control our universe. We do that by either allowing that Spirit to permeate our consciousness or by refusing to let it affect our Spirit of love and well-being. Because we live in a Spiritual universe, we can literally change the universe. Each one of us can. We can listen to the words that come from others and those words that come into our own minds and immediately sense the quality of Spirit that the words reflect. Then we can either allow negative spirit to continue or we can listen to the language of Spirit and lift our vibration into the Spirit of love. That means we can pray without ceasing by monitoring the Spirit without ceasing.

God as Essential Being

The ultimate facet or experience of God is the realization that God (Spirit) appears as individual being. The word "individual" is one of those words that have come to be accepted as exactly the opposite of its root meaning. It comes from the Latin word "individualis," which means "indivisible, inseparable, one with." God is individual being, which is to say that we are one with and inseparable from God. Our individual or essential being is what Jesus was trying to explain when he said,

As thou (Holy Spirit) *hast sent me into the world, even so have I also sent them into the world. And for their sakes I sanctify myself, that they also might be sanctified through the truth. Neither pray I for these alone, but for them also* (anywhere in the world) *which shall believe on me* (believe the same things I stand for) *through their* word (in whatever religion they follow); *That they all may be one, as thou, Father* (Spirit), *art in me, and I in thee, that they also may be one in us* (inseparable): *that the world may believe that thou hast sent me. And the glory* (the consciousness) *which thou gavest me I have given them; that they may be one, even as we are one: I in them, and thou in me, that they may be made perfect in one; and that the world may know that thou hast sent me, and hast loved them, as thou hast loved me.*[20]

In this he was saying that because of individual being God, didn't love him, Jesus, any more than anyone else, nor us any less than he loved Jesus.

Behind our masks hides our individual being, that part of us that is indivisible with the divine. As evolving humans we wear many masks. The word "persona" means mask in Greek, and our community of attitudes and personality traits are our masks. Most often we confuse ourselves with our masks. A mask covers something. That something is our essential Self. I capitalize the word "Self," because that is the Self that is made in the image of God—pure, complete, unconditional, unmasked, individual, and divine.

After experiencing God as individual being, it stands to reason that when we are in the Spirit or when our consciousness is exemplifying the qualities of God, the masks are removed, personality has dissolved into our essential being, and our egos no longer identify with the masks we have worn. In that state, we have come full circle and not only experience God but are also aware of how God appears in the flesh objectively as our own selves.   In that consciousness, there is no sense of separation, our egos are unmasked, and we realize that we are that one essential being. Then we can understand that Moses was talking of essential being when he said I AM THAT I AM, and why that is the first and only fully capitalized sentence in the Bible.[21] Though metaphysically or mystically we give Jesus credit for projecting the I AM consciousness into our experience, Moses planted the seed. Even though Jesus said, "*I have manifested thy name unto the men which thou gavest me,*"[22] Moses was the first to say "I AM" is the name of God. Exodus 3:11-14 tells the story:

> *And Moses said unto God* (unto his Spirit), *Who am I, that I should go unto Pharaoh* (the symbol of material power), *and that I should bring forth the children of Israel* (spiritual nature) *out of Egypt* (spiritual darkness)? *And he* (Spirit) *said, Certainly I* (your essential being) *will be with thee; and this shall be a token unto thee, that I* (Spirit or true identity) *have sent thee: When thou hast brought forth the people out of Egypt, ye shall serve God* (Spirit) *upon this mountain* (this high place of consciousness). *And Moses said unto God, Behold, when I* (the consciousness of essential being) *come unto the children of Israel, and shall say unto them, The God of your fathers hath sent me unto you; and they shall say to me, What is his name? what shall I say unto them? And God said unto Moses I AM THAT I AM: and he* (Holy Spirit) *said, Thus shalt thou say unto the children of Israel* (those with spiritual intuition)*, I AM hath sent me unto you.*

The minute one has the slightest experience of one's essential beingness, the word "I" takes on a new and sacred meaning. By accident or intent, in the English language the word for "I" and the mathematical symbol for one, "I," are the same. To experience "I" is to experience "I-ness." The minute we begin to become aware of how constantly we misuse our essential name, we are on the road to illumination. But we are blasphemous as long as we continue to identify with the various masks we wear or the materialistic attitudes that we live behind, and in that frame of mind claim that we are the I AM, that we are Gods. Every time we say "I," referring to anything other than our essential being, we are confusing our masks with the reality of ourselves. As long as we believe in personal powers or personal accomplishments as anything other than expressions of our divine essential being, we are taking the name of God, the I AM, in vain.

On the other hand, Jesus didn't just tell us that we should love God and our neighbor. He said we should love our neighbor, *"as thy self"* and that when we do we will find that the love of God, the love of neighbor, and the love of ourselves are a Trinity—that God, neighbor, and self love are like unto each other.

The Anointing

*I*n those moments when we are aware of our essential being, we are in that state of illumination the Scripture refers to in a number of places as "the anointing." There is no passage so significant in the whole Bible as one in the Old Testament that foretold the meaning and possibility of the anointing, which is Christ consciousness. This Scripture was Jesus' favorite, and mine, too, for that matter. It is the sixty-first chapter of Isaiah, the one Jesus quoted when he entered the temple after he had been baptized by John, after the dove had descended on him symbolizing his "Christing," and after he had proven himself on the mountain by resisting the temptations.

As recorded in the fourth chapter of the Gospel of Luke, when Jesus came down from the mountain:

> *And Jesus returned in the power of the Spirit into Galilee: and there went out a fame of him through all the region round about. And he taught in their synagogues, being glorified of all. And he came to Nazareth, where he had been brought up: and, as*

his custom was, he went into the synagogue on the Sabbath day, and stood up for to read. And there was delivered unto him the book of Esaias. And when he had opened the book, he found the place where it was written, The Spirit of the Lord is upon me, because he hath anointed me to preach the gospel to the poor; he hath sent me to heal the brokenhearted, to preach deliverance to the captives, and recovering of sight to the blind, to set at liberty them that are bruised, To preach the acceptable year of the Lord. And he closed the book, and he gave it again to the minister, and sat down. And the eyes of all them that were in the temple were fastened on him. And he began to say unto them, This day is this scripture fulfilled in your ears.[23]

Alas, they did not understand that Jesus was not talking about himself, but about his experience of the power and presence of Spirit. When Jesus quoted Isaiah, *"The Spirit of the Lord God is upon me; because the Lord hath anointed me to preach good tidings unto the meek;..."*[24], those who still lived by the law thought he was claiming to be God and they couldn't take that. *Of course he was,* but not in the way they looked at it. What he was saying was *that when the Spirit is on us, we will realize we are the children of God; we are anointed.* "Anointed," in Latin means, "smeared upon"; so when any of us are enveloped or smeared upon by the Spirit, we are Messiahs—but not until then.

After Jesus left the earth plane, his disciples often talked of the significance of his anointing. In Acts 10:38 we read, *"God anointed Jesus of Nazareth with the Holy Ghost and with power: who went about doing good, and healing all that were oppressed of the devil: for God* (Spirit) *was with* (appearing as) *him."* Also, II Corinthians 1:21, *"Now he which stablisheth us with you in Christ* (the anointed one), *and hath anointed us* (also), *is God."* That is to say, when we are in that anointed dimension of Spirit or God that Jesus achieved, we will realize our oneness with and as God. The anointing is God doing things through the flesh, doing those things flesh cannot ordinarily do.

On the other hand, when we are not in the Spirit of the anointing, it would be blasphemous to claim we are God appearing as us. When we are anointed, we experience a different state of consciousness than our ordinary humanness, and at that moment could rightly say we re-present God. The anointing is the same consciousness that Jesus was in when he said, *"I and my Father are one."*[25] Whenever we are in the Spirit of God, we are the way God appears on earth. When Jesus was baptized and the dove descended on him, that experience represented his anointing. When we are smeared upon by that Spirit, we, too, are the physical objectification of that subjective state of consciousness as well. The anointing represents that moment when our consciousness has matured into its union with the level of spiritual awakening we call the Christ. It is true that when the anointing is on a person, that person needs nothing from outside of his or her own consciousness, no external power, no human teacher. As the First Epistle of John 2:27-29 clearly announces:

> *...the anointing which ye have received of him* (the Spirit) *abideth in you, and ye need not that any man teach you: but as the same anointing teacheth you of all things, and is truth, and is no lie, and even as it hath taught you, ye shall abide in him* (in the Spirit of love). *And now, little children, abide in him; that, when* he (the I Am)*shall appear, we may have confidence, and not be ashamed before him at his coming. If ye know that he* (Spirit/God) *is righteous, ye know that every one that doeth righteousness is born of him* (of the anointing).

When we also experience the anointing we will have fulfilled our destiny. The very fact that we can comprehend what the anointing is means that sooner or later we, too, can walk in it. When Paul said, *"I can do all things through Christ, which strengtheneth me"*[26], he was talking about the anointing. The Christ is God consciousness. The anointing is what happens to us when we are in that consciousness. If every time that the word "Christ" appears in the New Testament, we can think of it as the anointing, we will understand it in a new way. If every time we think of Jesus we think of him as the anointed one, we will not only know Jesus in a personal way, but we will know that "there, by the Grace of God," we can go.

The Triune Life

*A*fter all is said and done, we still cannot describe God. To describe God is to reduce God to no more than a human concept, and that God would not be worthy of worship. A finite mind cannot encompass infinity, but by polishing as many of the facets of the diamond as we can, it is possible to experience its glory. God is beyond our intellectual knowledge of God, but, thank God, though we cannot think God, there is a process whereby we can experience the anointing. That process is the three-stage formula that is fulfilled in every creative act, no matter how impressive or how insignificant. Every time a creative act has taken place, the Trinity has been experienced.

Like everything else, if the Trinity is explained in purely objective terms, as it is in many traditional churches, it becomes illogical, and it is no wonder that many today reject the concept. Without the Trinity being interpreted subjectively as the principle of creativity, it becomes a half truth, and all half truths not being fully true are lies. When the Trinity is seen objectively as God being a Father-figure outside and beyond ourselves, as Jesus being His *only* Son, and the Holy Ghost as an exclusive experience that happened two thousand years ago, its relevance to our daily lives is left unexplained. When the symbolic nature of the Trinity reveals that all three elements of the Trinity take place within every one of us in every creative act, the full meaning and grandeur of the Trinity becomes a pattern for us to live by.

Subjectively, the first part of the Trinity is God, the invisible cause of all that is created. Secondly, the Son is the material offspring or creation of God, and thirdly, the Holy Spirit is the creative energy that produces the effects. Divine idea, through imagination and consciousness, is made flesh as human beings, and the Spirit is the Holy energy that makes it possible. Just as cause and effect are one, these three are one and there is no division between the source, the energy, and the creation. This is the cornerstone of the Christian message and how we can live life creatively as what I call "The Triune life."

When I wrote my first book over three decades ago, my working title was *The Triune Life,* but my editor was not happy with that title. He rightly found it too overloaded with theological baggage. Besides that, the book I had written, which I finally called *The Double Thread,* led up to the Trinity, but it was basically about how you arrive at the experience of Trinity via the two commandments—the double thread. It didn't fully reflect Trinity consciousness. I wasn't spiritually mature enough at that time to write about what happens after one has achieved Trinity or Fourth dimension consciousness, because I wasn't there yet myself. God works in mysterious ways. Though I was intellectually convinced that at the end everything would come together to create ascension consciousness; my concept was ahead of my own developed spiritual evolution. When I went through the manuscript again, I saw that the real substance and value of the book was that it offered an explanation of the tools—the two commandments—needed to break through to the Triune life.

Actually, nowhere in the Bible does the word, Trinity, appear. However, according to Matthew, the last instructions Jesus gave his few remaining disciples before his own ascension was the formula for the Trinity or ascension consciousness:

> *Go ye therefore, and teach all nations in the name*
> *of the Father, and of the Son, and of the Holy Ghost:*
> *Teaching them to observe all things whatsoever I*
> *have commanded you: and, lo, I am with you alway,*

even unto the end of the world.[27]

Apparently, almost four hundred years after Jesus left the earth, St. Augustine used that Scripture from Matthew as his basis for creating the traditional concept of the Trinity, the objective interpretation of the Trinity that has remained over the years and which many object to today. Subjectively, Jesus' final words as quoted in Matthew were all-inclusive. He tells his disciples to inform all people that the name of God is I AM, the creative center in all people.

If that is understood, *"I am with you alway,"* means that the anointing is with you in every way, *"even unto the end of the world."*[28] He was saying that if the formula inherent in the Trinity is fulfilled and experienced, one enters a new reality— the Triune life. The Trinity isn't this new reality but if we successfully integrate the three parts of our own being, we enter the Triune life, which is a totally different dimension than a life centered on human survival.

When experienced, this Trinity of conditions produces a new life, a child of the process. In other words, when the three are united, a fourth presence comes into being. This new creation is the product of the ascension consciousness arrived at through the integration of the three parts of the Trinity. At that time the objective and the subjective are both honored and understood, because cause, effect, and Spirit no longer exist as separate from one another. Whether we realize it or not, this integration of the three parts of the Trinity takes place in every artistic accomplishment, every musical composition, every scientific discovery, and every place where acts of love become objectively evident.

Just a few years ago when people talked about the body, mind, and spirit as the holistic approach to life, they were looked at askance by the general public, but today even the staunch medical establishment accepts and respects the part the mind and the spirit play as an important agent in the healing of the body. It isn't yet realized that in prescribing the mind, body, and spirit approach, one is prescribing the Trinity: mind (God), body

(Son), and Holy Spirit (the healing energy).

When we holistically experience that "God IS appearing AS that which I AM", we are fulfilling the two commandments by loving God, our neighbor, and ourselves, and when we experience Trinity consciousness for ourselves, we realize that it is also the truth of every creation. When we experience Trinity consciousness in ourselves, we are anointed and we step into the Triune life. That life is the ascension consciousness that heals the sick, opens the eyes of the blind, and repairs the brokenhearted. When this Trinity experience takes place, we are re-created in the image and likeness of the anointing. We are born again. We not only experience the ascension consciousness; we become the presence of ascension consciousness, a totally different being than we were before.

Chapter 4

THE IMPERSONAL I

I am thy shield, and thy exceeding great reward.
                                            Genesis 15:1

And God said unto Moses, I AM THAT I AM: and he said, Thus shalt thou say unto the children of Israel, I AM hath sent me unto you.
                                            Exodus 3:14

Fear thou not; for I am with thee: be not dismayed; for I am thy God: I will strengthen thee; yea, I will help thee; yea, I will uphold thee with the right hand of my righteousness.
                                            Isaiah 41:10

I am the Lord: that is my name.   Isaiah 42:8

I am the first, and I am the last; and beside me there is no God.
                                            Isaiah 44:6

I am the door: by me if any man enter in, he shall be saved, and shall go in and out, and find pasture. The thief cometh not, but for to steal, and to kill, and to destroy: I am come that they might have life, and that they might have it more abundantly.
                                            John 10:9-10

I and my Father are one,…   John 10:30

And I, if I be lifted up from the earth, will draw all
men unto me.   John 12:32

I am the way, the truth, and the life.   John 14:6

… ask anything in my name, I will do it.
                                          John 14:14

I *have overcome the world.*   John 16:33

And now, O Father, glorify thou me with thine own
self with the glory which I had with thee before the
world was. I have manifested thy name unto the
men which thou gavest me out of the world: thine
they were, and thou gavest them me; and they have
kept thy word.   John 17:5-6

*T*here is no way that I, as Walter, the author of this
book, can put into words what I would like for this
chapter to offer. If possible, it would be by far the
most important chapter in the book for it is the central mystery of
life. I quoted the above Scripture because I feel that Jesus came as
close to voicing it as anyone ever has, and yet even he could not
make it understandable, because the only way one can realize it
is by actually experiencing it. I said before that absolutes do not
exist at the personal level. At best, they can be sensed, but not
intellectualized. Yet the intent of this writing is to offer all sides
and show that it is all God. When we transcend egotism, the
miracle of the impersonal nature of self or God can actually be
experienced.

Just by one's being in the presence of a great Master like
Jesus, spiritual consciousness can somehow be imparted to a
few by a kind of divine spiritual osmosis, or what the Hindus call

"darshan." Even Jesus could not give it to the masses; otherwise he would never have had to be crucified. Egotism, which is a personal sense of self, intellectual incredulity, and assumptions of self-depreciation make it almost impossible for one to step across into a conscious awareness of this secret of secrets that lies hidden in the Ark of the Covenant.

Legend has it that if a human being laid his eyes on that which was in the Holy of Holies, in the Ark of the Covenant, in the secret place of the Most High, that person would surely die. It's true. They would. If one experiences even the tiniest vision of one's impersonal God Self, one's old self ceases to exist and one never sees one's self in quite the same way ever again. Certainly, one will continue to wear the old mask as long as one has yet to fulfill one's purpose in the world. One will even forget from time to time that one is not the mask, but deep inside the memory of one's impersonal essential being will never completely fade. Instead, it will inspire and transform one's life.

When you read the Scripture at the beginning of this chapter, you cannot but have been aware of how desperately Jesus, John and the prophets, who had seen their spiritual nature, wanted to share it. However, it is ultimately impossible to put the name of God into words. In fact, it cannot be put into words, but it can be put into one word, "I."

"The Kingdom of heaven is like unto a merchant man, seeking goodly pearls: who, when he had found one pearl of great price, went and sold all that he had, and bought it."[1] This pearl is the realization of the impersonal nature of one's true being, and one has to sell every other desire in order to purchase it. With all of his ingenuity, man has been unable to make a synthetic pearl that has the wonderful inner luminosity of a perfect pearl. We look at the pearl and forget that it would not have come into being except that an oyster had to overcome an irritant that somehow got under its skin.

There is a saying that claims that "the perfect state of man is the state of divine discontent," because those who are never quite satisfied by the world's toys find themselves pushed to realize their true identity. They are those who will eventually possess the pearl of great price—the I AM.

At the end of the road, the ultimate prayer becomes the contemplation of Moses' revelation, I AM THAT I AM. But what is that I AM? Obviously it is not my physical presence, though my presence is the result of the "I" of my being. It is not my mind nor sense of individuality. In fact, the "I" is not anything that can be seen or localized. "I" is all that has brought me to where I AM at present, and it is all that will take me on into eternity. "I" is the energy or Spirit that has been active as my being at every moment. It was myself as a child and it was myself as every experience that followed in my life process, developing me into that which is present today — THAT I AM.

"I" is the "process" that I AM. This process has healed every wound. This process that I AM has straightened all the crooked places. I am not just a person; I am the process that is living me. All I need to contemplate is my existence as the process that I AM, and I must fully and completely trust it. In this light, I can see the words, I AM, before my eyes and feel them in my heart. Because all the world and everything in it makes up this that I AM, I need think of nothing else but that I AM.

This is what Jesus meant when he said that he was the way, the truth, and the life. *The way, the truth, and the life is the process you are as well.* This process is your I AM. This divine process is the way your life has been and is to be.

I'll give you a challenge. Get a *King James* Bible and underline the word "I" every time Jesus says it in the Gospel of John. If you can do it without missing any, you are exceptional. In four short chapters, Chapters 14 through 17, Jesus says "I" some one hundred and twenty times. Does that mean Jesus was an egomaniac, always talking about himself, as so many people we know do? Hardly. Jesus was not talking about his personality. He was referring to his impersonal and universal essential being—of himself as a spiritual energy, the secret that is in the Ark of the Covenant. He was referring to the I that is within and "as" every one of us, the divine nature that is the pearl of great price.

We can't think of what to do to buy the pearl, but we can hear it from within. God says:

Get quiet. Listen. Really listen to that still small voice which I am. Sit quietly. Close your eyes to the pictures you see with your eyes and with your mind. Look unto Me, the I THAT I AM.

Allow my word, this pearl of great price, "I," to permeate your being. Feel it. Feel it to the roots of your soul. Dare to know that I AM God. Speak the word. Say it over and over knowing you are talking of the true nature of your being. Let every cell in your body respond to the I that is its being. Feel It breathe your Self into your whole being. Realize that for the first time in your life you are depending on no one and nothing other than the I of your own being.

In all the teachings you have turned to, in all the lectures you have attended, in every religion you have studied, you have ultimately been disappointed because something was missing. At times, you have thought you had found the secret, only to eventually be disillusioned. You have believed in your masters and have been confused when you found they were not perfect. You have looked everywhere but where I AM, the I of your own being. I, alone, your I, is your only teacher. Turn to me.

I, the I AM of you, is the way, the truth, and the life of you. I am not your mind or intellect. They are just ways I use to speak to you. Even your personality is my way of communicating with the world; so free yourself from personal sense and its egoism. Use your ego as your servant to serve the I Am that you are. Put aside personal concepts, personal opinions, and impersonalize the human picture. When you find your Self, you will not be egotistical because you will see that God is Self, your Self, my Self, all

Self. I am the Self and the Self is I.

I am come into your consciousness now because my time has come and you are ready to experience the God that I AM within your being. Now you can see that I have been with you always and that you have never really been aware of this impersonal universal Self that is the meaning of your being. As long as you search for the truth you will not find it. When you stop and realize that I AM the truth, you will be it.

Use your imagination. Listen to the I of your divine Self. Be still and know that I is your name, the name of God. Get acquainted with your Self. Stop believing that you are just a body, just an intellect, just a person. Know that you include your body, your intellect, and your person, and that I am that which encompasses your whole universe.

Surrender and obey. Surrender all that you thought you were. Listen, to the still small voice of your I and obey it. Do not let your intellect talk you out of it. Obey its instructions even though they make no sense to those of this world, because it is I.

Place your trust in me, the I of your being. Do not reject or condemn how I appears to you as those in your life and the experiences that you face. Realize that they are I appearing as aspects of your own consciousness. You do not know anything you are not conscious of; so now realize I is consciousness. I is what I am.

If what I am saying to you is too hard for you to follow right now, just feel what you can of the mystery of your Self, of the word "I." Keep turning to the I of yourself and it will purify your whole being.

Now you may see that I have been with you always. I have been in every experience, every mistake, every mis-step, every falling short because I have always been leading you to myself, your Self. It has always been I who has kept you searching, searching for your awareness of the I of yourself.

This is not someone else talking to you. It is your own Self. Listen, feel, be. I am the air you breathe, the life you live, the love you love. Though you have not known it, every time you have said "I," you have subconsciously known that I am the infinity of your being and of all others as well, for there is only one I and you are that I. Do not try to convince yourself of this. Do not rationalize it. Feel it. Know it.

Realize that you have not bought the pearl of great price with your effort because it is a gift your Self is giving to you. Take it. Respect it. Honor it and let no one tell you that what I is telling you is not the truth.

When I say that this is the impersonal I, I am not putting down the personal I that appears as your personality. I am only saying that your essential being is all that God is and God is universal, not limited to a body. I includes the body. Where you differ from others is that each person is a point of light where the impersonal I appears individually. You are your individual point of light. I is God appearing as your individual being.

I am always there to hold your hand in time of need. If you make your bed in hell, I will be there because there is nowhere you can go where I am not. Use your imagination. Image me as the I of your being and I will be it unto you. By creating your personal being in my image and likeness I am saying that the I of your whole self is divine. There is no other. My will, the I's will within you, is your will. Now you can distinguish the true from the false.

Anything that does not reveal that I am the truth of your being is a false picture. Anything that tells you that I am not your true nature is a liar. Anything that tells you that God is other than the "I" of your own being is a thief that steals your true identity from your consciousness. Anyone who tells you that your desires are human and selfish is wrong. I am the cause of every desire and every desire will lead you to me. Let yourself become free of limitation for all that I have is thine, and the earth and its fullness are yours. Be still and know.

Be not deceived. I appears as your humanity as well as the impersonal Self that is your cause. You cannot go wrong as long as you realize that I, the impersonal nature of your being, is wholly conscious within and it appears both as the one that is doing or acting and the I within that is inspiring the action.

Be not afraid to enter into the thick of the material world. Do not be afraid to express your humanity, for I am revealing my truth through your humanity. Just always remember it is I. Through the word you close the gap between your humanity and your divine I. When you realize that I am expressing myself in the world as your personality, you are loving your Self, the I that I AM. There is no other way.

I Am In Your Temple. I have told you that your body is the temple of the living God, which I am. So now put aside all the words that I have been using and let us enter the temple. Symbolically see yourself preparing to enter the temple as you did before going to church every Sunday as a child. Take a mental bath by cleansing your mind and sense of self. Feed yourself a breakfast of the best thoughts you can. Feed yourself the realization of your I. Dress your consciousness in your Sunday best. That is to say, clothe your personal sense self with the loftiest and most loving concept of self I can reveal to you, and then close your eyes, close out the outside appearances, and reverentially enter your temple, your body.

Listen as I, the priest of your Self, tells you that your body is the temple of the Holy Spirit. Approach the altar within where you can encounter this Holy of Holies, the I of your self. Kneel; submit your sense of individual self before the altar, and the priest of your Self will come to meet you. See it.

Realize that you are here to take communion, to commune with your Holy Self, your higher consciousness, your priest Self. Your priest Self offers you the bread and the wine with the words, 'This consciousness is the body of the Christ. The bread that feeds you is the I of your being. The wine that flows through your being is the spirit of love that flows as Christ consciousness. Do this in remembrance of me, the I that was before the world was. Remember me by being a member of my I.

Fear not, it is I. I have come that I might have life and that I might have it more abundantly. I, your I, and my I, is the Way, the Truth, and the Life.

Dare to believe that this I, your I, is the same I that was in Jesus, in Buddha, in Krishna, in every saint and master. Dare to believe that it is your I. Dare to believe that when you are completely in that I, you are not only one with Jesus but appearing as Jesus.

Know that whenever you say the word, "I," you are speaking the name of God. Lift up your I into the high point of your awareness. See this I as a sacred little baby born within you, seemingly so innocent and helpless but actually all-powerful and made of pure light. Know that I have given you this sacred being. Honor it. Tend it. Love it. Nurture it. Know there is no other, none better, none more powerful.

This I that you are is the secret of life and of love. I am the energy of the universe and I am you when you abide in my word. That word is "I." Honor it, keep it sacred, but never, never forget that no matter where you go, I will be there because wherever you go, I go with and as you. All you have to do is remember me. I...I...I...I...I.

Be not confused. There is no difference between you and the temple of your body. From the outside, the temple is what and who others think you are. Those who love you know that within that which appears as you is the child of God, the I that you are. Your temple protects you from those who are not aware of the true you that lives in the temple.

Rejoice that your I has this protection from those who have not realized their own I. Rejoice that the world does not even know your body is a temple, because that way you can smile and know your essential being is safe within.

Now get up from the altar. We, your I and your human identity, have communed. You are once more clean, whole, and ready to go back into the world for I have not come to take you out of the world but to keep you from harm in the world. Rejoice in your secret, that you are both priest and supplicant, that you live in the house of God.

Go back into the world knowing I AM THAT I AM. Be happy to re-enter the world because you now possess the pearl of great price, the realization of your own I.

Realize that what is in the world is not inferior to the pearl within because that which is in the world is the outer expression of the I that is within. Rejoice that your name is writ in heaven, and return to the level of human awareness rejoicing.

I AM.

Part Two

The How
PRACTICAL MYSTICISM

$\mathcal{C}$hapter 5

THE NECESSITY OF INCLUSIVENESS

For as the body is one, and hath many members, and all the members of that one body, being many, are one body: so also is Christ. For by one Spirit are we all baptized into one body, whether we be Jews or Gentiles, whether we be bond or free; and have been all made to drink into one Spirit. For the body is not one member, but many. If the foot shall say, Because I am not the hand, I am not of the body; is it therefore not of the body? And if the ear shall say, Because I am not the eye, I am not of the body; is it therefore not of the body? If the whole body were an eye, where were the hearing? If the whole were hearing, where were the smelling? But now hath God set the members every one of them in the body, as it hath pleased him. And if they were all one member, where were the body? But now are they many members, yet but one body. And the eye cannot say unto the hand, I have no need of thee: nor again the head to the feet, I have no need of you.

I Corinthians 12:12-21

*I*f anyone thinks or talks about what it means to be spiritual, they are not being spiritual. They are being psychological—logical about the psyche. Some mystics, like the great Ramana Maharshi, stop talking altogether in order to just let the experience of their love or their presence make its statement. All teachings as such, and all writings about mystics or the mystical life, are of the intellect. Hopefully, they are spiritually inspired, but they are nonetheless channeled through the mind. Fortunately, though all words are of a psychological bent, if it is realized that the information in this section of the book is my attempt to make logical interpretations of some necessary spiritual principles, it is possible to read between the lines and take advantage of their help.

Personally, I myself, would much rather soak in the poetry of mysticism, hear about the I AM, and let the rest go. But unless we have a conscious realization of how the mind works, it isn't possible to hold on to or repeat cherished spiritual experiences with consistency. Therefore, I am offering some mental or metaphysical tools in this section, which will lead to the more inspirational third section. One such helpful concept crystallized itself for me late in 1989.

In the summer preceding the beginning of the final decade of the twentieth century, I agreed to speak at a Unity Church in Kansas City for the advent of the hundredth anniversary of the founding of Unity. In asking me in advance for a title for my talk, the minister requested that it have something to do with Unity. I don't like to anticipate the subject of a talk ahead of time, because that would mean it was predetermined by an intellectual decision, rather than by its being drawn from the consciousness of those present or one that would come from the spirit of the moment at the moment. That's why I usually offer some ambiguous title that I can fit anything into, such as "The Search for Self Love" or "The Celebration of Life." This time, wanting to include Unity in the title but without thinking, I heard myself say, "Inclusive Unity." I guess my subconscious mind knew more than my conscious mind did, because when the day came for me to speak, I realized I could not have planned a more significant title than one that highlighted inclusiveness. At that moment it was revealed to me that inclusiveness is a spiritual matter. It represents the paradigm shift that is now taking place in the mind and spirit of humankind, individually and collectively. The time has come when we can and must interact with the universe, and that only happens when inclusiveness becomes a synonym for God.

The social and spiritual importance of inclusiveness was reinforced by something that happened at the beginning of the final decade of the twentieth century, an incident that ended the cold war and signaled what is going to happen throughout the twenty-first century. When the significance of what this occurrence symbolized is acknowledged, it will not only change how society is constructed, but it will be the end of conflicting religions and of global war. That incident was the fall of the Berlin Wall.

Walls exclude, by either keeping people in or keeping them out. When the world celebrated the destruction of the Berlin Wall, which separated the Soviet Union and its satellites from the Western world, it signified the beginning of the end of exclusiveness. It symbolically put us on the road to the realization that all people now have to be included in the family of mankind, the consciousness Jesus called, "*My Kingdom.*"[1] Exclusion is the opposite of the Christ message, which tells us that "*He maketh his sun to rise on the evil and on the good, and sendeth rain on the just and the unjust," excluding none.*[2] It also says, "*Inasmuch as ye have done it unto one of the least of these my brethren, ye have done it unto me.*"[3] and, "*He said unto them, Go ye into all the world, and preach the gospel to every creature,*"[4] not to an exclusive few. I am sure he did not mean force it on them, but he did mean for them not to exclude anyone. Spiritual nature tells us that we will achieve our ends, not by subtraction but by addition, by inclusion rather than by elimination or segregation.

Inclusiveness sounds like one of those simple words we think we understand and nod at, but when the truth is known, inclusiveness is bringing on a revolution in consciousness that will transform the world in unimaginable ways—and us as we currently conceive of ourselves. Revolutions are not easy to understand because, like a wheel, when that which was at the bottom comes around to the top, it is upside down. It becomes the opposite of what it was before its number came up.

Revolutions redefine both individuals and institutions. When this one is over, we may be surprised to see that almost all, if not all, of our current attitudes and institutions are now obsolete. That is because they are, without exception, based on and operate out of our habitually thinking exclusively—"me" and "mine" instead of "us" and "ours." It will be the end of "My nation right or wrong and to heck with the others," "My business regardless of yours," "My religion, and though I will patronize yours, mine has exclusive rights to the true answer."

Currently, the reason many establishments, religions, and individuals are having a hard time understanding why their old ways no longer work as they used to is because exclusive interests are no longer viable. Until organizations and individuals are motivated by ways that do not reject but include the ideas and beliefs of others, they have yet to recognize the paradigm shift that is well under way. Confusion, personal and collective, exists because the old system no longer applies, and the new one has not fully evolved. In fact, when inclusiveness is fully understood and practiced, it will not only eliminate exclusive national interests but exclusive religions as well. They won't be needed.

Objectively, exclusive interests have to end, because the world has become increasingly crowded and its resources appear to be limited. The exclusive interests have to end because the world's economic systems have become co-dependent, and because of the communications explosion they have to end, as the world's politics no longer stop at borders. Exclusive interests also have to end because unless the world's environment is understood and responsibility for it is internationally shared, the world will asphyxiate itself. We cannot have "our" exclusive ozone layer. Not only that, we now have a technology that can make the whole world heaven if it is shared inclusively with Love, rather than wasted on wars that are designed to exclude.

Subjectively, our thinking of exclusive thoughts has to end for spiritual reasons. When we are consciously aware of being included in the family of all humankind, our Spirit shouts that it is inclusively all God. We no longer make such exclusive statements as, "East is East and West is West and never the twain will meet," or "man is man and woman is woman and they will never understand each other." Instead of looking at different customs, different nationalities, different religions, or different individuals in terms of what we do not like about them—we must now concentrate on what we have in common with them. We must figure out how we can include their virtues in our awareness, both objectively and subjectively, both humanly and spiritually.

The reason I am bringing up what it means to be inclusive in the "how to" part of this book is because the universe is listening, and once we express the Spirit—the spirit of inclusiveness—we will be able to communicate with It and with our whole selves.

Our Inclusive Selves

We are promised that one day we will realize that we are made in the image of God, and we spend our whole lives searching for what that means. When that day comes, we will understand that because God is infinite and all-inclusive, so are we. We are so used to thinking of ourselves as being what we see in the mirror that it is difficult for us to really be aware that we are microcosmic holograms of a macrocosmic infinite inclusive "beingness." As infinity represents total inclusiveness, and infinity can't exist minus anything, once we learn to think and feel inclusively we will realize our oneness with infinity, and we, too, will no longer need to exist minus anything that we need or image. We can have it all.

The other side of that coin is that we have been led up the proverbial garden path because our advisors and others have told us there are things in ourselves that we should exclude. We are told that we should eliminate fear, should shun doubt, should avoid getting angry, should not desire anything, and should not be passionate. *Balderdash!* Because our true nature is infinite, all aspects of our nature are forever included in our infinity, and for a good reason. When you are standing at the edge of a high cliff, I hope you have some fear. Fear is God's signal sent to protect his physical incarnation.

At times, we should all have doubts. Having healthy doubt spurs us to seek the truth that will make us free. We should even include anger in our make-up. Jesus was justifiably angry when he chased the moneychangers out of the temple. If anything, we should increase our passion. Kill passion, and you deal a deathblow to your creativity. Passion is energy, and until we passionately desire to experience God, we never will. Ordinarily we try to get rid of our sometimes disturbing human feelings because we have not properly understood their purpose and how they fit into God's all-inclusive nature.

Instead of trying to get rid of or exclude those sometimes disturbing human feelings, we should honor our wholeness by including them in order to see what they are telling us. It is all God. Nothing happens by accident. Our feelings are signals, and it is a mistake to ignore them until their purposes are revealed. Once revealed, their energies can be redirected if they turn out to be inappropriate. Resist not evil. Rather than eliminate—replace. Once we stop trying to eliminate undesirable attitudes, and instead replace them with desirable attitudes, we discover that we never have had a problem with what we feel, but rather with how we use or are being used "by" what we feel. Jesus was plenty angry when he chased the moneychangers out of the temple, but he used his anger and wasn't used by it. After expressing the anger that was included in his infinite nature, he let it go. It had served its purpose. *"...forgive them; for they know not what they do."*[5]

Love It All

*T*he first part of the inclusive Scripture I quoted at the beginning of this chapter basically told us two things: How we need to include an infinity of different characteristics within ourselves and how together we make up the one body of humankind. The verses that followed were more psychological and are even more important spiritually for us to hear.

> *Much more those members of the body, which seem to be more feeble, are necessary: And those members of the body, which we think to be less honorable, upon these we bestow more abundant honor; and our uncomely parts have more abundant comeliness. For our comely parts have no need: but God hath tempered the body together, having given more abundant honor to that part which lacked: That there should be no schism in the body* (in your consciousness)*; but that the members should have the same care one for another. And whether one member suffer, all the members suffer with it; or one member be honoured, all the members rejoice with it.*
>
> I Corinthians 12:22-26

Inclusively we can become aware that every aspect of our personality is necessary, even those traits we think of as our weaknesses. As Paul said, *"My strength is made perfect in weakness."*[6] Instead of dishonoring those parts of our constitution that we want to change or denying their existence, we should see how those energies can be redirected so that they can contribute to our strengths. Then we will be that much closer to reflecting the image of God. Once we take the approach of trying to include our so-called faults by seeing the reason they came about in the first place, we can positively transform them through calling on our strengths. Then we will no longer be a house divided. When one part of our personality suffers exclusion, all the rest of us suffers, but when we see how the energy expressed by our faults can be transformed into our virtues, we honor ourselves and joy replaces self-rejection.

In the Prodigal Son story, the father didn't exclude the errant son on his return. If the Prodigal Son had not gone through what he did, he would not have become a conscious being and been welcomed home. Instead, his father killed the fatted calf in his son's honor and made him feel welcomed. We have to do the same with those errant parts of ourselves—face up to them and realize they are there to push us into becoming more conscious beings. Then we can include them so that we can transform them. We don't need to concern ourselves with our good points because, as the father said to the other son, "*Thou art ever with me.*"[7]

Because the most sensitive and potentially creative parts of our nature can be used equally—either constructively or destructively—we have been taught to suppress or get rid of them. As dramatic as it may sound, what I am talking about is a matter of life or death. "*The branch cannot bear fruit of itself except it abide in the vine,*" otherwise, it is cut off and dies.[8] When we exclude any part of our being because we have not understood its divine nature or purpose, we are in danger of killing our wholeness. When we truly believe that God is the only power in and as our presence, we will realize that at those times when we exclude any aspect of our bodies, minds, or spirits, we are in danger of denying God. Instead we can turn to God as our Omniscience, our access to infinite knowledge, and find out what those feelings and attitudes we have wanted to exclude are for—what they are telling us, and how we can fulfill their purposes. When we do, we will be more fully alive, and we will realize that *our oneness with God is our oneness with all spiritual being.*

The Ways

*O*ur need to be inclusive applies to the outside of our lives as well as the inside. As long as anything or any condition is present in our lives, it includes a purpose. Though we resist what we consider to be evil, we must realize that the rough spots and illnesses would not have been included in our lives unless there was something to be revealed through them, something that would make us become more fully conscious beings if we can hear what they are telling us. If something is included in our awareness, good or bad, it has information, and it will most likely stay with us or repeat itself until we include it and discover its purpose.

Many have tried to brush duality under the rug by claiming that evil is an illusion, or they have tried to exclude evil by un-seeing their problems—it does not work. I am not saying that evil or disease is good. Good and bad are both exclusive words. They both divide our understanding of omnipresence. Use one and you exclude the other. I am saying, however, that *there is only one life source, one life energy, and the only way we can arrive at an experiential conviction of this truth is by including every experience and person in that oneness.* When we include everything, everyone, every appearance, and every idea in God, we affirm that God is the only power, the only presence, and the only intelligence. The secret is that once we become aware of what a difficult situation is trying to tell us, its purpose has been fulfilled. It then goes away, and we call what has taken place a healing. It may only be telling us that we have forgotten the nature of error, that error is a "nothingness" claiming to be a power, but until we have consciously included this information, the problem remains. That is because it has not satisfied the reason for which it has come into our consciousness to begin with.

Because God is the only power, by including our difficulties and fears, we can release them and embrace God. To include is to embrace. When we embrace infinity—the universe—we are embracing God and ourselves.

Exclusion and Forgiveness

*F*orgiveness is the most important single act anyone can do to bring peace to his or her soul, harmony to life, and love to God. Surprisingly, it has little or nothing to do with another person. Though forgiveness may include an external act, it is basically an internal matter. To be forgiving is just what the word says—to be "for giving." Spiritually, there is only one thing we can give another person, and that is *freedom from judgment.* Whenever we give, we release and thereby allow God or Love to be all-inclusive. Any time we no longer hold on to any thing, any person, or any concept (even good ones), we have forgiven them and accepted their oneness as a part of God's allness. There is a Hermetic teaching which found its way into Christian Scripture that explains how holding on excludes. Jesus called it the keys of the Kingdom, "*Whatsoever thou shalt bind* (exclude) *on earth shall be bound* (excluded) *in heaven: and whatsoever thou shalt loose on earth shall be loost in heaven.*"[9] It also means that whatsoever you release (forgive), you free subjectively in heavenly consciousness, and whatsoever you judge you bind objectively.

Everything God has created has a place and a purpose. When you are aware of this fact, you no longer live by the law of survival which claims some things are good and others bad, and you have become a forgiver. When you no longer try to totally eliminate anything, you are affirming that it's all God. The only security or happiness one ever achieves comes about by realizing that God is all, and that everything and everyone is included in that allness. When that happens, there isn't anything left to forgive. When we no longer believe that it is necessary to exclude our hurt feelings, but rather believe we can include and replace them with the Spirit of Love, we will know true forgiveness. What I am talking about is a spiritual matter—a matter of Spirit. Whenever any aspect of wholeness is excluded, the Spirit of Union and fulfillment is impossible. The Spirit of Forgiveness is present when our release is all-inclusive and there is nothing more to let go of at any level.

It sounds strange, but we also have to forgive God. While simultaneously realizing our fulfillment comes from God consciousness, we have to release God from our wants and expectations. God is all and God is perfect, because God is perfectly all-inclusive. Everything is included in God. By realizing that everything is perfectly part of the divine plan, we forgive God, we release God. If we trust and live by this realization, it follows that we can forgive and release every person and every thing, because it's all in God's hands. That is why to be forgiving is the surest way to heaven.

Exclusivity and Loneliness

It wasn't too many years after I had made contact in meditation and learned the principles of metaphysics that I was able to transmute most of the problems I faced into harmony and abundance, but there was one nagging lack that at times insisted itself —loneliness. Looking back, every one of the major mistakes I have made in life, or what might have been called my sins, have been related to moments of loneliness. Somehow it was a stumbling block in my quest to live by Spirit. Allowing myself to feel lonely may not have seemed to have been a sin, but entertaining a sense of separation from God is the father of all sins. By feeling lonely, I was excluding myself from union with God. This drop from feeling included in God is another explanation for the fall of man. We may have once lived with a constant awareness that we were included in all that God is, but somehow in the process of evolving conscious awareness, we fell from that realization. The result was the birth of a kind of spiritual loneliness, a loneliness that has nothing to do with other people but rather with our feeling excluded from God.

When we examine all the popular sins, all those listed in the law courts, we find that every one of them in one way or another relates to the primal fear of loneliness. A man robs a bank because, at one level, he feels that money will buy him all the things he thinks he needs in order to be included in companionship and not have to face loneliness. A person kills someone else, not to get rid of that person, but because he or she feels that that other person stands in the way of the good that will keep him or her from being lonely. We look at our surface problems and take them at face value. If we look deeper, we may find that at some existential level, we fear that some negative result might cut us off from others in some way. As long as we subconsciously associate loneliness with being excluded from God or from others, it is obvious how our having felt excluded effects our lives. Every suicide is attempted as a way of ending loneliness, of the feeling of being excluded from life. But there is only one way to erase loneliness: We have to think inclusively, include everyone, and include ourselves in all that God is.

Though the following two words, aloneness and loneliness, sound similar, aloneness is the opposite of loneliness. Aloneness means just how it is spelled—"all-one-ness." True aloneness is all-inclusive, because it includes everything in Godliness. On the other hand, loneliness is exclusive. It is selfish. When one is lonely, one is selfishly allowing one's self to feel excluded from God.

If exclusion is the fall of man, then inclusion is the ascension of man. When we are totally aware of the all-inclusive nature of life, we ascend out of the darkness of separation and we no longer sin, no longer feel separated. I am only interjecting this now because "*God is not mocked.*"[10] I found that whenever I have felt lonely, there was something I could do about it—*I could consciously include myself in God.* And, boom! Loneliness turned into "all-one-ness."

Inclusive Love

*W*ithout a doubt, at the birth of Christ consciousness a new kind of love was introduced to humankind, an all-inclusive, spontaneous, altruistic universal love—Agapé love. In terms of our Judeo-Christian myth, Christ Love initiated a new dimension at the time it was introduced by Jesus. Like any seedling that matures and finally bears fruit, we are now, after 2000 years of the growth process, at the ripening century of "Agapé" love. How is Agapé Love different from the love that preceded it? Before, love was limited. It was personal and exclusive. It was reserved for one's own race, biological family, or life partner; it wasn't all-inclusive. Love was the product of a material or physical process and was limited to one's specific social or family inheritance.

When Jesus was asked about his family, his mother and brother, he explained what Agapé Love is. He spoke of family subjectively rather than in terms of the old objective family. He said, "*Who is my mother? And who are my brethren?*"[11] and then answered his own question by adding, "*Whosoever shall do the will of My Father which is in heaven,, the same is my brother, and sister, and mother,*"[12] meaning his family was universal. He told his followers, "*By this shall all men know that you are my disciples, if ye have love one to another,*"[13] and underlined love's inclusiveness by adding, "*And the Lord make you to increase and abound in love toward another, and toward all men…*"[14]

Certainly, there have been hints of and signs of this Agapé love ever since Jesus demonstrated it, but only now has the fruit appeared on the branches of the universal tree. The old love was the fruit of exclusion. Family loyalty came before loyalty to the family of all humankind. Now we are in the century where the fruit of inclusiveness binds all life into one, and that one is God.

The chapter in the Bible that is known as the "Love" chapter is the Thirteenth Chapter of First Corinthians. I will quote the Scripture using the word "love" in place of the word "charity," as is done in most Bibles other than the *Kings James*. As God is Love, I will capitalize the word.

> *Though I speak with the tongues of men and of angels, and have not Love* (Agapé Love), *I am become as sounding brass, or a tinkling cymbal. And though I have the gift of prophecy, and understand all mysteries, and all knowledge; and though I have all faith, so that I could remove mountains, and*

have not Love, I am nothing. And though I bestow all my goods to feed the poor, and though I give my body to be burned, and have not Love, it profiteth me nothing. Love suffereth long, and is kind; Love envieth not; Love vaunteth not itself, is not puffed up, Doth not behave itself unseemly, seeketh not her own, is not easily provoked, thinketh no evil; Rejoiceth not in iniquity, but rejoiceth in the truth; Beareth all things, believeth all things, hopeth all things, endureth all things. Love (being inclusive) *never faileth: but whether there be prophecies, they shall fail; whether there be tongues, they shall cease; whether there be knowledge, it shall vanish away. For we know in part* (exclusively,) *and we prophesy in part. But when that which is perfect* (inclusive) *is come, then that which is in part shall be done away. When I was a child, I spake as a child, I understood as a child, I thought as a child* (exclusively): *but when I became a man* (anointed), *I put away childish things. For now we see through a glass, darkly; but then face to face: now I know in part* (exclusively); *but then shall I know even as also I am known* (included in God). *And now abideth faith, hope, and Love, these three* (the triune life, faith in God, hope in material existence, and the Love that makes it happen); *but the greatest of these is Love* (inclusiveness).

Inclusive Relationships

*E*arlier I said that the inclusive approach was eventually going to change our way of living in unimaginable ways. How Agapé love will affect our personal relationships is one of the most revolutionary changes that will come about. To some it will seem to destroy the institution of marriage; to others it will re-define and enhance it. This impending change is also the reason why there are so many divorces, and why so many of us have a hard time finding a single lifetime mate. Fundamentally, most contracted unions have approached marriage exclusively and objectively, as though a single specific partner were responsible for fulfilling all of our emotional and physical needs. The minute the label of husband or wife was applied, we were well on our way to what the *A Course in Miracles* calls a "special relationship." A special relationship comes into being when one's partner is expected to exclusively be all-in-all, and when one looks to that particular person to fulfill all one's needs—rather than to God appearing in or as that person.

Traditionally, husbands are supposed to perform certain designated acts designed to fulfill all his wife's needs, and the wife is supposed to fulfill the whole range, if not all of her husband's needs. Subconsciously, the partners in a special relationship feel guilty about having needs to begin with, because at some level they realize they are made in the image of God and should therefore be complete. Partners project their guilts onto their partners —blame them for not fulfilling their needs—and usually end by creating an exclusive co-dependency. By expecting a particular person to provide and include the fulfillment of all of one's needs, one creates a special relationship that is doomed to failure in this rich and expansive day, in which we are beginning to consciously experience our spiritual connection with all of humankind. Special relationships deny the infinity of our natures.

I am not saying that marriage isn't a wonderful institution and is not one that can work beautifully. It can, if it is a "Holy Relationship." Holy means just what the word says—whole and inclusive. In a Holy Relationship one's focus is not on the objective level of a particular personality. Rather, it is on the God in one's partner, and inclusively in others as well. Personal love is no longer reserved exclusively for one particular person alone. Without lessening or dividing one's love for a particular person, one can share and express equally valid, but different, aspects of love for others simultaneously.

Holy Relationships are inclusive relationships. God consciousness fulfills all of our needs; however, not necessarily all through just one person. Our "live in" mate, our marriage partner, may be our particular soul mate, may be the one who nurtures us, may represent our best friend, and may be the channel through which our most intimate needs are fulfilled. However, there may be some other person who provides us with intellectual stimulation, another who fires our creativity, another with whom we can share athletic activities in ways that our marriage partner cannot. It may be the same for our marriage partners. We may not be able to fill all of his or her needs. When the marriage is broadened into a kind of inclusiveness that does not exclude having some of our needs being fulfilled by others, it will be a Holy Marriage, and not one based on jealousy, resentment, or on one person alone.

In the future, when we understand how we relate to others inclusively, we will no longer expect our needs to be fulfilled by people, but by the God in or as others. Then guilt will be laid to rest, understanding shared by our partners, and exclusive co-dependency will be a thing of the past. It's all God.

*C*hapter 6

CREATING OUR OWN REALITIES

IMAGINATION, PERCEPTION, AND PROJECTION

Judge not, that ye be not judged. For with what judgment ye judge, ye shall be judged: and with what measure ye mete, it shall be measured to you again. Matthew 7:1-2

Be not deceived; God is not mocked: for whatsoever a man soweth (in thought), *that shall he also reap. For he that soweth to this flesh shall of the flesh reap corruption; but he that soweth to the Spirit shall of the Spirit reap life everlasting.* Galatians 6:7

And the Lord said... now nothing will be restrained from them, which they have imagined to do... Genesis 11:6

Then said he unto me, Son of man, hast thou seen what the ancients of the house of Israel do in the dark, every man in the chambers of his imagery? Ezekiel 8:12

*N*elson Mandela made a statement in his inaugural address, whether original or quoted, that has resonated around the world. He said that we did not have to fear not being powerful enough, but rather that we fear being too powerful. I might add that our fear will remain until we realize what that power he was referring to is and how to control it. Mandela wasn't talking about the power of our arms and armaments but of the power of consciousness inherent in every human being—our God power.

Because of our oneness with God, God's power is our power. We use that power every day in hundreds of ways, both constructively and destructively. Until we are conscious of the nature of our power, and until we learn how to use it for the good of all, we will continue to witness what is called man's inhumanity to man. When we understand the ways by which we are already intentionally or unintentionally using this power, we will not only be able to make of life what we wish it to be, but we will finally understand how creation came into being as outlined in the first chapter of Genesis. When Genesis 1:26 says "*And God said, Let us make man in our image, after our likeness: and let them have dominion over...all the earth,*" the key word is not "dominion;" it is "image." Creation is "imag-ination," image initiation. Because at every waking moment we are imaging, we are expressing this God power at every moment. *Every time that we interpret and activate the images that come into our minds, we are effecting the universe.* What a tremendous responsibility we have! The creative and destructive power of imagination is awesome. That is why it is important to constantly be aware of its workings, and for us to take time to understand the metaphysics of personal power.

As incredible, mundane, and illogical as it may sound, our lives are literally the products of our imagination. That's what Albert Einstein was trying to tell us when he said, "Imagination is more important than knowledge." It is. We human beings have dominion over the earth and all the creatures on earth, because the power of imagination is the one thing that separates us from all the other physical life forms. Animals can procreate, they instinctively build nests, and evolve ways to hunt for food, but without conscious imagination they cannot conceive of (giving birth to) new forms, something we humans do daily.

On the other hand, it is obvious that we humans can and do give form to anything and everything we can imagine. In the 1930's, when I was a boy, we thought it was fantasy when Buck Rogers went zooming off in space or that Dick Tracy owned a wristwatch television, but it wasn't long before imagined fiction became material fact. Like it or not, we must become constantly aware that we give form to anything we imagine. "*In the beginning was the Word* (imagined idea), *and the Word was with God* (in consciousness), *and the Word was God* (the creative power of all life.)*[1] That is why Mandela thought it was important to say that we have a power greater than any power man has been able to conceive of up until this time, even a greater power than atomic energy. This power is the power of imagination. After all, the splitting of the atom came out of man's imagination.

When we become constantly aware of how we use this incredible power, and stop dis-empowering ourselves by misusing or letting others usurp our power, we can begin to consciously use our imaginations to transform our world and our lives. Then we will be living up to our spiritual inheritance. If at an early age we had learned how our every-day imagination fashioned our lives, we would have been saved a lot of painful lessons brought on by our unbridled imagination. Therefore, the greatest gift we can give our children is to instill in them the significance of imagination and how to use it unselfishly.

Imagination, like truth, does not do anything by itself. It has to be programmed and energized. As the first chapter of Genesis points out, at the beginning of creation God "*said*" and then "*saw*." Initially, the concepts of light, land, water, grass, and all the other material forms outlined in Genesis came into consciousness, and when the energy of perception was activated by imagination, those forms were projected into being.

There are three words that are the keys to the power of

imagination, three words that modern psychology has successfully used in order to help people understand the workings of their minds. Metaphysicians have used the same three words in teaching people how to pray successfully—*concepts, perception,* and *projection.* It may seem pedantic at this point for us to take the time to define these three words, but intellectually they constitute the foundation for mindfulness.

The Prison of Concepts

*C*oncepts are imagination's fuel. It has been said that we are prisoners of the mind. Actually, we are not so much prisoners of our thoughts as hypnotized by the concepts programmed into our minds by our imagination. Brain researchers tell us that our every thought is no more than a chemical reaction that passes through a pathway or channel made up of receptors and connectors that leads us to awareness. They also say that when a particular thought or concept is repeated often enough, it forms a groove, and after that, future thoughts automatically return to the familiar grooves in the brain made by concepts that have often been repeated. Thoughts not only return to those grooves but by repetition they dig the grooves deeper and deeper so that it takes great effort and counter-repetition in order to reverse or change those particular ways of thinking. Social anthropologists point out that many of the ethnic hates and class prejudices that should be obsolete in this modern world remain virulent because hate-filled groups have been conditioned since childhood by repeated prejudicial concepts passed on generation after generation. By the time one is an adult, one's thoughts automatically return to old hateful concepts, and it is almost impossible for future generations to think any other way. Thoughts automatically travel familiar (family-conditioned) grooves and the victims don't even know why they have those feelings.

Up until now, psychotherapists have often begun their therapies by regressing people into their childhood experiences. Some mystics fear this technique because they believe that the past no longer exists, and by returning to it one may just be anchored to past conditions, but there may be another explanation. The thought grooves with which a person was conditioned in childhood may remain in the present, and by going back to one's childhood it may be possible to discover how present feelings were established and then know how to spiritually recondition them.

With the advent of mass media, fascist dictators, advertising agencies, and our political parties know that if a concept is repeated often enough, over and over, and with enough energy, sooner or later it will wear a groove in the mass brain whether it is true or not. The public will then become hypnotized by it and believe that an oft-repeated concept is truth.

In a lighter mood, perhaps the best way I can illustrate how we personally create our reality out of our concepts is to repeat a story I heard. In the day when doctors still made house calls, a man called his physician and begged him to come to his home immediately because his wife was very sick. The doctor arrived with his black bag and told the man to wait outside his wife's room. After a few minutes, the doctor came out looking perplexed and asked, "Do you have a cork screw?" Of course the man was curious, but he didn't question the doctor and went and got him a corkscrew. After another wait the doctor came out again, looking frustrated, and asked the man to get him a screwdriver and a hammer. By this time the man was really upset, but nevertheless he went and got what the doctor asked for. Finally, ten minutes later the doctor came out all sweaty and disheveled with a frantic look in his eye and asked, "Have you got a hack saw and a chisel?" The husband couldn't stand it any longer and pleaded, "Doctor, doctor, what is wrong with my wife?" The doctor replied, "I don't know. I haven't been able to get my bag open." So much for the power of conceptualization.

All of us are loaded with conditioned concepts that lead us around by the nose. To the degree that we are still under the first law of human nature—survival at any cost—we are hypnotized by our concepts. All our habits are examples of deeply worn thought grooves that have taken us over. For instance, one of them is the concept that we have to eat three meals a day. We are so hypnotized by it that when the clock tells us it's time to eat, our saliva glands start working and our stomachs growl. Concepts can kill. Smoking is an example. After one has finally replaced the smoking habit with a smoking-free habit, it becomes hard to remember why it was so difficult to stop. It wasn't that the cigarette had any power. Cigarettes can't think. The concept of habitual smoking programmed into the brain was the control factor.

Fortunately, there is one sure way to change an undesirable habitual concept. It is not by believing you have to resist an evil concept but rather by replacing it with a better one. Resistance just deepens the groove, but by repeating a more desirable or enlightened concept often enough, it will eventually become automatic and the inferior concept will be involuntarily by-passed. The way to stop smoking, drinking, overeating, or any of the other habitual concepts that have imprisoned us is not to give them power by making the bad habit a moral issue, an issue of will power. That just deepens the grooves and dooms us to failure. *Don't resist—replace.*

The way for you to by-pass an old groove is to repeatedly replace the habitual negative thoughts with thoughts of how good it is to feel healthy, what a joy it is to breathe clean air, how good it is to be slim, how rewarding it is be to like what you see in the mirror, and how great it is to once more be in control of your life. Keep that up until a new groove is established, and you become your mind's master. Remember, we are infinite; so nothing ever completely goes away. It just becomes dormant and inactive in the subconscious; however, when and if it does reappear, you can remember and switch back into the new groove.

The reason we keep going over and over our spiritual studies, reading inspiring books, and repeating affirmations may seem to be just a mental exercise, but by repeating spiritual principles often enough, we eventually create a new and better groove of receptors and connectors. When we experience the new channel with its spiritually superior content, we rightly believe we have had a spiritual experience, even that we are born again. We can experience truth or God, but we cannot honestly voice it because words are concepts, and all concepts are limited. However, through our newly developed capacity to think multi-dimensionally and simultaneously, we are able to include a whole assortment of different concepts about something at the same time. In doing so, we can get a feel for a total truth that is beyond any single concept. We may even approximate ascension consciousness, at which time we go beyond all concepts. Until we experience that level, it is important to be aware of how often we are led around by our concepts.

The minute an experience has turned into a thought, it has been objectified into a concept. Because all concepts are objects, even subjective ideals, once thought, become concepts. Yet there is nothing wrong with our having concepts as long as we recognize them for what they are and we do not lock ourselves into them. As human beings, our concepts are our communication tools. When we go beyond good and evil, we can use concepts and not be used by them. If we interpret life through the language of the Spirit inherent in our concepts, rather than by the concepts themselves, they become the way we translate imagination into form. Understanding the nature of concepts helps us because when some disturbing concept appears, we can remind ourselves that it is only a concept, a limited viewpoint, and not the whole truth.

Even after the resurrection, Jesus was still at the level where concepts existed. That is why he said, *"Touch me not: for I am not yet ascended."*[2] Until our ascension, or when we are in ascension consciousness, we still deal with concepts, but when we are in ascension consciousness, we are beyond all divisions, all separations, and all the judgments that come from concepts, and we are then able to see that it is all God.

Our Conceptual Clothing

*O*ur concepts about ourselves have a purpose: they are our garments. They are what we clothe ourselves with in the human scene. We wear garments for a self-protective reason: to protect our identity from unenlightened thought just as our material clothing protects us from the elements. When the inquisition asked St. Joan if the Virgin who came to her wore clothes, she said, "Of course, how else could I have seen her."

A thousand people may know you. Each one has a different concept of who you are. Which is the true you? None, and, unfortunately, unless you conceive of yourself as being the presence of God, your concept of your self is as erroneous as other people's concepts of who you are. On the other hand, the concept of self you have created for yourself is the costume you wear in the world. That is OK as long as you do not fool yourself into believing you are your concept, and lose sight of your spiritual inheritance. Like an actor in a summer stock company, you can wear many different concepts of yourself as long as you realize they are all costumes.

That reminds me of another story. At the time I produced the play, *I Am a Camera* on Broadway, which made a star out of Julie Harris, I noticed that Julie was happiest when she had a part to hide in, a concept to fit into. Off-stage she was uncomfortable. When her name went up in lights, Julie, being surprisingly shy, didn't know how to handle her new status until she found an off-stage part to play. Quite deliberately she created the concept of a gracious young star and began to act it. That became her public mask.

When I keep repeating, "It's all God," I am advocating a kind of reverse hypnotism, replacing a material concept with a spiritual one. The first law of human nature may be a hypnotic state that we have inherited from past lives. If so, we have to undo or replace it. How? By repeatedly imaging a spiritual concept of who we are until the new concept becomes automatic. If we tell ourselves over and over for enough times that we are made in the image of God, that will create a new habit. Then we will live, with the practice of that habit, a much more loving and truthful one than we had of ourselves in the past.

Ah, we have come full circle. What I am saying is that there is a whole different way of living. It is ascension consciousness which results from a conscious awareness that we can use all concepts and not be used by any of them. Ascension consciousness happens when you become free of all concepts—but being free of concepts does not mean that you try to live without concepts. It means that you are free of continuously repeating concepts, free of being hypnotized by them, free to use them without being used by them. Lama Govinda put it succinctly in his book on creative meditation when he differentiated between objective concepts and subjective knowing. He wrote:

> *A typical property of our intellect is its striving after objectivity. This is justified and useful as long as we are dealing with objects or things, i.e., with something that is limited, delineated, circumscribed, and defined conceptually. But this objectivity fails us whenever we are concerned with questions of vital importance—questions concerning the very essence of man and the deeper meaning of individual existence. The only way out of this dilemma is to replace the intellectual attitude of objectivity by subjective experience.*"[3]

Principle and Perception

*N*ow we come to the subtle, but necessary, metaphysical difference between concepts and perception. Though they are often used interchangeably, concepts and percepts are not the same. Concepts are objective; they have taken form. How we perceive of circumstances is subjective. Our perceptions dictate the spirit that is inherent in our concepts. Just as "*in the beginning is the Word, and the Word is made flesh,*"[4] in the beginning are our perceptions and those perceptions then become our formed concepts. We are all made in the image of God, but as long as we entertain false a perception of who we are, we can't live it. Spiritually speaking, in order to change ourselves or change someone else, it does not mean we have to change who they or we are. We have to change our way of perceiving who we or they are.

Webster's Dictionary says that a concept is something that is conceived in the mind, and that to perceive comes from a Latin root word, "percipere," which means "to take hold of." By perceiving them, concepts become objects you take hold of. What you take hold of becomes that which is real to you. It follows that how you perceive reality actually creates your reality. Again, a Trinity experience takes place. Your perception is the father and your spirit is the mother that conceives and gives birth to the son, your concept. The three are one. As such, a concept does not exist apart from how the mind perceives it and how the spirit animates the concept.

A great number of metaphysicians and others unwittingly make a wrong turn by perceiving humanhood as something separate and apart from God. When we judge anything in the visible scene as anything other than a materialized conception, we are conceiving of an effect as something other than cause and are placing ignorance before truth. We are denying that an immaculate conception is possible. Because Jesus' birth was perceived of and conceived in the pure spirit of Love, it became known as the Immaculate Conception.

I am pounding away at the importance of perception and concepts because there is an ancient mystery school secret involved with the power of concepts. As is the case with most alchemists' secret, where they transmute base metal into gold, it is so simple that we cannot believe it: never deal with a problem at the level of the problem. *Change your concept and the appearance will change.* If through our perceptions our conceptions come out of pure Love, they will be Immaculate Conceptions, and whenever Immaculate Conception takes place, the Christ is born.

Personally, I don't want to save the world. I don't think it needs saving, but when I see someone crying out in pain while continuing to hit their thumb with a hammer, I naturally feel inclined to say "Stop. You don't need to do that. Change the way you perceive of the situation that causes you pain and your imagination will stop creating it." Though it may not be as obvious as a hammer blow, when the Scripture says "*Judge not that ye be not judged,*"[5] it is saying that we become what we perceive and conceptualize.

We hear that we should not judge, but few people tell us why judgment is something to be avoided. It is a mistake to judge because when we judge we are acknowledging that the concept we entertain has power, and, by doing so through our perception, we give it power. We become what we judge. There are no two ways about it. *Whatever law we perceive, we dignify and empower.*

God's creations are actual and not changeable; so we have a yardstick by which we can check to see if our concepts reflect reality or if they are judgments. Behind all appearances there is an unchangeable reality; therefore, if a concept can be changed it is not to be taken as ultimate reality. When our scientists tell us something has to be seen in order to exist, they confirm that what we perceive with our eyes is a creation of our minds or consciousness, rather than a true fact. Mystics are individuals who are so subjectively aware of the truth of being that though they see material objects they do not believe that cause is material. They have found that by changing their perception of what claims to be taking place, the forms that appear change accordingly. That, of course, is the secret of spiritual healing.

Spiritual healings are the result of altered perceptions. By double thinking, we can constantly remember reality (it is all God) and we can act upon that truth rather than re-act to the changeable concepts with which we are confronted. *The way we can be in the world and not react to it is to constantly perceive that within every person, place, or situation is something spiritual that is unchangeable. Within every form or concept, there lies hidden something that is permanent—the presence of God, Spirit, or essential being.*

If the unchangeable in a person is perceived by you, that person, in turn, will express that unchangeable Self outwardly. You may think that they have changed, but what has actually changed has been your perception of them. For instance, I have my concept of who you are; so does everyone who sees you. Each of our concepts is an illusion because each person perceives of you differently, but there is something in you that is possible for us to perceive that is the same for everyone, something that is unchangeable. That something is the reality of your essential being. God is unchangeable; therefore, when I love you, when I perceive the unchangeable reality of you, I see God. If I can perceive of and deal with the changeable you without losing sight of the unchangeable spiritual reality of you, I am not only in love with you, but I am also not being fooled by an illusory concept of you.

In dealing with the concept of illness, it is all right to let someone tell you their problem once in order for that person to get it off their chest. But if you let them repeat it continuously, you may make healing impossible. That is because in order to have a spiritual healing, your job is to reject the concept of illness they have presented and substitute one of wholeness. If your perception of someone becomes locked into a concept of illness rather than the purity of that person's essential being, the problem would only be compounded. When you have experienced someone's essential being as being free of limitation, you will have loved that person into health.

Sometimes we hear *"your faith hath made you whole"*[6]—faith in what? If you have faith in a concept of your own essential being as Spirit, the objective concept that has tried to make you believe otherwise departs. To have faith in yourself is to experience your concept of God as your own reality. When God is perceived as All, healing takes place. Even the staid American Medical Association now generally concedes that how we perceive our lives creates our lives and our health. It has been proved that our attitudes greatly affect the efficacy and success of the healing process. Our attitudes are the perceptions that encode our concepts and condition results. We are as healthy as the health of our attitudes.

If we want to empower our lives, we must realize that our perceptions are learned. They are created by personal experience, by family conditioning, by the influence of collective consciousness or ignorance, and, if one believes in reincarnation, one's concepts may be carryovers from past lives. No matter how concepts came about, we are not helpless victims. We can become aware of our perceptions and re-train them into righteous judgments. Meditation is the process whereby you take a mental bath, clean yourself of dualistic images and misguided perceptions, and return to the void—to the womb of creation. Once there, you can build new or more exalted perceptions of what is to be, and those concepts will become reflections of themselves. Jesus had the capacity to enter the consciousness of God, ascension consciousness, which is so all-inclusive that it cannot be broken down into concepts. It was his capacity to transcend this world, the world of concepts, and touch that silence which in turn resulted in his life being lived by Grace. Grace is a different level than law. It is a level beyond concepts. Jesus most often lived in that anointed state of consciousness; however, just like you and me, he was not there all the time until the ascension. Jesus' final achievement was that he went beyond all concepts and merged with the eternal silence, where he became completely and eternally one with all that is. The "silence" is a kind of higher mental frequency where all concepts are no longer distinguishable because they have been combined into a oneness, and it is all God.

Projections

*N*ow we get down to the nitty-gritty with a word that both lets us off the hook and puts us on it—projection. Projection lets us off the hook because what other people see and say about us are their projections and not necessarily true. It puts us on the hook because what we see in others may only be the result of our projections, which reflect our consciousness and are not necessarily the truth about them. Modern-day psychotherapy first popularized the word "projection" as a way of explaining paranoia—how people project their fears onto others and onto situations. Our projections were soon identified as the way we have laid our own shortcomings onto others. Eventually blaming everything on projections became the ego's maddening way of getting us to ignore other people's criticisms, "That's your projection," or "You are projecting." Nonetheless, there is no word that better explains how we energize our concepts and create our reality than that they are our projections.

It's like this: when you go to the movies, what you see on the screen is a projection. As such it is not reality but an illusion. If you don't like the picture, you won't get anywhere by trying to rush up on the stage and attack the screen. To change what you see you have to get involved with the projector and/or the projectionist. Our minds are the projectors, we are the projectionists, and the concepts we put into the projector and energize dictate the images on the screen. The pure unconditioned screen is the only thing that is real and permanent. Unless we put something in the projector and energize it, there won't be any image on the screen. When we attack or resist appearances, we are trying to erase the picture on the screen. The only way we can actually do it is to turn off the projector or change the projectionist.

When Mary Baker Eddy gave us what she called "the scientific statement of being," she said, "There is no life, truth, intelligence, nor substance in matter."[7] In claiming that, she was saying that there is no life, truth, intelligence, nor substance in what we project on the screen. Those images are imitations of life. On the other hand, many modern psychologists, the *Course In Miracles*, and most mystical teachings, explain that everything we see, absolutely everything of *"this world,"* in the way we see it, is a projection of our own consciousness. We are never actually dealing with a person, place, or thing on the screen outside of ourselves but rather with our projections. If we want to change the projection, we must do it within the projector. We must change the film, and that means to change our minds.

Though psychotherapy first used projection as an explanation for conduct, it is nevertheless the basis for spiritual healings and for how the word is made flesh. As such, the entire human scene is a projection, and as no two of us project exactly the same image, there are as many worlds as there are people, and none of them is reality. The concept of projection I have been proposing is no different from the ancient Hindu concept of Maya, than Buddhism's concept of illusion, or the "*this world*" Jesus contrasted with "*My Kingdom.*" When Jesus said, "*Judge righteous judgment,*"[8] he was saying "Project a spiritual interpretation of reality, not a materialistic one." In other words, when you primarily project the subjective or spiritual nature of your concept, that is what will appear on the screen of your life.

For thousands of years the Hindus have said that we make a mistake when we believe what our senses tell us, because our senses lie. The railroad tracks do not join in the distance, the clouds do not sit on the horizon, yet we believe our eyes and project our false, purely objective concept on reality. What we consider to be reality is, in fact, our own individual projection. We may or may not be affected by what others project onto us, but we do act out of our own projections.

Of all the "how to's" that can change your life, the most important one is for you *to pray without ceasing.* That does not mean you go around saying prayers all day, but it does mean that to pray without ceasing is to constantly monitor your projections and the energy you put into your projections without ceasing. If you constantly project Love, Love is what your life will be.

By the same token, when you no longer see through a glass darkly, but face to face with Spirit, it becomes much easier for you to forgive others who judge you. You will realize that it isn't you that others are seeing when they judge you, but most likely they are judging qualities within themselves that they are projecting onto you. Whenever someone gives you unasked-for-advice, you can bet your bottom-dollar that they are projecting their own guilts and shortcomings onto you. *We only see in others the notes we have in our own scale.* Saints see no evil in others because there is no evil within themselves to project onto others.

When I say that our projections put us on the spot, it is because when we feel we are surrounded by petty feelings of greed, dishonesty, deception, or such, we have to make sure we are not projecting our own weaknesses. As we are infinite, all emotions or defects are potentially possible somewhere within us; so the way we know if we are projecting negatives is for us to go into our closet and pray. Our meditations are the confessionals where we confront what our projections are telling us about ourselves. When we listen, we can transmute any negative projection into one of creative love.

If we are at peace, it is because we have peace within ourselves to project. The only way we can manifest peace on earth is to first become peace ourselves, not by demanding that it come to us, but rather by peace being projected by us. To pray for peace as though it can come from outside of us is to be at war with ourselves. But if we pray for the experience of God consciousness, we will bring peace to the world because that is what we will project.

Word Power

*O*ur spoken words are our projections. James, the brother of Jesus, who being Jesus' brother probably knew him better than anyone else, wrote a brief Epistle that gives us probably the most important "how to" advice on projection in the whole New Testament. He wrote:

> *If any man offend not in word, the same is a perfect*
> *man, and able also to bridle the whole body.*
> *Behold, we put bits in the horses' mouths, that they*
> *may obey us; and we turn about their whole body.*
> *Behold also the ships, which though they be so*
> *great, and are driven of fierce winds, yet are they*

turned about with a very small helm, whithersoever the governor listeth. Even so the tongue is a little member, and boasteth great things. Behold, how great a matter a little fire kindleth! And the tongue is a fire, a world of iniquity: so is the tongue among our members, that it defileth the whole body, and setteth on fire the course of nature; and it is set on fire of hell. For every kind of beasts, and of birds, and of serpents, and of things in the sea, is tamed, and hath been tamed of mankind: But the tongue can no man tame; it is an unruly evil, full of deadly poison (if misused).   James 3:2-8

If any man among you seem to be religious, and bridleth not his tongue, but deceiveth his own heart, this man's religion is vain.   James 1:26

Of course, it isn't the physical tongue that betrays us but rather the perceptions, concepts, and projections that roll off of it. Our tongue most often betrays what we have in our own hearts. Most of us want to be loving—we want to let Spirit live our lives—but we betray our own selves by not being conscious of what our words project, and, conscious or not, words become flesh.

Once more, it is not the language of words that matters but the language of spirit. If we use our tongues to speak the language of love, we will no longer betray our hearts, and our words will affirm that it is all God.

Chapter 7

SPIRITUAL ANDROGYNY

There is neither Jew nor Greek, there is neither bond nor free, there is neither male or female: for ye are all one in Christ Jesus.

Galatians 3:28

So God created man in his own image, in the image of God created he him; male and female created he them.   Genesis 1:27

When a bit of Gnosticism leaked into Paul's teaching so that he could say that when we reached Christ consciousness—the anointing— we would be neither male or female, he wasn't talking objectively about our physical bodies. He wasn't saying that our masculine or feminine traits would no longer physically exist. He meant that if we were born again into a new sense of existence, we would accept the infinity of our consciousness and live at a level beyond either/or. In modern language it would be like saying that we would no longer be a right-brain person or a left-brain person, but that our new consciousness would make of the twain one, therefore no longer the same as the old. Unfortunately, the word "androgyny" has only been conceptualized objectively rather than having been conceived of and dignified with what it symbolizes spiritually. Until now androgyny has always been associated with social misfits. It is unfortunate because until we recognize, understand, and welcome the androgyny of our own souls, we will never truly experience our omnipresence or trust omnipotence.

Traditionally, when we read in Genesis 1:27, "*male and female created he them,*" we interpret it to mean two physiologically different sexes.   Perhaps the "them" meant   having the characteristics of both male and female. Rabbi Cooper writes:

> *The Midrash Rabbah says, 'When the Holy One created Adam (ha-Rishon) it was androgynous. God created Adam ha-Rishon double-faced, and split him/her so there were two backs, one on this side and one on the other.' The idea that Adam and Eve were co-equal at birth is not a Kabbalistic secret; it was openly discussed in ancient Midrashic literature. Moreover, it was known two thousand years ago that the idea that Eve came from Adam's rib was a common misunderstanding. The Torah is unambiguous on this point. It repeats a second time, 'Male and female It created them,' and goes on to say, 'and blessed them, and called their name Adam on the day they were created.' Whenever the Torah repeats something, the emphasis always suggests deeper implication. Here, it is impossible to ignore that the creation of male and female was simultaneous.*[1]

Therefore, creation would have to be androgynous.   Because what happens in consciousness always shows up at every level, it's no accident that at the same time that we have begun to recognize the need for an understanding of spiritual androgyny, our scientists have also pointed out that embryos are initially sexually androgynous. After a certain point, an embryo starts to more fully develop the characteristics of one sex or the other, but until that time it is androgynous. It is also noted that the physical signs of the opposite sex remain in an atrophied state in both the matured man and the matured woman, showing that both sexes are still included in all of us. In other words, *we were conceived androgynous, and when we return to our spiritual innocence, our souls will express their original inclusiveness.* In a number of cultures, including that of American Indians, homosexuals are honored as divine or super human beings. Most likely that is because androgyny is seen by those cultures to be Godly.

Androgyny is not an idea. It is an experience. It is a soul experience. *The soul is without form or gender, though it expresses itself infinitely and can be observed everywhere. The key is to double think; at which time one looks at uniqueness and is simultaneously aware that within each appearance spiritual infinity exists.* A mystic thinks androgynously. It cannot be any other way. A mystic does not think sexually one way or the other but androgynously, transcending anything that divides or limits. Once androgyny is experienced, "both/and" replaces "either/or" in thought and deed. Choice is no longer between this or that, but is rather a matter of listening to what the Spirit dictates at the moment.

Androgyny frees the soul from the responsibility of having to judge. An appreciation of androgynous perception is a necessary precursor of universal love and of universal equality. In fact, equality cannot be experienced until and unless an androgynous state of consciousness that includes our own being and all other beings has been realized. Everyone who has loved, who has risen above judgment, who has felt the presence of the Christ has experienced androgyny, if not consciously, then subconsciously. It is important, however, that one recognizes this quality of soul within one's self and in others in order for one's Christlike androgynous vision to be conscious and permanent. Once androgyny becomes conscious and becomes the lens through which life is envisioned, once androgyny is freed from morality and a sexual connotation, the ascension beyond conceptual judgment becomes a possibility.

Androgyny is the mystical marriage where the universe is integrated within the individual. Androgynous consciousness frees one to marry the universe in a total aloneness, all-one-ness. When people recognize the fact that because the Christ is all-inclusive and universal, the slightest experience of the Christ is a peephole into androgyny. After that, we can expand our awareness until we see ourselves in everyone—both male and female— until we are in love, literally in Love, with the universe. It's all God.

The Science of Complements

Let patience have her perfect work, that ye may be perfect and entire, wanting nothing.

James 1:4

*A*s I said in the Introduction, life's most vital secrets go unobserved, not because they are complicated but because of their simplicity. Believe me, of all the "how to's," while we are still talking about the letter of truth, there is one subtle, but all important, double thread prerequisite to all the others that is so obvious that we miss it: *Everything at the finite level needs a complement to complete it.*

The word "complement" comes from a Latin word which means "to complete." At the level of the finite—the third-dimensional level of time and space, the "*this world*" level that Jesus talked of—no thing and no idea stands by itself. Everything needs something added to it in order for it to be made whole, to be healed. At the human level, everything needs something to complete it. A right-brain idea by itself is a half-truth, but when it is complemented by its left-brain equivalent, it becomes a concept that transcends either idea alone. When our masculine side complements our feminine side and vice versa, we become something greater and different from either by itself. In practical application, it is wonderful to have an inspired creative and innovative business idea, but if it is not complemented with a logical and feasible economic plan, it will come to nothing. All the business sense in the world won't make a success without the complement of a useful idea. Knowledge needs experience and vice versa. Knowledge that is not complemented by experience is fruitless, and experience is meaningless unless it is complemented by the knowledge of what has taken place.

From the beginning, the whole purpose of this writing has been to demonstrate how important and necessary it is for us to assimilate or combine the virtues of the traditionally objective, institutional, or material approach with the virtues of the subjective, intuitive, or spiritual approach. They are necessary complements to each other. In the Yin and Yang of human third-dimensional existence, everything needs a complement to make it whole. Absolutes are true at some abstract or theoretical, fourth dimensional, subjective, or spiritual level, but at the objective level of personal sense where we spend most of our time, everything needs the addition of something else in order to complete it or make it work.

Paul pointed out the need to complement speaking in tongues with the addition of understandable content:

> ...Except ye utter by the tongue words easy to be understood, how shall it be known what is spoken? For ye shall speak into the air....
> Therefore if I know not the meaning of the voice, I shall be unto him that speaketh a barbarian, and he that speaketh shall be a barbarian unto me.[2]

On the other hand, any language that is not complemented by spiritual content is also meaningless. There is not a single thought or thing, be it material, social, or spiritual, that stands by itself at the level of the intellect. That is why any statement that anyone makes can be contradicted. Speak any truth without adding its complement and its exceptions can be pointed out. One of the problems with our instantaneous society and quick-fix mentality is that we often do not take time to look for or add the complements to a statement that will make a half-truth whole. If there is anything in this book that you disagree with, it is most likely because I have unwittingly left out its complement, an addition that would make it a whole truth.

The science of complements may sound simplistic, but, in fact, we must be aware of its importance if we want to assure success and eliminate the last traces of guilt from our consciousness. Failure to achieve our goal is almost always due to the fact that we have not asked ourselves what complement had to be added to our concepts in order to make them work. It is popular in business today to make mission statements, because in doing so, complements that are needed to accomplish the goal are often recognized in the process of objectifying the mission.

Jesus almost always included complements. He gave us two commandments because both were needed to complement each other. He didn't just say for us to love God alone. He added that we should love our neighbors or the world of effects as well. Neither of Jesus' two commandments is sufficient to fulfill the law by itself, but when they complement each other, ascension consciousness is possible. Unless God (Love) is expressed in material terms, it is sterile, and actions that are not based on Love (God) are futile. Complementary wholeness is what James was talking about when he said, "...*be ye doers of the word, and not hearers only deceiving your own selves.*"[3] Hearing needs the complement of doing, and doing is fruitless without hearing how to do what needs to be done.

The secret of the science of complements is that this approach eliminates the necessity for resisting evil. Evil never starts out as evil. It comes about because something desired had not been complemented with the right way of accomplishing it. Some good thing is desired, but unless the desire is complemented with the right way for it to be attained, wrong action follows. For instance, a thief subconsciously senses that it is his or her right to be heir and joint heir to all that the world has to offer. However, by not understanding that supply does not come from outside but comes from one's own giving, the thief goes about trying to manifest his riches in the wrong way. One tries to take rather than give.

At every occasion and with every thought, we can take the time to meditate and ask ourselves what complement is needed in order to complete what we wish to accomplish. If it is a matter of love, we can ask ourselves what action is needed to complement our desire to love so that it will manifest. When we have an objective goal, we can ask ourselves what subjective or spiritual principle needs to be expressed, because that which is in our consciousness will dictate the success of our results. When complements are included, duality ceases to exist. As a bonus, if in our disappointments we find what missing complementary principle was responsible for our failure, we can learn from our negative experiences rather than being used by them.

The Obscenity of Absolutes

*A*bsolutes are the enemies of complements. To think in terms of absolutes defeats the science of complements. Absolutes do not exist at the less-than-absolute level of this world. It is surprising how many traps we lay for ourselves and for others by habitually using absolute words about human conduct or situations where complements are necessary to make things whole. Spiritual reality is unchangeable, so at the spiritual level absolutes do exist. But to us as human beings change is constantly taking place; therefore, there are no absolutes at the personal dimension. When we and our spiritual advisors unthinkingly and habitually toss around such absolute words as "always," "only," "never," "none," we make ourselves vulnerable to becoming guilty for being unable to back them up. Humanly, there is never a never, never an only, never a none, and every time we use those absolute words we are laying a trap for ourselves and lying to others.

We do indeed make greater progress than we otherwise would when we aim at absolutes, but if we believe that absolutes are possible to achieve at the level of human nature, we and our teachers set us up for both failure and guilt. Alcoholics Anonymous avoids this pitfall. They tell a recovering alcoholic not to say, "I will never take another drink," because they know that such an absolute statement will doom that person to failure.

Instead, they tell them just to say, "I won't take a drink for the next twenty-four hours."

For that matter, a guilt trip was laid on all of us when we were told that Jesus was perfect (another absolute word) and that we should be like him or feel guilty. Subjectively, he was indeed perfect in that he was spiritually all that a growing, evolving human being could or should be, but in this world's terms he wasn't flawless. He stumbled, cried, got angry, and though he said "judge not," he scolded the Pharisees and Sadducees. You might say that when Jesus condemned the fig tree for not having figs, even though it wasn't its season to bear fruit, and then went into the temple and chased the moneychangers with a whip, that Jesus was having a bad day. But, in truth, that was part of his divine perfection because by his not being absolute and getting angry at the moneychangers, he set in motion the conditions that led to his crucifixion and ultimate triumph over death.

Paradoxically, the word "absolute" comes from a Latin word which means "to free, to let loose," and yet it has come to mean exactly the opposite because absolutes eliminate alternatives, and without alternatives we are prisoners. In fact, that is one of the wonderful things about the Christian story. It offers us alternatives. We can be both man of earth and man of God—in the world and not of it. The reason absolute words defeat us is because they imply either/or. For instance, with all good intent to dedicate one's self to the fullness of God, one might make such an absolute statement as, "I won't look to the human scene for anything." By that statement, one creates the duality of either/ or. If that person had said, "I won't look to the third-dimensional world for anything without realizing that it is God appearing at that level," their statement would not have been absolute. It would not have smacked of rejection because at the spiritual level, where absolutes do exist, it is indeed all God.

Yes, I am again making a case for inclusiveness. Yes, I am asking you to accept the divine paradox of the double thread. The paradox, similar to the two commandments, is that absolutes do not exist at the personal level, but because they do exist at the spiritual level there is no ultimate duality. That paradox is resolved when we double think and no longer expect absolutes to exist in our human lives while we simultaneously know absolutely that spiritually it is all God. Objectively, it is absolutely true that I have no life of my own. Subjectively, it is absolutely true that I am life eternal. When I complement those two would-be absolutes with each other, I arrive at ascension consciousness.

Now I am going to sound as if I am contradicting all I have just said. There is an absolute. By its nature, all-inclusiveness is absolute. When the nature of God and the nature of error are included, when the divine and the human are included, when every dimension, every idea, the subjective and the objective, the within and the without is included, it is absolutely all God—no ifs, ands, or buts. When all ways are included in the infinite way, we arrive at the absolute. It has to be because there isn't anything else. It's absolute because no way and nothing is excluded.

In the past, those teachers who put down what they called "absolutists" had a point. The absolutists they were talking about denied the human scene or that evil had to be actively dealt with. In doing so, they were like ostriches with their heads in the sand. In order to be an effective spiritual healer, just knowing that it is all God is not enough. Spiritually, you have to recognize the powerlessness of evil in order to get rid of it. The new absolute is absolute because being all-inclusive there is absolutely nothing left out. By including all the many levels of multi-dimensional being without the need to eliminate any, it is possible to be spiritually absolute and see that it is all God.

The Limits of Law

*E*ver since rational thought evolved in humankind, the search has been for laws to live by so that choices wouldn't have to be made. Choices put too much responsibility on the individual. Man set up laws to live by because he didn't love himself. He didn't trust that he could decide what was the loving thing to do in every situation. He believed that if there were laws to follow he wouldn't have to be responsible for himself. Except for those who understood that Jesus was telling them that there was another way to live, which was by Grace, to this day human beings seek laws to follow in order to avoid feeling, to avoid thinking, and to avoid having to make decisions. Many people depend on dictatorial leaders and bullying ministers to tell them what laws to live by in order for them not to have to be responsible to Spirit.

The body of laws that we have on our books, which by their nature are absolutes, have been created by good intention. No one is arguing about that. By and large, laws, including the Ten Commandments, have been put in place in order to keep destructive or inhuman things from happening until the spirit evolves in individuals to the point where they can know what it is to live spiritually—by Grace.

Because the Christ message of Grace is one that incorporates alternatives rather than absolutes, Jesus gave us the two complementary commandments of love and action that would fulfill all the good intentions of the law down to the last jot and tittle. In that he was saying that if we approached the law objectively, we would inevitably sin, fall short, but if we did the subjective loving, compassionate, generous thing, if we lived by Spirit rather than by absolute laws, even the Ten Commandments, the law would automatically be fulfilled.

No wonder Paul confuses us. He was a master at setting up specific and absolute laws of conduct and implied that if we did not follow them absolutely, we would be sinning. Yet, surprisingly, he turns right around and in his Epistle to the Romans he made some seldom-quoted Scripture denouncing the law or absolutes as the very cause of sin.

> *For the promise, that he should be the heir of the*
> *world, was not to Abraham, or to his seed, through*
> *the law, but through the righteousness of faith. For*
> *if they which are of the law be heirs, faith is made*
> *void, and the promise made of none effect: Because*

the law worketh wrath: for where no law is, there is
no transgression.   Romans 4:13-15

...I had not known sin, but by the law: for I had
not known lust, except the law has said, Thou
shalt not covet. But sin, taking occasion by the
commandment, wrought in me all manner of
concupiscence. For without the law sin was dead.
For I was alive without the law once: but when the
commandment came, sin revived, and I died. And
the commandment, which was ordained to life, I
found to be unto death. For sin, taking occasion
by the commandment, deceived me, and by it slew
me.
                                   Romans 7:7-11

The Devil And

When I say "the devil and," I am defining what the devil is, not leaving a sentence unfinished. The word "and" itself is the devil. By the devil I am referring to anything that encourages us to believe in or accept duality or a sense of separation rather than the realization that there is but one life and one presence. The word "and" deceives us. We spend our lives trying to experience our oneness with the allness of God, but the minute we think in terms of "and" we are already in danger of accepting either/or. Unless we are grounded in double thinking and are able to see the multiplicity of this world, while simultaneously feeling that it is all God, "and" can make us a house divided.

The nature of thought divides one concept, one idea, one observation from another and multiplicity is defined by "and." "And" creates the whole objective universe because things have to be objectified in order to be differentiated. Nevertheless, our goal is to experience infinity and God as all, without any differentiation. When that happens, deep in our consciousness there is no "and." The triune life remains a concept rather than an experience when we put an "and" in between Omnipresence, Omnipotence, and Omniscience, as though they are three rather than one. Omnipotence, which is God or cause, Omniscience, which is the consciousness or Spirit that incubates creation, and Omnipresence, which is the Son or material result, are all one with no "and," three "as" one rather than three "in" one.

Let me show you how often we are led astray by "and" so that you can be aware of what you are saying when you subconsciously use the word. We spend our lives saying that we want to be instruments for God, that we want to be channels for God, that we want to do God's will. Hidden in each of those statements is an implied "and" deceiving us into believing in the duality of a God other than our own being. In order for us to be instruments, there would have to be two—God "and" us. In order for us to do God's will it would mean there is an "and," God's will "and" ours. When it is realized that God's will is our will, there is no "and."

Every spoken absolute implies an "and." When the Nicene Creed said that Jesus was the "only" Son of God, it separated us from Jesus. He was the only Son "and" we were not. Try for a moment to think without using the word "and." Subjectively it is possible but objectively it isn't. As a human being "and" is needed to identify and individualize objects. However, if you are anchored in the Spirit of Love it is possible to say "and" while simultaneously remembering that God is appearing as all that is because it is all God.

Integration

What I have been leading up to by suggesting that you appreciate the necessity of your being aware of the importance of complements, by your recognizing the androgynous nature of your soul, and how by misusing the word "and" you may unwittingly create duality, has all been in order to lay the groundwork for the importance of integration.

After I wrote *The Double Thread*, people would say, "Oh yes, I understand. What you are talking about is balance, that we must balance our spiritual with our material selves." At the time I agreed because I couldn't think of a more appropriate word, though I didn't feel balance was quite what I really meant. Finally, I realized that balance implies duality, a compromise between two differences. The word I was looking for finally came to me: "integration." I realized that the ascension consciousness wasn't arrived at by balance but by integration. When one's consciousness is still at the third-dimensional level of cause and effect, of either/or, balance is a valuable goal to achieve. However, when one arrives at the anointing, where it is no longer God "and" but God "as," then integration has taken place.

Integration comes from the Latin word "integrare," which means "to make whole, renew, untouched, entire." As long as we still think of ourselves as departmentalized, categorized, or subdivided, we are neither whole nor integrated. The magic we experience after making contact with our God Self comes about because when it happens we have personally experienced divine integration. Integration is a positive approach to life. It, like inclusiveness, is a matter of addition, not elimination. When that takes place, we find that integration offers us a new freedom that we were unable to understand or experience until we went beyond the borders of the either/or thinking.

Integrity is the same word as integration. Look at those you feel are spiritually mature, those you believe have integrity, and you will see that they have the ability to integrate their subjective spiritual principles with their objective material achievements. Those who have integrity demonstrate inclusiveness. Those who have gratitude acknowledge integration.

Ken Wilber, who has inherited the California spiritual/intellectual Mafia's crown from Allan Watts, has written an article for the *Noetic Science Magazine* expressing the need for integration at the psychological level. The article was titled, "How Big Is Our Umbrella?" In it Wilber lists a dozen different schools of consciousness. His premise is that we have to integrate all of them into a union in order to comprehend the facets of the consciousness diamond. In the inclusiveness paradigm, he was on the right track, but though he pointed out the "what," he didn't specify how we go about doing it unless he intended to imply that integration is the way.

In follow-ups to the article, several authors and scientists commented on Wilber's premise. Author/scientist Alwyn Scott implied that Wilber was suggesting reductionism (rather than integration) as the way and questioned it. He felt that even his trying to reduce the meaning of consciousness to the dozen ways or levels of consciousness that can be identified suggests that our ever being able to contain consciousness in a single envelope would be impossible. However, Scott stated, "For a truly integrated theory of consciousness to emerge, we must transform ourselves into a culture where people typically listen to each other and give intuition a seat above the salt, a culture in which the immensely multifaceted nature of consciousness can be imagined." I agree, but as a prelude to his social or objective approach, we must first spiritually integrate the community of personal identities we include in ourselves.

Duane Elgin, author of *Awakening Earth*, took the concept of integration a step closer to what I feel is the answer by saying that we have to develop a new expanded mind. However, he too reduced it to being a collective endeavor without saying how we individually could set about doing it.

Rather than reductionism, Jeanne Achterberg, author and psychologist, came even closer to a spiritual integration, because she sees it as a matter of expansion, at which time as a whole we would individually expand to include the different aspects of consciousness. However, she didn't suggest how we were to do it.

Peter Russell, author of *The Global Brain Awakens* and other books, perpetuated the "what" but not the "how" by pointing out our need for "A new super paradigm" in order to understand consciousness, one that approaches it totally rather than breaking it down. He proposed one that synthesizes the seemingly incompatible worlds of science and spirit, "not so much as a larger umbrella as a new umbrella." Right on—an ascension consciousness umbrella.

Finally, in the Noetic Science article,[4] Will Keepin, who is an environmental scientist, looked at the subject of integration socially. He sees this integration possible only if we have spiritually oriented communities that are grounded in ecological or scientific realities, as well as spiritual, I might add.

If I had been asked to offer my two cents to that article, which I wasn't, I would have said that all those learned authors were on the right track; they were all adding facets to the one diamond, but perhaps they were missing one link. Through evolution we are now ready to bring into play something which will accomplish all Wilber would like to see without eliminating any approach. The " how to" not only comes about through our experiencing our infinite nature via prayer and meditation, but also through our consciously employing our newly evolved ability to double think in order to integrate. Without losing sight of any aspect of life, we can finally understand and integrate all the dimensions of consciousness, because we now have the ability to think a number of things simultaneously without excluding or losing the place or value of any.

Integration does not mean we have to homogenize all the different aspects of consciousness into a mental smoothy where individual tastes are lost. We don't have to synthesize the aspects into a single formula. Through the spirit of a unity through a diversity of awareness, we can integrate all aspects under one umbrella. By honoring each aspect simultaneously and actively, we can transcend the limitation of present awareness and experience life as an integrated interplay of consciousness. No longer limited by linear thought, we can now "cluster-think." That means we can see the whole without losing sight of any of the parts. In the "spirit" of integration, we will realize that it is all God.

The Principle of Priority

*T*he road to the spirit of integration and wholeness is paved by the principle of priority. "Priority" is such a flat and seemingly uninspiring word, yet how we prioritize is probably the most influential, practical, and spiritual reason for our successes and a lack of prioritizing the cause of our failures. Success may not be a matter of either/or, but it most certainly is a matter of prioritizing. We can talk all we want to about our spiritual values and our materialistic goals, but if our priorities are in the wrong order, there isn't any God out there that will make things come out as we wish. Prayer may help us see our mistaken priorities, but that may be like closing the barn door after the horses have gotten away.

In my theatrical life the biggest failure I had at that time came about because I got carried away and forgot my priorities. Ordinarily the first thing a producer does is to take an option on a play; the next thing is to sign a director and star; after that it is time to lease a theater and set a rehearsal schedule. Even though the theater would not be used for months ahead, the right time to lease a theater comes after the other priorities are in line.

I produced a play written by John van Druten who had given Marlon Brando his first acting job in John's play, *I Remember Mama*. At the time we were producing the play, Brando had become a big movie star and though he had not returned to Broadway since his success in *A Streetcar Named Desire*, he read the script and said he wanted to do it. Contracts were not yet signed, but feeling Brando would make the play an assured success, I jumped the gun, did not follow the right priorities, committed myself to a theater, and announced an opening date. Brando stalled and stalled and stalled, disappeared, reappeared, disappeared again, and as rehearsal time grew near it became obvious that because I had leased the theater there was nothing we could do but go ahead with the best substitute we could find. Because my priorities were in the wrong order, compromise became the name of the game. We signed an actor who wasn't up to the part, and the whole production went down the drain.

Priority is also an important ingredient in personal relationships. Couples do not stay together over a long period of time unless their values are the same, which is to say that they do not stay together unless the priorities they place on their values are similar. When there are long-standing relationships you can bet your bottom dollar that no matter whether the couple approach life in a dog-eat-dog fashion or in one of gentleness and love, they stay together because they share the same priorities. Where your heart, your priority, is, there is the coin of your soul. If a couple or even a business partnership is in trouble, the first place they should look is at their priorities and either reach agreement on the order and value of their priorities or face the writing on the wall and shake the dust from their feet.

The importance of priority goes all through the Bible. The very first words in the Bible announce priority, "*In the beginning God,*" and all through the New Testament Jesus repeats the importance of priority. When asked, "Which is the great commandment," he outlined his priority by saying, "*Thou shalt love the Lord thy God with all thy heart, and with all thy soul, and with all thy mind. This is the first and great commandment. And the second is like unto it, Thou shalt love thy neighbor as thyself.*"[5]

In saying that the whole law is fulfilled by his two commandments he nevertheless gave us a priority—love Spirit first and then effects. Jesus said, "*Take no thought, saying, What shall we eat? or, What shall we drink? or Wherewithal shall we be clothed? (For after all these things do the Gentiles seek:) for your heavenly Father knoweth that ye have need of all these things. But seek ye first the kingdom of God, and his righteousness; and all these things shall be added unto you.*"[6]

In saying that, he wasn't putting down the Gentiles as a people but rather he was again telling us to prioritize and put cause before effect. He was saying that *the principle of life would manifest abundance, fulfillment, and everything we need if we would make Spirit our first priority.* He even said that if we put the spiritual first that Solomon, the epitome of luxury, would not be clothed any more glamorously than we.

Simple as it may sound, the spiritual revolution that is taking place in our government and economic structure today is taking place over a change in priority. In the past we have said, "In God we trust," but if the results we wanted were not soon coming, we would send in the CIA or drop a few bombs. Who were we kidding? In the past our first priority has been to get results rather than act out of the Spirit of Love. But the wheel is turning, and more and more we should look for politicians who will give top priority to the subjective values that founded our nation on spiritual principles. When I say that, I am not talking about moral concepts made up by human beings but by the Spirit inherent in our actions. Partly because of the growing influence of the collective consciousness, each of us has as great, if not greater, influence on the future than our politicians. That is because each of us who put Spirit first by our example helps transform the collective consciousness. At least, we can if we pray without ceasing which is to say if we make love, compassion, honesty, generosity, and all the other spiritual principles our top priority without ceasing.

Priority does not mean that we consider only the Spirit, but it does mean that before we proceed at the material or objective level we stop and think of what our top priority is and how it affects matters. To put Spirit first is to be spiritually objective. The story of Mary and Martha is another example of Jesus' teachings on the importance of priority and the precedence of subjective values over an objective approach.

> *Now it came to pass, as they went, that he entered into a certain village: and a certain woman named Martha received him into her house. And she had a sister called Mary, which also sat at Jesus' feet, and heard his word. But Martha was cumbered about much serving, and came to him, and said, Lord, dost thou not care that my sister hath left me to serve alone? bid her therefore that she help me. And*

Jesus answered and said unto her, Martha, Martha, thou art careful and troubled about many things: But one thing is needful: and Mary hath chosen that good part, which shall not be taken away from her.[7]

Martha, representing the objective side of ourselves, took the Christ into her house, her consciousness, but there was another side within her, representing the subjective Mary-side of ourselves, that was contemplative, that sat listening to the Spirit. Martha, perhaps the workaholic-side, complained. Jesus had compassion but pointed out that Martha's priorities were reversed. She had let the objective world of effects, of things, take priority over Spirit, but though things will be taken away, Spirit is eternal. He wasn't being an absolutist by denying that things were necessary, but rather that it would be a better way to live if action was first complemented by Spirit.

The Mary and Martha story points out another priority that has commonly been reversed. We hear that "it is better to give than receive." Wrong! *Until we have received, we have nothing to give. Our first priority is to seek God, seek guidance, seek Spirit, and when we have received we will not only have something to give but will know by example how to give and in what spirit.* There is only one love, one healing, one Spirit. It is all God's love and healing. We express it. However, we cannot express it unless we have first received it. I believe that the number one priority at the beginning of each day is for us to meditate or pray in order to receive guidance from our higher consciousness. To say that we are virtuous because we meditate every morning is like saying we should be admired because we eat breakfast, lunch, and dinner. All those who meditate regularly know how wonderfully and necessarily they are fed by the Spirit. Priority comes from a Latin word meaning "prior to." If we "*seek first the kingdom,*" prior to our actions we can make this world into "*My Kingdom.*"

All you have to do is to listen carefully to people in order to know their true priorities. If you are going to give a talk and someone says, "I really want to hear you tonight, but I can't. My bridge club meets tonight," what that person is really saying is, "I would like to hear you but playing bridge is my top priority."

By the same token, we do not have to mentally decide the rights and wrongs of others' religions or teachings. All we have to do is to observe how they treat others, whether they are giving the Spirit of Love top priority rather than their judgments or their actions. *"Ye shall know them by their fruits,"*[8] could read, "Ye shall know them by their priorities."

Today many are crossing over into a new priority. In the past most people primarily saw themselves as human beings and secondarily as having a divine potential. Now many are at the place where they can actually experience the fact that they are first and foremost consciousness or divine beings and that secondarily they express themselves as material beings. In the past we thought that ascension meant leaving the body behind, but now we can ascend in consciousness without having to leave the body. We can realize that we are our first priority, consciousness or cause, which then expresses itself as a body. When we fully see ourselves primarily as consciousness, we can take up or lay down our bodies at will. We can come and go because time and space no longer limit us. Death ceases because there is nothing in consciousness that dies. *"Seek ye first the kingdom of God,"* and you will be able to see that it is all God.

Chapter 8

THE I THAT IS US

And God said, Let US make man in OUR image, after OUR Likeness...   Genesis 1:26

And after six days, Jesus taketh Peter, James, and John his brother, and bringeth them up into an high mountain apart, And was transfigured before them: and his face did shine as the sun, and his raiment was white as the light.   Matthew 17:1

All power is in the word. Whenever we use a word, that word begins to create itself in form. Even when we desire to do good works, we are unable to accomplish our purpose if we know the truth and yet do not use the right words to convey it. Jesus tried valiantly to share his vision but unless he was misquoted, which is highly likely, there are stumbling blocks in the words that are attributed to him. Because Jesus used ordinary language to explain extraordinary possibilities, such as our eventually being able to come and go from our bodies, most who heard him thought he was "mad." For instance, in referring to his life he said, *"No man taketh it from me, but I lay it down of myself. I have power to lay it down, and I have power to take it again. This commandment have I received of my Father."* The Scripture goes on to report, *"There was a division therefore again among the Jews for these sayings. And many of* then said, He hath a devil and is mad; why hear ye him?"[1] No wonder they thought he was mad. He spoke subjectively and they heard him objectively.

There are a number of times in the Gospels when either those who quoted Jesus did not understand what he was saying or else Jesus did not fully explain that he was talking from a subjective level that those who heard him were unable to comprehend. At one minute Jesus would say, "*I can of mine own self do nothing.*"[2] At the next minute, as far as we know, without explaining that he was now talking about a different and mystical dimension of his being, he would further confuse them by saying, "*I and my Father are one.*"[3] When he added, "*He that hath seen me hath seen the father,*"[4] those who heard him most likely knew Joseph personally; so naturally some of them thought Jesus had lost his marbles. From their objective and literal point of view, it sounded as though he was saying that he was both Joseph and himself. Unless he complemented his statement by explaining that his material self and his spiritual cause were one and the same, they were naturally perplexed.

At face value, the eighth chapter of John illustrates what I mean. It clearly shows how Jesus, speaking from what we would today call his right brain or subjective consciousness, was totally misunderstood by the left-brain-Pharisees he was talking to. In the twelfth verse he says, "*I am the light of the world.*" To us it is obvious that the "I" he was talking about was his subjective divine identity, but the Pharisees, who only understood left-brain objective stuff, answered, that he was bearing record of himself and his record was not true. Of course, it wasn't true to them. They thought by saying "I" he was referring to his body, his personal sense self. By adding, "*Ye judge after the flesh; I judge no man,*" [5] Jesus hinted that there was another identity, but he did not explain what that other subjective identity was. His next words must have really confused the Pharisees, "*And yet if I judge, my judgment is true: for I am not alone, but I and the Father that sent me.*"[6] Naturally, the Pharisees looked around, and not seeing Joseph, thought Jesus was out in left field.

By saying, "*I am not alone but I and the Father who sent me,*" he really meant that he, as you and I, could be seen in two ways —as a physical presence and as a divine God self-creating consciousness. In adding "*I am one that bear witness of myself, and the Father that sent me beareth witness of me,*"[7] he was saying that the physical bears witness to the Divine and the Divine, the Higher Consciousness, bears witness to the material. No wonder that the objective-minded Pharisees, if the Scripture is accurate, thought he was possessed by a demon, which is to say, "insane."

Assuming Jesus was accurately quoted, if Jesus had fully explained what he meant when he used word "I" subjectively at one time and objectively at another, those who heard him might have better understood. Most of us today are just as confused as they were then when we hear or use the word "I." At one moment we say "I" subjectively, meaning our Spirit or consciousness, and at another moment we use "I" to refer to our personal-sense self. The difference is that Jesus had attained ascension consciousness; so when he said "I" he most likely meant it both ways at the same time.

There are a number of valuable teachings today from which we can benefit, but we have to be careful how we interpret their use of pronouns. For instance, I can show you one short paragraph in *A Course in Miracles* that is very helpful; however, it uses the word "you" forty-four times. Half of the time it is talking about you as the Son of God, and the other half it speaks about the personal sense "you" without pointing out when its meaning shifts from the Divine to the personal. It might help if someone were to go through the manuscript and capitalize "You" every time it means the "Divine You" and leave "you" in lower case every time it meant material sense.

I know that I keep repeating myself about our need to reverse our usual priority, but that is what the new paradigm is all about. We have to stop thinking of ourselves primarily as egocentric humans and begin to automatically think of ourselves as primarily spiritual beings and secondarily as physical ones. Eventually we will be able to see the two as one, and when we do, the most important step we can ever take in life will have been taken.

Our habit of denying our divinity runs deep. When we hear someone make a statement such as, "So it is that we, insignificant you and I, who of ourselves are really nothing, can become the source through which infinite wisdom flows," we have to watch out. At first the statement sounds OK, but if we are not careful, we automatically buy into limitation and think of ourselves primarily as insignificant beings rather than as beings made in the image of God. We may at times confuse ourselves with our egos; however, it does not make us any less the children of God. Confusion is temporary but our reality is eternal. To believe that we must see ourselves as "nothings" in order to see ourselves as "God beings," is the same as saying we must believe in a lie in order to realize a truth.

When I have attended an Alcoholics Anonymous meeting and on the roll call heard someone say, "My name is Joe. I am an alcoholic," I can't help but wish that he had a sense of the double thread. Instead of denying the Christ-I of his eternal being by confusing it with the roel he is playing in this life time, it would have been more spiritually accurate if he had said, "My name is Joe. He's an alcoholic." By answering the roll call in that fashion he could have had it both ways. *He could have recognized that the character he is playing in this lifetime drama can't drink, but his eternal being is free from addiction, perfect and beyond human limitation.* It sounds as if I am splitting hairs, but I hate to see people locking themselves into laws that are less than the Christ of their being. Jesus didn't become the Son of God when he realized he was nothing. He became the Son of God when he realized he was everything—when he realized he was one with all that God is. He acknowledged the eternal nature of his being when he said, even *"before Abraham was, I am."*[8]

If God is omnipresence, we are presently the sons and daughters right now, but, as I reported in the first part of this book, when Paul said, *"For what I would, that I do not; but what I hate, that do I,"*[9] he was contradicting omnipresence. His statement showed that Paul wasn't talking about the same sense of self that Jesus was when Jesus said, "*I and my Father are one.*"[10] Paul was seeing himself as human, not divine. If Paul had said, "That which Paul would not do, he does, but I am the way, the truth, and the life," he would have shown that he had made what I call "the metaphysical leap."

The Metaphysical Leap

The metaphysical leap is what happens to us when our priorities shift and the invisibles become as real or more real to us as the visibles. After experiencing the metaphysical leap, we become simultaneously aware that we have a physical presence or self and an essential spiritual or invisible presence, as though we have a Self that is observing our self. Once that leap has taken place, life is never quite the same because all kinds of alternatives become possible. Material limitations are no longer so inhibiting, and the invisible power of consciousness to transform the visible material scene becomes an experiential reality. Those who have made the leap can tell very quickly if someone else has made it or not. There is a kind of secret or inner language that identifies those who do not take appearances too literally.

We who have made the metaphysical leap may constantly confuse our families and our friends. Unless they have also experienced it themselves, they will think that we are hypocrites. That is because at one minute it will seem that we are approaching life objectively or materialistically, and at the next minute we seem to have chosen to be spiritual and unrealistic about what is taking place, depending on how we want to play it. However, for those who have experienced the leap, life becomes much easier to handle, because they are consciously aware of the two ways of I—the singular visible one and the multi-faceted plural one. In fact, "I" is no longer single, but being consciousness as well as body, "I" becomes a "we" or an "us."

The first step we must take in order to live our lives without confusing our identities is to recognize that at the earth level, the level of personal sense, we have two basic co-existing selves. Our visible personality is our mask. It is a concept; therefore, it is limited and fictional, like an actor temporarily playing a part in a soap opera. Our other self is invisible, infinite, eternal; therefore our true self. Secondly, we can understand that the false "I," our lower self or outer self, exists only for us when we are on stage, in the human scene. The other and true "I" is the Higher or Divine inner Self. It exists eternally. Thirdly, we can learn to stand aside and become aware of our Divine Selves observing our personal sense selves.

Unless you and I are so grounded in our ability to consciously double think and consciously realize that our two I's, the divine and its appearance as our physical selves, are One, when we use the word "I" we are blaspheming. When you say, "I don't feel well today," whom are you talking about? God? When you say, "I had a flat tire this morning," you are using the name of God in vain. You didn't have a flat tire, your car did. If you confuse your small "I" with your spiritual "I" you constantly project limitation on yourself. When you think, "I haven't," you place yourself under the law of lack and you are therefore setting your self up to manifest lack.

Until I made the metaphysical leap and was able to make sure which "I" that I was referring to when I used the word "I," I figured out a way to help keep my selves straight. I started to think of my human or outer self by my given name, Walter, the one that was given to me when I showed up with a material body. "Walter of his own self can do nothing," and that's the truth. Walter has no power because Walter doesn't even exist except as this limited, finite, and therefore unreal, concept of self that I am appearing as. My other self could say, "I can do all things," because that one is my inner self, the Christ presence which is evident when my humanity isn't claiming to be me.

Seeing Walter as my child has been invaluable. In the past, when I have said that I haven't had any children of my own I have lied. As of this writing, I have an almost eighty-year-old child named Walter. Sometimes I have to spank him, sometimes I have to nurture him, sometimes listen to him, sometimes talk to him. However, as long as I can remain objective about the difference between my subjective eternal Self and this temporary personal self that I also inhabit in this lifetime, I can be constantly aware of which me is in the driver's seat.

Maintaining this double sense of self is necessary in every facet of our daily lives if we want to avoid duality. For instance, before I became a producer, I was an actor. I found that there had to be two me's on stage. One me was physically there saying the lines and expressing feelings, while there was another me talking to myself, "Someone in the balcony coughed," "Raise your voice," or "The scene is dragging. Pick up the pace." If either me was absent, the performance would have been unprofessional, to say the least.

If, a few years ago, in referring to myself, I had said, "I am God," I hope someone would have locked me up because at that point I would have still been identifying myself egotistically. Today, I can say it because through double thinking, I can simultaneously know 100% that I of my own self , as Walter, can do nothing, and at the same time I can know 100 percent that spiritually "I can do all things through (my) Christ (consciousness) which strengthens me."[11] Nothing is either/or, for it's all God.

The Explosion of Self

*I*n explaining what introduced the metaphysical leap to the collective consciousnes s, it may help to explain something that happened in 1945. This experience made it possible for us to finally be aware of the reality and importance of the invisible nature of our multi-dimensional being, something that we were ever able to before. It put the invisible within us on an equal footing with the visible. That was the day the world's consciousness was transformed, if not exploded, when it became public knowledge that the atom had been split. When we heard about it, none of us had any idea what the splitting of the atom would symbolize, how it would affect every aspect of life on earth both spiritually and materially, and why we would be able to know ourselves more fully because of it.

Previous to the splitting of the atom, humankind had for centuries speculated about invisible or spiritual things, but the speculation was mainly superstition or fantasy. When the chips were down, human consciousness was "man-ipulated" by the first law of human nature—material survival predicated on the belief that reality could be touched, tasted, or smelled. We thought that knowing ourselves went no further than knowing our outer human or psychological nature. When the atom was split by something invisible and immaterial in the consciousness of humankind, the invisible was at last put on an equal footing with the visible. The power of the invisible Spirit to affect material appearances was at last affirmed in the collective consciousness.

The splitting of the atom was a spiritual act because the intangible Spirit in human consciousness had split the very substance out of which all material form is composed—the atom. The dropping of the atom bomb showed us that there is enough energy or consciousness in a single atom to destroy (or create) a city. Fantastic, but no longer fantasy. This literally earth-shaking phenomena has been responsible for more of the spiritual confusion and social chaos that exists today than anything else. To illustrate the reason, we have to approach the splitting of the atom both subjectively (spiritually) and objectively (materially).

Subjectively, two thousand years ago a state of consciousness we call "the Christ" was crystallized in a man named Jesus of Nazareth. This consciousness eventually and inevitably led not only to his death and resurrection, but his resurrection also exemplified a state of consciousness that ultimately made it possible for us to split the atom. Jesus realized that all matter was spirit, or energy, and that all matter, when lifted to the speed of light, becomes light, and he demonstrated it in two dramatic ways.

By taking Peter, James, and John up to the Mount of Transfiguration, Jesus intended to impart to them the principle that Spirit and matter are in reality the same thing. Therefore, matter can be transformed into pure light or Spirit if and when one's consciousness lifts it to that vibration or speed. He could have said, "All right, fellers, in two thousand years a guy named Einstein will come along and produce a mathematical formula explaining that if any material object reaches the speed of light it becomes light, but right now I am going to personally demonstrate it for you." Anyway, right in front of Peter, James, and John, Jesus raised his consciousness to the vibration of light and translated himself—his material body—into pure light. In doing so, Jesus not only demonstrated that he and we are not only much more than material bodies but also that the Christ man, the new man, is consciousness.

We are consciousness that manifests itself in form, even in different forms. In other words, Jesus empirically proved that our Divine Selves are the two I's, that *we are spiritual or energy-beings manifesting as bodies, not just bodies manifesting Spirit.* I guess Jesus' disappointment was in thinking or hoping that his disciples were at the point where they could comprehend what he was demonstrating for them. Perhaps that is a dilemma every visionary faces when they have concepts that are in advance of society. Jesus should have been aware that though his disciples, Peter, James, and John were the pick of the crop, they still looked at life objectively in material terms, but he so longed for companionship that he hoped they could comprehend what he was revealing, just as you and I do when we try to share our visions with others.

When Jesus saw that Peter, James, and John did not fully understand what had taken place, it must have hurt. Now he knew he had to face the fact that he had no choice but to demonstrate the power of consciousness the hard way—on the cross. He figured that by going through the pain of crucifixion he could show that the Spirit in man could even create a new body. Objectively, when Jesus manifested a living material body from one that had been dead, he proved that third-dimensional, spiritual, or subjective awareness could be consciously demonstrated and lived. He proved that time, space, and the physical body were not the ultimate reality. He showed that in the presence of illumined consciousness material sense was not a power.

Whether or not the crucifixion and resurrection happened the way our myth explains it is irrelevant. The principle that consciousness or Spirit can transform the material world, heal broken bodies, and manifest anything man can imagine has been proved over and over. In other words, when Jesus resurrected or produced a new body through the power or energy of Spirit, he planted a seed in the collective consciousness. When that seed matured it proved the principle, which two thousand years later had evolved to the point where human beings are not only able to split the atom, but can clone life, heal every disease, and ultimately end the strangle-hold material limitation has had on humankind. No wonder society in general is confused. Our social structure continues to be based on the pre-atom-splitting paradigm, which is that material power is king. However, now a Christ level of consciousness has been empirically demonstrated, a fact which has fermented and matured to the point where it affects everything today, and, because we have not understood or accepted it, is also responsible for much of our current transitional chaos. I call it transitional because we are in transition now from the objective approach to the subjective approach, from the material to the spiritual, and that has introduced confusion in everything from governments to personal relationships and our own understanding of who we are.

Let me simplify. This world consciousness is the level of appearances, of the physical or material. It conceives of everything through the senses and believes that reality is visible. Ascension consciousness, "*My Kingdom*," transcends time and space. It is aware of forms, but experiences them through a different dimension than the one of which we are ordinarily aware. It literally sees forms as consciousness simultaneously expressing itself as—not "in" but "as," those forms. When we realize that there is no power in material forms as such, but rather that the power is in the consciousness that created those forms, we will realize that the way to change a form is to change the consciousness which manifests itself as the form. This ascension or Trinity consciousness completely annihilates the old belief that there is cause in effect. That is why I claim that the resurrection set the stage for today's splitting of the atom. It is also the secret of and basis for the principle behind spiritual healing, at which time material form is transformed by the energy of Spirit alone.

Anyway, the splitting of the atom released a genie that had been bottled up in ignorance since the beginning of time which has claimed materiality as the only reality. The problem we face today with that gene on the loose—and it is an all-pervading problem—is that our whole social structure is based on the old paradigm of putting material concerns before spiritual ones. Governments, institutions, schools, and even religions, were founded on laws that approach life primarily materially and objectively. From earliest childhood right through the rest of their schooling, we still condition our children to think in terms of linear third-dimensional cause and effect consciousness. That is why many parents now home school their children and why a transformation is taking place in many churches.

Though both the objective (material) and the subjective (spiritual) approaches are valid, the way you can tell which is being practiced is by noting how people pray and how they refer to God. If their prayers are directed to a God outside of themselves, if their prayers are petitionary, as though they are asking some being apart from themselves to fulfill them, they are objectively oriented. If when talking of God people feel they are talking to something other than that which is within them, they are conceiving of God objectively. When morality is equated with specific conduct, rather than the spirit expressed by the conduct, that, too, is a primarily Old Testament approach. Any religious study or psychological approach which assumes that a person is inherently a physical being manifesting Spirit, rather than Spirit manifesting as a physical being, is demonstrating a pre-atom-splitting, pre-resurrection, pre-ascension approach. All of us at one time or another look to something apart from ourselves at one time, and within at another, but now we can know which is appropriate and avoid the failure that comes about when we confuse the two.

Energy

$\mathscr{I}$f we analyze what the splitting of the atom meant in terms of our seeing ourselves as energy, we can better understand who we are and how it affected our daily lives. First of all, Spirit is an energy. That is why it can change appearances. Second, if all we see with our eyes is spiritual—Spirit appearing at the material level—then it follows that Spirit and energy are the same word—Spirit and energy are synonymous. One is its subjective nature, Spirit, and the other is how it appears objectively, as energy. If you are spiritual you are spiritual energy expressing itself. Every time you hear the word energy, think of it as the objectification of Spirit, because that is what Spirit is—divine energy.

Though Deepak Chopra, Einstein, and others tell us that 99 percent or more of the things we see are made up of empty space (consciousness), the rest is atoms in different configurations. As atoms make up everything that is, and as atoms are energy, then Spirit (God) is omnipresent, everywhere. *There are no things or actions that do not represent the presence or movement of Spirit/ energy.* Consciousness is energy and there is consciousness in every physical form. As Teilhard de Chardin said, even a rock has consciousness. It may be a denser or slower rate of vibration or Spirit than other ascending forms, but everything is consciousness expressing itself. That belief lays the groundwork for the realization that we are all of the same substance, that God Consciousness is in and as all of us. Although Spirit is the highest dimension or level of existence, it is also the condition of all existence. As such, it does not of itself change or grow, though it appears in an infinite number of different configurations.

As I said earlier, scientists today tell us that every thought represents an electrical charge. When you say a single word or think a single thought, a chemical/electrical charge of energy or Spirit stimulates a series of connectors which end up as the word that comes from your lips, and by doing so it, too, releases energy. Thought is energy. It takes energy to think. We might be frightened that we might run out of energy except for the fact that each human being is made up of trillions upon trillions of atoms and each atom potentially has enough energy to light the world. When we absorb that idea and become consciously aware that we are powerhouses of pure energy, we need no longer "dis-empower" ourselves. We begin to realize how much more we are capable of accomplishing than we have previously realized.

How can our knowing we are bundles of energy help us in a practical way? Let me give a personal example. Until I was forty I had horrendous migraine headaches. Unless I was in the long run of a play or involved in some other continuous activity that daily required the output of a lot of energy, I would have these migraines. Every month or so I would have an excruciating headache which would leave me unable to think or function. After I learned to meditate and began to become spiritually aware, sometimes I could catch an attack early as it started to come on and could, through meditation, redirect it, but most often I couldn't. Nothing would bring an end to it. I even tried codeine and other pain killers, but to no effect; so I soon gave up on that and would just meditate and ride it out. Eventually I would vomit until I was exhausted and then sleep for ten hours. I would wake feeling released from the pressure and be fine until the next one hit.

When I reached forty, I had a spiritual experience when I was temple hunting on the island of Sri Lanka. Because of that experience, I finally stopped looking outside of myself for a teacher, teaching, or anything else, and came to realize that I had to live by that which I had within myself. I was still enormously beholden to my teachers and to the writings that were a source of inspiration, and I appreciated all I had yet to learn, but I knew that the future had to flow out from within my own soul. Months passsed and I suddenly realized I had not had a single migraine since my experience in Sri Lanka. From that day on I never had another.

You might ask, "What does that have to do with energy?" I feel that the realization I had in Sri Lanka was my first act of pure self-love. I had been looking outside myself for guidance, and in doing so I had deprived my Spirit/energy of an outlet. I was bottling it up within myself leaving it no way out. As a result, that self-induced and self-contained energy took the form of my migraines. The door was closed and the energy was trying to batter its way out. After Sri Lanka, I never had another headache, because by then trusting my own inner source I was able to let it flow outwardly as spiritual energy. On my return home to Key West, where I was living at that time, within a year I had become a key figure in starting the restoration society and a highly successful business, which led to my being made the Citizen of the Year. Shortly thereafter I began to write and speak to groups for the first time.

Yes, everything is energy and everything is Spirit—every act, every feeling, and every thought. After we have made the metaphysical leap, we can see ourselves as energy, or Spirit, as easily as we can think of ourselves as bodies. Consciousness is energy and we are consciousness. When that is realized, a new morality comes into play based on how we use our energy or spirit. Do we use it to heal or destroy? Do we allow our lips to energize unloving projections or do we transform appearances by expressing ourselves as the energy of Love?

The Inner Self

*O*ften today you hear the two basic selves being referred to as the "Higher Self" and the "lower self." The only problem with calling the divine self the Higher Self and the human self the lower self is that the words higher and lower convey a sense of superiority and inferiority rather than just different parts of one whole. We must always remember that our two selves are one Self which is seen from different dimensions, from the so-called fourth dimension of Spirit and the third-dimensional physical level of effects. As such, they are equally important and equally necessary.

In place of higher and lower, I like to think of my two selves or two minds as the "inner" self or mind and the "outer" self or mind. In that way the two are One, just as the outside of a cup and the inside of a cup are both the cup and both equally necessary in order for the cup to exist. Once we accept the Inner Self as our divine perfection—our God-self—the Scripture makes sense when it says, *"If I make my bed in hell, behold, thou art there"*[12] or when it says *"I will go before thee, and make the crooked places straight."*[13] No matter where you take your outer material body, your inner self goes along with it. That means you are never alone and are never deprived of both divine help and divine intelligence. You can be in hell but you are not separated from God because your Higher Consciousness is within you no matter where you go.

Until you actually experience the presence of God within and as yourself, you continue to think of God as being outside of yourself, and no matter how strongly you believe in God, you still create duality by denying that you include God within yourself. Once you have experienced your true identity as God being, at which time there is nothing other than God, you will realize that God is your own Higher, Inner-evolved Self. After that, you no longer need to pray to God, seek God, or do God's will because your own Higher Self that is God is right at hand, and is doing all that God wills. However, just as you have sought God in the past as though God were outside of yourself, you now need to seek for and listen to your own Higher Self in much the same way that you have always sought God.

In fact, you still do all the things you previously did in the past when you turned to God for guidance and truth, but now you do it in the name of "I AM," your infinite Higher Self. You ask your Higher Self to illuminate your materialistic sense of self. When

My Higher Self, which art heaven consciousness, wholly be thy recognition. The kingdom of my Higher Self come, Its guidance be done at the outer material level as well as at the inner spiritual level. My Higher Self, fulfill for me all my daily needs, body, mind, and Spirit. Release me when I have not listened to my Higher Self as I release others who are not listening to theirs. Lead me not into the temptation of believing my lower self is all; deliver me from the evil of believing I am not already One. For this realization of my Higher Self is Heaven, the only power, and the glory of all being.

The Higher Self is God—and *is you.* Now when you pray, your prayer becomes your own objective or lower self attempting to access your own higher Christ mind. You are not seeking an outside God, but the God within. Such an approach is not egotism, and it does not make God any less God, any less universal, any less Omnipresence, Omniscience, and Omnipotence. It just keeps you realizing that *you are one with all that God is.* As long as you still think of your higher mind in terms of your personality, it does indeed become egotism, but it is possible to see your Higher Mind impersonally as the presence of the divine within. Everyone has this inner self because it is consciousness itself. It is Spirit, and Spirit isn't limited by anything material, including our bodies.

Always remember that your lower objective mind can of itself do nothing, but do not confuse it with your Inner mind. Realize that your own Higher mind is divine and that it has the power to set all laws aside; it can move mountains, it can heal all ills, and it can open the eyes of the blind. Then let meditation be a surrender of personal sense, the surrender of your lower or outer mind to your Higher Self. Let your outer self say, "Speak, Inner mind, thy servant heareth," making your objective self the servant of your divine capacity until you become the prayer you are praying.

All that God is I AM. Listen to those words. Repeat them over and over until they preface your every act. Mean them, but be sure you are applying that meaning to your own Higher Self. Contact it. Wait on it, and do not limit it. Your oneness with your Higher Self affirms your oneness with all spiritual being and idea because it is not limited by a body or personality. When you are in your Higher Self, prayer is not something you do; it is something you are. Think back to the very beginning of your life and you will see that there has been an ongoing process at work growing you, leading you, perfecting you, and fulfilling your every need. *You are not a body; you are that process, and it will continue.* See it as one continuous Self that will lift you into heaven. You are that Divine Process. Acknowledge it, meditate on it, and be grateful for it is all God.

Our Divine Humanity

*A*ncient mysticism and modern metaphysics has tried valiantly to explain that there is only one true identity or process. However, in expostulating on the illusory nature of human personality, they have nonetheless perpetuated duality. Perhaps what metaphysics has stumbled over in trying to eliminate illusion is itself the illusion. It isn't that personality is other than our reality but rather that our concept of personality, being other than God, is the illusion. We will never break through to ascension consciousness as long as we have to excuse our humanness, denounce it, or un-see it, and we are kidding ourselves at those times when we say that God is Omnipresence and Omnipotence and that our humanity is something we have to eliminate. Our full, complete, and perfect identity, like heaven, exists right now or it never has and never will. If it is not, it is not because it does not exist; *it is because we do not see it.*

When we reach illumination, we will see that our humanity is our divinity—in disguise. Sounds blasphemous to say that our humanity is spiritual, doesn't it, but wait! *The greatest act of love we can do for another person is to help that person find*

God; therefore, our humanity has been our most profound lover.
Man doesn't move without something motivating him, and our
humanity has certainly motivated us to find God. It has made it
imperative. Look back at every problem you have had, and you
will see that every failure, and every success has been a projection
of your humanity, and every human experience, good and bad,
has been there to push you into becoming a conscious being.

I agree that our humanity is not easy to cope with. It is not
always fun. It is definitely something we need to work through,
to use rather than be used by, and eventually to overcome, but it
is our need to get on top of it that pushes us into ascension; so
in that respect our humanity is love propelling us on to heaven.
Until we see our humanity as the flip side of our divinity, we will
remain a house divided. Any teaching that outright condemns
our humanity, or makes us think that because we are human we
are sinners, is stabbing us in the back. When Jesus rejoiced, "*I
have overcome the world,*"[14] he wasn't putting down his humanity
but was saying it had served its purpose—lovingly.

The Dehumanization of Jesus

*P*erhaps the greatest betrayal of our Western psyche has
been the dehumanization of Jesus. His whole life and
message was that God enters the human scene as a human being
and thereby eliminates the duality between the flesh and the
Spirit. If his humanity has to be sanitized to the point where we
are supposed to believe he didn't face the same temptations we
do, the one unique aspect of the Christian message has been lost.
As Teilhard de Chardin said in substance, if God incarnated as
Jesus, then all incarnation has to be of God, has to be divine right
now as it is. That's the heart of the Christ revelation, or should I
say, revolution.

The main reason that Christianity spread so quickly and with
such irresistible force among the ordinary people in Greece and
Rome in the first three centuries was not so much because of its
message but rather because of the unique aspect inherent in Jesus

being a God/man. For the first time ever, God was personalized in terms of the man on the street. The Gods that the Greeks and Romans worshiped before Christianity came into the picture were all depicted in royal garb, they were all super-beings with powers beyond ordinary human limitation. However, Jesus was not so exclusive. He walked with and as ordinary people did. He was God, but he was also a human being. He wore simple clothing and lived in near poverty, as the great majority did. He, though God, brought divinity to the human level. This was something completely new and obviously a greatly appealing drawing card.

Christianity spread like wildfire because of Jesus' humanity. Its appeal was that if Jesus, having all the qualities of everyday man, could triumph over limitation, then everyone could. When the Gods were off in the sky, aloof and inaccessible, there was nothing people could identify with, but when God walked among the people, they felt he cared, and this attraction became the fire that made Christianity so appealing. And, what is more, Jesus told everyone that they were also made in the image of God as he was. No religion previous to Christianity had offered so much.

Eschatology is a fancy word for that personalized Christian message of hope. Simply, it means "the good news" that in the end all will be saved. As I see it, the good news isn't the promise of achieving life in some future time, but that life is eternal now. The good news is that precisely because Jesus was human and became free of human limitation, we can do it too. But as long as Jesus is stripped of his humanity as though he were not like us, we cannot be like him. The Scripture does not erase his humanity, quite the opposite, but because we have been taught to think of him as being above making mistakes, we have become biased. When we read those Scriptures that show how Jesus vacillated between intolerance and acceptance, compassion and judgment, and brush over them, we miss the fact that he was like us. As a result, we feel guilty ourselves when we make natural mistakes.

Brought up in a home where I was told I should love Jesus, for years I felt guilty because I couldn't really identify with him. Without identifying with his humanity I couldn't actually feel love for this person I had never seen. Finally, one day I was thinking about the meaning of love and I thought of Jesus. I imagined what I would have felt if I were born into a world that did not know Agapé Love, where dog-eat-dog was the way of life. I would have felt if I were Jesus and no one understood what I was offering. When I stopped equating Jesus with myself and started thinking how I would feel if I were Jesus, he became a real flesh- and-blood person that I could feel love for. He became alive for me.

I can identify with Jesus' humanity in both a positive and negative way. He wanted so much to help people. He tried so hard to tell them to live subjectively, that his and their true being was Spirit, but he wasn't able to get his concept across in the way he wanted and was frustrated, just as you and I are when people don't get our meanings. If the Scriptures are accurate, Jesus was human enough to let his frustration take over by judging the Pharisees for their lack of understanding, which probably meant he felt he was a failure for not being able to get them to understand. Remember, this is the guy who said that everyone is made in the image of God, but at times he contradicted himself just as I do. This made me love him all the more because I could now say, "Thank you, Jesus, for sharing your humanity. The fact that you have faced the same frustrations I have and triumphed over them lets me know I can."

How wonderful it would have been if we had been taught to appreciate Jesus' humanity. It would have shown us that in the end he really walked his talk and not only forgave everyone but transformed himself into all that he said his true being and ours is and can be. Because Jesus was human, because he stumbled, because he cried, then whenever I stumble and cry I can remind myself that that was his gift to me, the gift of my potential, of my also being able to triumph over my shortcomings and become like Jesus, the Anointed One.

Part Three

The Why
Rethought Christianity

Chapter 9

EASTER CONSCIOUSNESS

Behold, I shew you a mystery; We shall not all sleep, but we shall all be changed, In a moment, in the twinkling of an eye, at the last trump: for the trumpet shall sound, and the dead shall be raised incorruptible, and we shall be changed.

I Corinthians 15:51,52

But we all, with open face beholding (ourselves) *as in a glass* (mirror) *the glory of the Lord, are changed into the same image from glory to glory,...*

II Corinthians 3:18

Peace I leave with you, my peace I give unto you: not as the world giveth, give I unto you. Let not your heart be troubled, neither let it be afraid.

John 14:27

Ye have not chosen me, but I have chosen you, and ordained you, that ye should go and bring forth fruit, and that your fruit should remain: that whatsoever ye shall ask of the Father in (as) *my name, he may give it you.*

John 15:16

...when he, the Spirit of truth, is come, he (your higher consciousness) *will guide you into all truth: for he shall not speak of himself; but whatsoever he shall hear, that shall he speak: and he* will shew you *things to come.*   John 16:13

Verily, verily, I say unto thee, When thou wast young, thou girdedst thyself, and walkest whither thou wouldest: but when thou shalt be old, thou shalt stretch forth thy hands, and another shall gird thee, and carry thee whither thou wouldest not.
                                                          John 21:18

Being confident of this very thing, that he who hath begun a good work in you will perform it until the day of Jesus Christ.
                                                    Philippians 1:6

The rituals practiced in our Christian tradition and their related Scriptures represent an ever-changing kaleidoscope of human experiences. If we only continue to repeat the way we have interpreted the message in the past, we get very little out of it that is new. If we have the courage to think for ourselves and draw out the meanings that are relevant for today, the traditions and Scriptures will become a treasure chest of self-discovery. Reinterpreting our Judeo-Christian myth is a way for us to talk to ourselves.

In this chapter, I am going to take just a few Scriptural passages, along with a couple of our rituals, to show how I wring my truths out of them. I am not saying that I have found "the" truth or that anyone needs to agree with me. I am simply including my interpretations as examples of how individualizing the Scripture has worked for me; so that you might take the same liberties that I have and find your own truth.

Our myth is one big spiritual jigsaw puzzle. Every piece represents a step in the evolutionary process. When the puzzle is completed, we will have been led to ascension consciousness. It starts with Christmas, the time when the birth of Christ consciousness is born in us, then takes us through childhood into the confusion of our spiritual puberty, and ends with the Easter experience that matures us into ascension consciousness. As such, Christmas and Easter are not two different occasions, but rather two poles of one continuous experience, the meaning of which finally comes into focus when the real significance of Easter is realized.

Forget theology; forget the objective way most people interpret the Easter story. Easter symbolizes that moment in our lives when it is revealed to us that we are Spirit or consciousness with bodies, rather than bodies with consciousness. Easter represents the breakthrough at which time we are freed from death and all material limitation, even from time and space. Easter proves that consciousness is the cause, the maintainer, and sustainer of our lives.

Jesus did not get off the cross and manifest a new material body by an objective physical act, but rather through the subjective energy and activity of his own consciousness. When he said, "*Destroy this temple* (this body), *and in three days I* (consciousness) *will raise it up*," he did not say, "Destroy this body, and in three days I will raise me up,"[1] because he knew he wasn't a body. *He had a body, but he was consciousness or Spirit.* He could make such a statement because he knew he was the I AM manifesting a body. His literally earth-shaking act did not take place because something outside of himself did it. He didn't resurrect just by an act of Grace. *He did it by an active, intentional, and conscious realization of his own. It was his doing that did it.*

It is quite legitimate to say that Jesus died for us as long as we mean that because of his Easter experience, he showed us there is no death. It was not that he thought a Barbara, a Tom, or a Walter was going to come along in two thousand years that he was going to die for. He did not do it for anyone. He did it for the truth of his own being, and in doing it, he paved the way for the rest of us. You might say he did it for the glory of God.

Let Easter remind us that it symbolizes the moment when our priority shifts from an objective, primarily materialistic, approach to life into a primarily subjective Inner Spirit as the power, presence, and intelligence of our lives and the universe. Easter does not ignore the physical or objective side—quite the opposite—but it does signify that the subjective consciousness in us is that which creates and gives life to what we see as an objective appearance. Easter says that *life is eternal and that when you turn to the Spirit, your material life is transformed and even resurrected.*

Your whole life and mine has been preparing us for this very moment in time—and that can be said about everyone on earth. All that has transpired in our lives has brought us both individually and collectively into this evolutionary Easter moment, at which time the old way is being crucified. We are being born again into a spiritual awareness, which, in turn, will become ascension consciousness. The reason I am bringing up the esoteric meaning of Easter is because every call I get, and almost all with whom I am in contact, are eagerly aware that some kind of profound life-altering change is imminent in their lives and in the world at large.

We have been given the tools to work with; so by understanding what Easter symbolizes, each of us can release our own sense of personal inadequacy and move joyously into this new dimension. In order for us to let go of our old limitations and to experience a conscious awareness of the divine process, it helps us to see how right now the earth is also in its Easter transition, materially as well as spiritually. For example, via satellite TV, we are now aware that there are more earth changes and catastrophes taking place around the world than ever before, some humanly engineered. Even California, the "land of milk and honey," has been plagued, in a single year, with fires, floods, earthquakes, El Ninos, mudslides, and social issues that appear to be out of control. Those apparent disasters represent and symbolize the breaking up of old thought forms—a kind of mental as well as physical Easter.

Each of us is confronted and confused by the challenge of change that is crucifying traditional ways in both the collective consciousness and in our own selves. Whenever the headlines scream disaster, the best way for us to help those in California, Bangladesh, or elsewhere, is for each of us to individually lift our awareness into the spiritual nature of what this Easter shift means and know that after the crucifixion comes the resurrection. We have to be able to see the omnipotence of God in all of life, or none of life will make sense.

Whereas in the past, Easter was individual, personal, and seen only as something that happened to Jesus alone, it is now— like the Second Coming—manifesting in the collective or universal consciousness, with signs following. In fact, it is happening so rapidly that the space between crucifixions and resurrections has narrowed to the point where they are not only taking place simultaneously, but they are so continuous as to be indistinguishable from each other. It's hard to tell the difference between crucifixion and resurrection because it is all one concurrent process. This current is growing stronger, and whereas in the past we have believed that swimming upstream against the current was necessary for self-preservation, by ceasing to resist the current and by flowing with it, we will move into final freedom. The breaking up of old forms is Easter's prelude to a new level of life on earth.

Death and resurrection does not happen once in a lifetime. Every time there is a divorce, every time a partner dies, every time one loses a job, or every time there is any shift in consciousness whatsoever, the old identity dies and a new one is born. Every shift in consciousness brings on an identity crisis. If we understand and welcome our personal Easters, we will be born again into a better place. Unfortunately, we have been trained to believe that crucifixion—the dark or shadow side—represents failure and should be avoided. Instead, when we see it as the flip side of resurrection, as no more than a stage in the creative and divine process, we will come out triumphant. If we can *"Let this mind be in you which was also in Christ Jesus,"*[2] we ,too, will have the capacity to lift ourselves into heaven.

There wasn't any God outside of Jesus that raised him up. It was Jesus' own consciousness that did it. As long as we conceive of crucifixion as separate from resurrection and, more importantly, without the ultimate reward of ascension, we are a house divided and we leave ourselves open to be conquered by ignorance. Not only that, but if we are able to think of our difficulties as our opportunities, we will no longer contradict ourselves when we say that God is the only power and that it is all God.

Understanding the nature of crucifixion does not mean we have to brainwash ourselves into believing that it's fun to be crucified or that we must un-see whatever it is that is putting us on the cross as though it is an illusion. The only illusion is our judgment. Crucifixions happen, but they happen as part of a divine plan that cannot be understood in the context of either time and space, or good and bad. When we realize that as part of the process, every creation goes through what "looks like" an act of destruction, we are halfway home. For instance, if you want to build a house, you have to crucify the trees before they are resurrected into a lovely home. If you want to paint a masterpiece, you have to destroy the tubes of paint. There are not two powers. There is only one power of creation that makes itself known through a process that we may ordinarily think of as crucifixion.

Thank God that life is one continuous death and rebirth process, because each of us knows that our greatest crucifixions have revealed our greatest resurrections and have brought us ever closer to the ascensions of consciousness that we call illumination. I have not met anyone yet who has been crucified by an addiction and risen above it, who hasn't said that their addiction turned out to be their greatest blessing because it led them to God. What we must realize today is that what is happening to us is our second life, the Second Coming of Christ—first objectively as Jesus and now subjectively as universal consciousness. The collective body of humankind is in its Easter experience. When it fulfills itself, it will bring the world into ascension consciousness, at which time we will realize it is all God.

Therefore, today we must call on the deepest level of faith in the invisible divine Easter process to which we can rise. We must be ready to fully trust, even though day after day we may not see visible signs or feel the presence of Spirit resurrecting our lives. At our low periods, we must remember that Jesus was three days in the tomb—in darkness. The tomb for the universal consciousness may be three days, three months, three years, or more. Time is symbolic, but be assured, everything is happening in divine order. Let yourself off the hook. That means that you are not to expect your human self, the personality you have assumed for this schooling, to at all times understand what is happening; do not expect it to be humanly perfect; do not expect to always avoid tough moments, to never be sick. Be kind to your child, your human self. Trust the process. Trust Easter. Surrender yourself to your Higher or Inner Self. Remember there is no God apart from your own Higher Consciousness, and it will transform any darkness into light. Know that when you refuse to see your Higher Consciousness as limited to your body, you free it from personal sense—and from the cross. Know that Easter proved that time or space does not bind you, for you are all that God is.

I know it is hard to ask, but be willing, at this universal Easter, to let yourself change, even if that change looks like death. Know that resurrection is assured, because death is not a reality, just a concept. It is a mistake to call death an end, because it is really the beginning of resurrection. Honor your fears as signals announcing the advent of Easter. Indeed, you and I are ready to be born again, and we will rejoice as we drop old concepts of self, dive right into the center of creation, and consciously enter the Easter cycle, knowing it is all God.

Dear Judas

*F*inally, and perhaps most importantly, our understanding of Easter is not complete without our loving the one who made it possible—Judas. As long as we think of Judas as a person, rather than what he represented, we cannot fully understand God's omnipotence or love.

Judas symbolizes that negative part of our own personalities which is necessary for us to have in order for us to catalyze the Easter process out of which we are born and without which we would never reach ascension. Objectively, there was a man named Judas who betrayed a man named Jesus and caused him to be put to death so that he might resurrect and ascend. Subjectively, out of Love there is a divine process at work in us that betrays our dependency on material appearances so that our inner Christ can prove that life is eternal. It is all one piece, and just as crucifixion is the other side of resurrection, the Judas characteristics in each of us that betray our divinity are the other side of our Christ.

Poor Judas! All these years we have condemned him as the one who loved Jesus the least, whereas, he was the one who loved him the most. That is why Jesus passed him the sop, and planted in Judas' mind that someone had to betray him in order for him to be able to fulfill his mission on earth. Jesus knew what price Judas would have to pay. He also knew that because Judas loved him more than anyone else, he would be willing to pay the price. Without Judas' sacrifice (in Latin, sacrifice means "to make sacred") Jesus would not be remembered today.

The crown of forgiveness is placed on our heads once we finally realize that those in our lives who seem to have betrayed us are our own Judas projections, projections that our consciousness has brought about in order to make possible our resurrection and our final ascension. Often, those whom we feel have betrayed us have done it out of a love that neither of us has understood or were capable of understanding at the time. What they did has pushed us into becoming conscious beings, into taking our next step, and that is Love. In turn, as our own Judases, they may have laid down their own lives for us, because *"greater love hath no man than this, that a man lay down his life for his friends."*[3] Forgiveness becomes possible when we transcend appearances and realize that those people who represent the Judases in our lives and those qualities within ourselves that seem to have betrayed us have been the divine process growing us into Christs. It's all Love.

Pentecost

And when the day of Pentecost was fully come, they were all with one accord in one place. And suddenly there came a sound from heaven as of a rushing mighty wind, and it filled all the house where they were sitting....And they were all filled with the Holy Ghost, and began to speak with other tongues, as the Spirit gave them utterance. And there were dwelling at Jerusalem Jews, devout men, out of every nation under heaven. Now when this was noised abroad, the multitude came together, and were confounded, because that every man heard them speak in his own language. Acts 2:1-6

And it shall come to pass in the last days, saith God, I will pour out of my Spirit upon all flesh: and your sons and your daughters shall prophesy, and your young men shall see visions, and your old men shall dream dreams. Acts 2:17

Though it sounds somewhat irreverent and similar to something a weird social anthropologist might come up with, in the truest sense of the word, Jesus was a "mutant." *Webster's Dictionary*, talking objectively, and not in terms of spiritual cause, says that a mutant is something or someone "with inheritable characteristics that differ from those of its parent." In other words, a mutant is a divine invention that has the ability to pass on its unique characteristics to future generations. In that case, all of those who have experienced the Spirit of the Christ and whose lives have been affected because of the Christ consciousness are consciousness-clones or offsprings of Jesus.

It is one thing for a master, such as Jesus, to bring forth an advanced state of consciousness, to perform miracles, to heal the sick, and to personally demonstrate new freedoms. It is quite another matter for the master's consciousness to be cloned in his or her followers so that they could go and do likewise. There are two incidents in Acts that showed that Jesus' followers could do the same things he did. These examples are far more personally important for you and me than anything Jesus did for his followers. They prove that we are heirs to His inheritance. The first incident mentioned in the Scripture, which demonstrated that the Christ Spirit was actually experienced by Jesus' followers, happened at Pentecost after he was no longer on earth.

We already know that Jesus lived a great deal of the time at a level of spiritual energy called the Holy Spirit. We know that he was able to heal the sick and break the limitation of material law because he had attained that transcendental spiritual ecstasy called the "anointing." However, until Pentecost, there was no proof that Jesus' anointing was other than unique to him. When his followers had the same visitation of Spirit that Jesus so often had, it was demonstrated for all time that his consciousness was alive in those that came after him. Because of what took place at Pentecost, we know that the possibility of having a charismatic experience has been passed down through the years, and that everyone can experience it, including you and me. Pentecost represented an evolutionary shift in vibration to a different level and experience of spiritual energy for humankind.

Let me reinterpret some of the Pentecostal passages that I quoted at the beginning of this section. When it says that those who were gathered together were *"all with one accord in one place,"* you might say that it explained what happens when the particles become the wave. The *"place"* was not a room. It was a shared state of consciousness, and the "*accord*" was a shared purpose. This sets the stage for the possibility of Pentecost happening today in the collective consciousness among those who are of one accord, in one consciousness. The "*sound from heaven as a rushing mighty wind*" was the thunder of silence, not auditory, but it was rather the movement of ascension consciousness rushing in like a mighty wind.

Metaphysically, "house" stands for consciousness; so when the Scripture says "*And it filled all the house,*" it filled all their consciousness. "*And they were all filled with the Holy Ghost*"— they were all filled with the spiritual energy that comes from a conscious experience of God or the presence of God consciousness, the anointing. As a result of the descent of the Holy Spirit, they "*began to speak with other tongues, as the Spirit gave them utterance.*" Subjectively, tongues and utterances symbolize the communication of different dimensions of awareness that the Spirit engenders. At Pentecost everyone experienced the Spirit in ways each could understand. "*And there were dwelling at Jerusalem Jews, devout men, out of every nation under heaven.*" Devout or spiritually men and women from all over the world can experience the same Spirit. "*Now when this was noised abroad, the multitude came together, and were confounded, because that every man heard them speak in his own language.*" Today we can all come together and no longer be confounded. That is not only because the English language is spoken around the world, but rather because everyone can understand and speak the language of Spirit or Love.

The Scripture goes on to say, "*And it shall come to pass in the last days, saith God, I* (the I AM) *will pour out of my Spirit upon all flesh: and your sons and your daughters shall prophesy, and your young men shall see visions, and your old men shall dream dreams...and I will show wonders in heaven above, and signs in the earth beneath.*" To me, that means in the last days of this Pentecostal stage of spiritual evolution that we are going through, ascension consciousness will be poured out on the entire visible world. The sons and daughters will voice truth, the young men will envision how truth will manifest, and the old men (I, Walter, for instance) will dream the dream.

It is happening. The Pentecostal Spirit is beginning to affect the collective consciousness. Certainly, it will take a number of years for the Spirit to be evident in the lives of everyone on earth. However, it is breaking through, and it is up to us now to recognize it and to help it along by accepting it and not to be so sophisticated as to fear its happening to us individually as well.

We have experienced Pentecost in the past without realizing it. Every time we experienced a healing that seemed to miraculously set aside the law of material powers, we have had a Pentecostal experience. Every time we have experienced what " *A Course in Miracles*" calls the "Holy Instant," or Joel Goldsmith referred to as the "click," we have experienced a sample of Pentecost. Our ability to deliberately induce the Holy Spirit will increase, and future generations will not have to develop Pentecostal energy because they will be born with it.

The Second Easter

After Pentecost, the next experience that showed Jesus' state of consciousness was alive in his disciples took place a year after the Easter we currently celebrate. The reason I call it "The Second Easter" is that this one is more significant for you and me, as potential inheritors, than the first one, because it proves that we, too, can overcome our crucifixions.

The only place in the Bible where the word Easter appears is in the twelfth chapter of Acts. It says that Herod, the same authority that had Jesus crucified, decided that, once and for all, he wanted to put a stop to the word that was going around about Jesus' having resurrected. Hoping to do so, he took Peter, Jesus' most prominent disciple, and put him in prison, "*intending after Easter*"[4] to crucify him as well. However, though guarded by four quaternions of soldiers and bound by chains, Peter showed that he also had the Christ consciousness in him. *"And, behold, the angel of the Lord came upon him, and a light shined in the prison: and he smote Peter on the side, and raised him up, saying, Arise up quickly. And his chains fell off from his hands.*"[5] To me this means that, as angels are individual truths that come into consciousness, Peter's consciousness became so illuminated that he got up, and the chains fell from his hands without personal effort. Peter's consciousness led him "*unto the iron gate which leadeth unto the city; which opened to them of his own accord,*"[6] which I take to mean that iron, the symbol of material power, opened before the presence of Peter's Christ Spirit. Thus Peter, like Jesus, had his own resurrection. Through his inherited Christ consciousness, he had triumphed over the same powers that had tried to get rid of Jesus. Or should I say, he had our resurrection, because the fact that Peter triumphed shows us that we, too, can resurrect from all those people and things that claim to have power over us. We can when and if we also experience Christ consciousness.

The Communion Ritual

Throughout this book I have repeatedly made a correlation between the subjective and the objective approaches of the two commandments that Jesus said would solve all life's problems if reconciled. Countless lives were lost over the church's inability to look at the communion ritual both ways. During the Middle Ages, the Western world was split in two over the meaning of transubstantiation—over whether the communion service was to be understood objectively or subjectively. Even today, there is a schism between the Catholic and Episcopal dogma on one side, and the Lutheran and Protestant-based concept of the communion service on the other side.

It is hard for us today to understand why such a fuss was made over the issue. However, if we can see what actually lay at the root of the situation, we might wake up to the fact that just about every problem we have in our own lives today stems from the same conflict. In all walks of life, if the rationale for both the objective approach and the subjective approach had been simultaneously appreciated and viewed from their individual standpoints without either excluding the other, we would have a very different world today. First of all, before attempting to justify the sacraments, the whole subject of rituals has to be touched upon.

Most of the rituals in our Churches are hangovers from pagan days. Because rituals appeal to, and are necessary for, those who need an objective act in order to relate to inner meanings, the Church took over old rituals and reinterpreted them in light of the Christian message. For instance, pagan blood sacrifices of first-born goats and lambs were reinterpreted in the sacraments to mean that the shedding of Jesus blood symbolized the sacrificing of the first-born Lamb of God.

Unfortunately, along the way the rituals themselves became more important than what they symbolized, and superstition replaced understanding. For that reason, many have rejected ritual all together, and once more the baby has been thrown out with the bath water. Again that is a pity, because on our way to ascension consciousness, we continue to be both man and woman of earth and man and woman of God. The man and woman of earth have need of an earthly example of the embodied Spirit to identify with. Rituals offer that, even though the spiritual significance of the ritual may be subconscious.

In fact, I doubt that the Church itself would exist today had rituals not been the glue that kept its followers personally, if not superstitiously, involved from birth to death. The souls of all the different religions—Hinduism, Buddhism, American Indian, and Christian—are defined by their rituals. If those who are more objective and physically oriented can experience the Spirit through rituals and have the right intent, rituals are perhaps indispensable. For others, who find pageantry, sound, and physical contact to be distracting, a solitary experience that is more easily experienced in the silence of meditation than in the presence of others is their form of ritual. The main purpose of ritual is to prepare the ground and activate the Inner Spirit so that one can then carry that Spirit into their silence where the still small voice speaks.

The purpose of ritual is to make the invisible visible, or, in reverse, to activate the invisible through a visible experience. If ritual becomes an end in itself, it becomes self-defeating, but if the inner meaning of the ritual is kept in mind while the ritual is being experienced, it can light the light.

I can understand why people have shunned rituals, because for many years I, too, felt that rituals and group activities distracted me from going within, at which time I could enter the silence. I felt that costumed processions, holding hands, chant ing, moving through an Indian medicine wheel, and other rituals, diverted my attention and kept me from going beyond the human scene. Finally, I realized that resisting all ritual could result in a Gnostic-like rejection of the human scene. Ritual has its place because sometimes a ritual can jump-start the spirit. It does not have to be either/or if we follow the priority Jesus gave us: "*Seek ye first the kingdom of God*,"[7] which means to keep one's attention first and foremost on the Spirit that a ritual intends to engender while simultaneously performing the ritual.

Rituals recognize spiritual union with others and reinforce Jesus' statement: "*For where two or three are gathered together in my name, there am I in the midst of them.*"[8]

Now, let us take a look at the ritual of the sacraments. Transubstantiation (from two Latin words, "trans" and "substantia," meaning "to transform") is what takes place symbolically or literally when a person swallows the bread and the wine. That can be taken in two fundamentally different ways. When transubstantiation is conceived of objectively—the way it is in the Catholic and Episcopal Church dogma—it is believed that the bread and the wine is transmuted into the very body of Jesus, that one is actually swallowing the body of Jesus. It is believed that when one does so, one is no longer a sinner, but has been cleansed and is now one with Jesus.

The other viewpoint is that when one swallows the bread and the wine, a subjective or symbolic experience takes place.

Instead of the bread and wine becoming the body of Jesus, the Christ comes into the material scene and becomes the bread and the wine. Symbolically, by swallowing the bread and wine one's physical presence becomes Christed.

When I say that in one approach the bread and the wine become the body of Jesus and in the other approach the Christ becomes the bread and the wine, it may sound as though I am saying the same thing. I am not. They are 180 degrees different. When we believe that the bread and the wine becomes Jesus, we are saying that our humanity is transformed into something divine and no longer exists in an inferior state. That approach may imply that our flesh, our humanity, is ordinary, not divine, and should be gotten rid of. It says that the flesh becomes the word, rather than "*the Word*" becoming flesh.

On the other hand, when it is believed that at communion the Christ becomes the bread and the wine, it means that the flesh has become spiritualized, that "*the Word*" has incarnated as individual being, that our humanity is divine when it is swallowed up by Christ consciousness.

Hear me! Both approaches are true and valuable. It is a pity that wars were fought and lives lost over the meaning of communion because if either approach is fully understood, the ends are the same. It is not either/or. *The unique aspect of the Christian message is that there is a bridge from God to earthly existence, and that it is a two-way street. The Word is made flesh and dwells among us; therefore, we can either objectively take the flesh to the Word or we can subjectively bring the Word into the flesh.*

On one side, because God incarnated as the man Jesus, all matter is spiritual. That means that we, right here, right now, at the level of personal sense, *are God appearing materially as our divine selves.* If the communion is seen exclusively, as though by eating the body of Jesus we become something worthier than we have been, our humanity is being rejected. On the other hand, if communion is only seen symbolically, that also is a denial that "*the Word*" was made flesh as Jesus—and ourselves as well. The virtue in seeing the communion objectively is that by objectifying Jesus it becomes possible to also objectify ourselves as God's presence. When that happens, we have accomplished what the communion service symbolizes both objectively and subjectively. Either way, it is all God.

The Fifth Chapter of II Corinthians

I habitually read the New Testament from beginning to end every year and have for almost fifty years. I realize that the words are just ink on paper, until I make them my own. Every time I go through the New Testament I find what an incredible source it is. To show you my process, I will take you verse by verse through one of my favorite Scriptures. For me, the most important chapter in the Old Testament, apart from the first chapter of Genesis, is the sixty-first chapter of Isaiah. In the Gospels, the most significant chapters for me are John 14 through 17, and the fifth chapter of Second Corinthians.

The reason the fifth chapter of Second Corinthians is so revealing is that it not only sums up the whole Christ message, but it also shows us that Paul finally broke through and personally experienced ascension consciousness. In this chapter, we are encouraged to believe that Paul, who really had to struggle with personal sense and his ego—as we do —finally made the transition from his humanity into his mysticism. If he did, so can we.

Starting with the last verse of the fourth chapter, I'll show you the way I interpret the Scripture verse by verse. (You may want to follow it in your own Bible.) He begins, *"While we look not at the things which are seen, but at the things which are not seen: for the things which are seen are temporal; but the things which are not seen are eternal."* Objective things that you can see with your eyes are temporal— temporary. Sooner or later they all disintegrate, but if you look at life in terms of consciousness, these invisible truths will be everlasting.

"For we know that if our earthly house of this tabernacle were dissolved, we have a building of God, a house not made with hands, eternal in the heavens." Metaphysically, house means consciousness, and tabernacle or temple is interpreted to mean body. Therefore, if our material body is destroyed, we still have a spiritual body, a consciousness not made by human hands, one that is eternally in divine order.

"For in this we groan, earnestly desiring to be clothed upon with our house which is from heaven:" And don't we all groan or anguish, earnestly wanting to be clothed with spiritual consciousness?

"If so be that being clothed we shall not be found naked." If we are clothed with spiritual consciousness, when we are up against it—when we are told we may have a critical illness, or when we are involved in an automobile accident, or if we are not clothed with Spirit—we are naked. Humanly, our clothes protect us from the elements, and when we are without them we are without protection, but if we have spiritual consciousness, no matter what happens, in the end we will come through protected.

"For we that are in this tabernacle do groan, being burdened: not that we would be unclothed, but clothed upon that mortality might be swallowed up of life." This verse has a subtle, but all-important, truth in it, one that can reverse an error that has tricked the majority of well-meaning seekers away from the truth and into bondage. It says that many of us in this tabernacle, in this body or spiritual quest, groan, that our mortality (from "mortise" which means subject to death) might be swallowed up of life. However, the secret is in the words, *"not that we would be unclothed."*

Most of us spend the majority of our time trying to get rid of, or take off, our faults and shortcomings. By doing so, we only affirm the power of those evils. Instead, if we would forget our weaknesses for a while and concentrate on being filled with Spirit, so that we are swallowed up of life, we would find the freedom we so long for. Instead of subtracting our faults, if we add to our virtues eventually the faults will be swallowed up by love.

"Now he that hath wrought us for the selfsame thing is God, who also hath given unto us the earnest of the Spirit." This is a wonderful verse. In a way, it lets us off the hook. It says that the creative source that brought us into life is God, and that same Spirit is what is giving us the earnestness to keep on trying. We didn't earn our earnestness. That which keeps us searching is a gift from God. No one stays on the path unless there is that in their own Higher Consciousness that keeps them on it.

"Therefore we are always confident, knowing that, whilst we are at home in the body, we are absent from the Lord:" That's it! If we believe we are just a body, at home with being no more than that which we see in the mirror, we are absent from appreciating our own divinity, absent from the I AM of ourselves.

"For we walk by faith, not by sight." We don't walk on human legs. We walk because it is in our consciousness to walk. We don't see with our eyes; we see with our consciousness. This knowledge is the "seed" we plant. Our faith is what moves us.

"We are confident, I say, and willing rather to be absent from the body, and to be present with the Lord." Ask yourself if you are willing to give up a materialistic sense of who you are in order to be present with the truth of yourself. I know I am.

"Wherefore we labour, that, whether present or absent, we may be accepted of him." We keep on trying because whether we are at the physical level or at the spiritual level, we want to express Christ consciousness.

"For we must all appear before the judgment seat of Christ; that every one may receive the things done in his body, according to that he hath done, whether it be good or bad." At the level of personal sense, we reap what we sow, and our consciousness is measured against the fullness of the Christ.

For the next six verses Paul lapses into personal sense and gets a bit confusing. He uses such words as *"the terror of the Lord,"* [9]which could be translated to mean that truth is unrelenting. It could mean we can't cheat on truth. We can't go behind the barn and say two times two is five and get away with it. He also makes another statement that is easily personalized in the old "Jesus

died for us" way. He says, " *If one died for all, then were all dead.*"
[10] However, that could mean that because Jesus proved himself
by successfully going through the crucifixion and resurrection, he
set an example that we can all follow.

"*And that he died for all, that they which live should not
henceforth live unto themselves, but unto him which died for
them, and rose again,*" may have been Paul's way of saying that
because Jesus proved the principle we no longer have to live
trapped in a material sense of self.[11]

In the next verse Paul shows that he finally got the message:
"*Wherefore henceforth know we no man after the flesh: yea,
though we have known Christ after the flesh, yet now henceforth
know we him no more.*"[12] Do you hear what he is saying? He not
only tells us that we should no longer judge people materially,
but that though he, Paul, had personally thought he knew Jesus,
he now no longer knows him. Paul had seen Jesus as a man, as
a personality, but now he finally sees that Jesus was not a person
– rather, a state of consciousness. He now sees Jesus as the
Christ Spirit appearing as the man, Jesus. By Paul's coming to
this realization via his own humanity, he shows that it is possible
to start from a judgmental and objective approach and break
through to a subjective viewpoint of life. If Paul could come
from a purely objective personal concept of God and Jesus into
realizing he had been wrong—that the Christ was a state of
consciousness appearing as a man—then all the rest of us can,
too. We can all change and wake up. We can see each other as
spiritual beings rather than personalities.

Paul goes on to add, "*Therefore if any man be in Christ, he is
a new creature: old things are passed away; behold, all things are
become new.*"[13] In saying that we would become new creatures,
he was announcing that we would be born again into a spiritual
sense of who we are. More than that, Paul said that all "things,"
all material appearances, would become new to us as well. That
is because we would now see things as consciousness appearing
in form and not just as material objects. "*And all things are of
God* (consciousness), *who hath reconciled us to himself by Jesus*

Christ, and hath given to us the ministry of reconciliation."[14]   To reconcile means to bring together into a oneness. In combining Jesus' name and His title, Jesus and Christ, he was making the man and His consciousness One and the same. That tells us that reconciling the human with the divine is the true meaning of the Christ message.

Paul goes on to say, "*To wit, that God was in Christ, reconciling the world unto himself, not imputing their trespasses unto them; and hath committed unto us the word of reconciliation.*"[15]   In this one statement Paul summed up the whole Christian revelation. He says that *God* (creative consciousness) *was in Jesus* (a human being) *reconciling* (making One) the material world with his Higher Consciousness, and he was saying that reconciliation comes about, not by telling people what is wrong with them, but rather by *reconciling* (making One) *their humanity with their divinity.* This one statement fulfills the two commandments. It tells us to love God by reconciling appearances and to love our neighbor as our selves by forgiving—by not imputing trespasses.

"*Now then we are ambassadors for Christ, as though God did beseech you by us: we pray you in Christ's stead, be ye reconciled to God.*"[16]   An ambassador is one who goes to a foreign country "re-presenting" his government. If we want to be ambassadors for higher consciousness, then that is what we do when we go among those whose consciousness is a foreign country to our own. We may not have to say anything, but we must live it. That is the responsibility we have if our lives are to be governed by the Christ and if we expect to be accepted in the family that knows it is all God.

Spiritual Business

*I*f it is all God, instead of thinking of commercial business as being other than spiritual, we have to re-think our Christian principles in order to discover how they translate at the level of the market place. In the 1980s and most of the 1990s, I had a retreat center in the Hill Country outside of San Antonio,

Texas. Midway through that time we were discovered by the Exxon Oil Corporation. When they began to send middle level management to us for leadership training sessions, I meditated to ask God what was going on. I had originally created the center for the purpose of providing a spiritual ambiance where not only my own seminars could take place, but where other spiritually minded groups could meet. I hadn't expected corporate America to become so interested in what we had to offer that they would become our main clients. After all, though we had well-equipped meeting rooms, we deliberately kept telephones and televisions out of the private rooms and specialized in quiet areas around the ranch where groups or individuals could go to meditate.

On contemplating what was happening, several surprising conclusions evolved. First of all, a divine paradox was revealed. Though the Fortune 500 companies were sending employees to the ranch because of the bottom line—in order to increase profits—they had consciously or unconsciously put their finger on some simple spiritual principles that will eventually revolutionize industry. They found that in order to increase productivity they needed to incorporate principles in their operations that the metaphysical approach to Christianity had put forth for years. Second, though my own success in the business world should have clued me in, I realized that *the spiritualization of our nation's corporations is the most important development that can possibly happen for the spiritual growth of the world as a whole.* Governments apparently are unable to help. Churches have not fully succeeded; however, the multi-national corporations that control the lives of countless millions have the power and financial wherewithal to bring on an incredible transformation of consciousness if—if it comes down from the top. For spiritual values to permeate a company, they have to start in the minds of management at the top of the corporate structure. Then those values will percolate down through the consciousness of the whole organization. When top management starts practicing spiritual principles, the rest will follow. It is the same principle as, *"I, if I be lifted up…will draw all men unto me."*[17]

I saw that in the new paradigm there won't be a place where Churches stop, and daily life or corporate America begins. The world of creative industry will be a Church—a new Church—and one that will actually do what Churches are meant to do in transforming consciousness. In fact, from what I observed, today established churches could serve a great purpose if they would design meetings that would be set aside to openly deal with the subject of how spiritual principles affect the business world, of one's attitude toward business, and the metaphysical principles that can make one successful in business.

Third, I realized that even though the groups that came to my center were not consciously aware of what was happening, they responded to the spiritual consciousness and presence that was at the center. Corporate groups were unable to tell where their programs stopped and the spirit of the center and its employees took over.

The fourth element, which I felt was responsible for the success of the ranch, was that the programs were both subjective and objective. They combined classroom instruction with outdoor experiential exercises that put into practice what was learned indoors. We included an elaborate challenge course in one of the canyons, with all kinds of experiential tests that were not only designed to increase one's self-esteem but which also demonstrated how groups were able to see the practical value of the principles in action.

On the other hand, though we conducted some of the classes ourselves, most of the groups came with their own instructors. After they left I often read the flip charts they left behind, and I was blown away by their spiritual content. Many of them not only insisted on the importance of self-worth, and the need to honor one's union with one's fellow workers, but they also showed an awareness of the importance of giving them real and often spiritual or creative purpose, rather than paychecks alone. They realize that rather than tear down self- respect, corporations now have to consciously build it up in their employees. Corporate America may not yet tell its people that they are made in the image of God, as we would in our Churches, but some of them do say the equivalent. They tell their leaders and their employees that they have perfection within themselves, and they explain that by their realizing it, they can express that perfection. They tell their employees that they have to honor their perfection before they can share it.

Finally, and more subtly, some of the corporate trainers explain the difference between craft and talent. They tell the employees that just repeating a job over and over in a satisfactory way is fine, but if one honors their God-given talents they can contribute new ideas, ways to help the company improve, and thereby they will personally succeed.

Perhaps top management was forced into it, but many of them now realize that the old vertical system, where orders were passed down from the boss at the top to those below, without concern for anyone's feelings or well being, no longer works. Now management has to become horizontal as well as vertical—like the cross. That means, that it *must have a sense of unity and oneness, at which time ideas come from heaven and are anchored in the earth, and where the two arms of Spirit and matter reach out to embrace all.* That realization establishes a harmony of oneness, where the good of one becomes the good of all.

The most successful book that has ever hit the business world has been Stephen Covey's, *The Seven Principles of Highly Successful People.* It has sold literally millions of copies, and many corporations have given it to their employees to read. In it, Covey says we go from dependence, to independence, to inter-dependence, and unless we become independent, we cannot become interdependent. That is pure metaphysics.

Unless we arrive at our own sense of divinity—that we are made in the image of God—we remain dependent on external circumstances and we fail to realize that our good comes from within our own consciousness. After we have realized our own Self-worth, we have something to offer to others. Then, at that level, we will recognize that because of our own omniscience and omnipotence we are one with all others—interdependent with universal omnipresence or Oneness. That applies practically to success in the business world, and it is also pure Christian metaphysics.

The right time to go to God, or to a lawyer, for that matter, is when you are starting a business, in order to see that you do it in a way that fulfills the law —not to get you out of trouble after you have made a mess. The right time to approach business decisions is after you have made your inner contact and received guidance from your own Higher Consciousness. *"Seek ye first the kingdom of God, and his righteousness* (the right or loving way)*; and all these things* (material success) *shall be added unto you."*[18]

For that matter, we should not be spiritual about business! Yes, that is what I said. We should not be spiritual about business. God appears at the level of business as good business principles. If, before contemplating business problems, we go within, drop all thoughts about this world, and contemplate spiritual principles until we experience the presence within, we will receive inner guidance, and that guidance will put us in contact with the source of good business principles. In that Spirit, we can forget about being spiritual and concentrate on right business techniques, because that is how God appears at that level.

If we try to get Spirit to make bad business principles work, we are barking up the wrong tree. That is why I say that we should seek first the kingdom and get into our higher spiritual consciousness. Then, without thinking of business one way or the other, our problems will either be healed or we will be told what to do to straighten them out. With confidence that God is on the field, we will be led to successful business solutions, because that is how God appears at that dimension.

With all the problems that arrived with running a business that had over fifty employees, one morning I faced a dilemma. I kept getting mad at myself, because that is the time of the day I set aside to meditate in order to receive spiritual inspiration, but no matter how hard I tried, I could not stop thinking of possible solutions to my human problems. I kept getting answers about what to do in the office. Finally, loud and clear, the inner voice said, "Who are you to outline what my instructions are to be about. You say that it is all God; so walk your talk. Whether my words are of spiritual principle, or of good business principle, it is all the same. My truth is expressed from different dimensions, but it is all my truth. This is how I chose to come to you today. Your intent is what is important and if your intent is to listen to the word of God, no matter in what form it comes to you, you cannot lose. First listen for the truth, and then do it."

The best possible business principle is to seek first the Spirit of God or Love, and then go about your business, thinking in terms of good God-given business principles, because that is how you will see that it really is all God.

Chapter 10

BEYOND THE BEYOND

There is an Oriental saying, "To one who has arrived, the way is foreign," meaning that once you have arrived, you will see that all you went through had little to do with your getting there. It isn't that everything from the past is valueless or unnecessary at its place and time in the evolutionary process, but old concepts take on new meanings after they have served their purpose. The Trinity experience hasn't fulfilled itself unless something additional and new results from it. The offspring of a Trinity experience is a fourth reality—ascension consciousness. This chapter does not refute the past, but tries to expand it, and, in doing so, shows how we can go beyond old automatic, and perhaps obsolete, meanings and therefore go beyond our old lives.

Zen masters give their students Koans—those verbal enigmas—not so much to reveal hidden truths as to shake the mind free of automatic assumptions. We are lulled by habitual thought, stuck on previously conditioned meanings, and are imprisoned by repetition. In the last chapter, I gave some examples of how Scripture and ritual can be shaken loose from old interpretations. By the same token, I say that if we don't look twice we may be tricked by love, deceived by religion, lied to by the truth, and betrayed by God.

For instance, love can be addictive. When we experience love, it is easy to lust for more of it. I say we can become tricked by love because in our drive to possess love, we may find ourselves rejecting our own and other people's sometimes flawed humanity. I know that when I discovered mysticism, I hungered for those moments when my teachers would tell me about the I AM, tell me of my oneness with God, when they exalted my own Christ consciousness, and when they lifted me beyond my humanity. However, when they started to talk about the nature of error, my responsibility to perform daily tasks in order to develop a Higher Consciousness, about discipline, and other mundane procedures, I barely tolerated their instructions, waiting for another gulp of love.

Until we evolve into the realization that Love (God) itself is all-inclusive, we cannot see that every act in life, no matter how mundane, is performed not only in search for Love, but is Love in action. Teachers who preach Love and reject humanity as though it is not worthy of being loved are being tricked by their misunderstanding of Love. They don't know the difference between real and illusory love. If there is a trace of judgment that implies that one person or one condition is more lovable than another, the trick has succeeded, and "would be" love has betrayed a would be lover.

Those who spend time inspiring love just for love's sake, as though unconditional love is a superior or an even more admirable state than love expressed personally, are advocating a mental narcotic as a substitute for the joy of loving. Lovers might benefit by aiming at an absolute of unconditional love, but the only way they will know how close they have come to it is by seeing how extensively their love has been expressed conditionally in the lives of those they love, and by seeing how far their circle of love extends. A syrupy "sweetness and light" public show of love is the surest sign that someone has been tricked by love, because that kind of love sticks to the surface and doesn't penetrate the soul. Tough love is often the most honest love, because it demands that a loved one live up to the Christ of one's higher being, breaks the hypnotism of duality, and thus frees the loved one to fly. *You will be tricked by love until you become consciously aware that both the good and bad—the rewards and the disappointments—are all Love.*

Religions, on the other hand, deceive by speaking half-truths. We are drawn to religion in our search for the truth because somehow we sense that the truth is hidden in our Scriptures, but what we do not know is that whereas truth is constructive, half-truths are destructive. By being offered half-truths, we are lied to by the truth. For instance, we are all familiar with the Scripture, *"Ye shall know the truth, and the truth will make you free."* We inscribe it over the doors of our universities and advertise our theology by its apparent wisdom. Wrong! That's a half-truth. Unless we include the verse that precedes *"the truth will make you free,"* it becomes a lie. What Jesus actually said was, *"If ye continue in my word...ye shall know the truth, and the truth will make you free."*[1]   The truth isn't going to make you free unless you live the truth. If we "continue" in the truth, if we live it, it will indeed make us free—not otherwise. The complement that makes a truth whole is the living of it.

All of our lives we have been deceived by another half-truth: Forgive seventy times seven. The Scripture actually says, *"If he trespass against thee seven times in a day, and seven times in a day turn again to thee, saying, I repent; thou shalt forgive him."*[2] Adding *"If they repent"* makes all the difference. When someone has not repented and we forgive that person, we have been deceived by a half-truth, instead of our helping him or her change; we have become enablers, encouraging someone to continue violating the Spirit. Enablers are worse sinners than the supposed sinners. A sinner is just harming him or her self, but an enabler is harming someone else other then one's self.

St. Thomas of Aquinas, one of the most, if not the most, influential theologian of all time, sometimes deceived his followers through a technique of mis-employed truths, and many have accepted his sometimes erroneous conclusions ever since. He would start with an indisputable truth, add a second obvious truth, then a third, fourth, and fifth truth, but on the sixth or later he would sneak in his own opinion or a subtle distortion.

By that time, his followers' acceptance had become automatic and routine, so they would go blindly along and were eventually deceived by an almost truth. For instance, if someone were to tell you, "two plus two is four. Four plus four is eight. Eight plus eight is sixteen. Sixteen plus sixteen is thirty-two, thirty-two plus thirty-two is sixty-three," by the time they were dishonest you might have stopped questioning them, and you would have been deceived by a string of truths that led to an almost truth.

Finally, all the tricks, all the deceptions, and all the lies stem from how we are betrayed by our concepts of God. We have reached out to the highest concept of God that we can imagine. We have trusted God to show us the way. We have been willing to offer our very lives to God, but as long as we believe that God is other than our own essential being, something outside of ourselves, either a judge or a power that we have to appease and appeal to by thought, prayer, action or desire, we have betrayed ourselves by our own concept of God. As long as we think of God as a punishing God, we have been betrayed by that God, because the real God is too pure to behold iniquity. As long as we think there is some place where God is not, we are betrayed by our concept of God. The only time we are not betrayed by God is when we see God in everything, in the void as well as in the visible, in the good and the bad, in the spiritual and the material, and ultimately as our own being. When we finally understand that it is all God, we no longer betray ourselves by a misconception of God.

Beyond Faith

And God said, Behold, I have given you every herb bearing seed, which is upon the face of all the earth, and every tree in the which is the fruit of a tree yielding seed; to you it shall be for meat.

Genesis 1:29

While the earth remaineth, seedtime and harvest, and cold and heat, and summer and winter, and day and night shall not cease.

Genesis 8:22

Now faith is the substance of things hoped for, the evidence of things not seen.

Hebrews 11:1

But they that wait upon the Lord shall renew their strength; they shall mount up with wings as eagles; they shall run, and not be weary; and they shall walk, and not faint.

Isaiah 40:31

Since recorded history, those people who have offered the most to society, who have added to the betterment of humankind, who have created inspired art, who have contributed to those scientific breakthroughs that have made life more manageable, have all claimed that life is meaningless without a faith in God. Ask them to define God and you would have as many different descriptions as there are people you have asked. However, they all have one common denominator—they all have faith.

Faith is not something you think or feel. It is something you do that can take you from finite limitation into infinite possibility. I, for one, found out a long time ago that I could not live without faith, but it took me even longer to realize that faith was not something that worked on me from outside of myself. My having faith was not as though I would blindly push a button that would turn on some outside godly resource. Faith is not an invisible servant that is there to do my bidding on call. Faith is something I must do—something I must do that empowers me.

Scripture tells you, "...*if ye have faith as a grain of mustard seed, ye shall say unto this mountain, Remove hence to yonder place; and it shall remove; and nothing shall be impossible unto you.*"[3] However, when you discover what faith is, you will find that misguided faith can also cause mountains to fall on you as well. Whatever you have faith in, you create—good or bad. When the principle of faith becomes a conscious activity, your destiny is in your own hands, and you no longer need to look to a God outside of yourself for protection or success. When you consciously know how and why faith works, superstition is replaced by knowledge and you go beyond having faith into being faith-full *"and nothing shall be impossible unto you."*[4]

What actually is faith? All of our lives we have been told we should have faith. Though Paul said that *"faith is the substance of things hoped for,"*[5] no one has told us what faith really is or how it works. Sure, the dictionary says that faith was derived from the Latin word "fidere" which means to trust, but what makes trusting work? Everything we have in life and every situation in which we find ourselves is the result of an activity of faith; so what is it?

Let me cut to the chase: *Faith isn't something we have; faith is something we do.* Faith is an energy. Faith is the power inherent in what we see or perceive. If faith is the substance of things hoped for, then faith becomes our "seeing" because what we image or see manifests outwardly in form.

Starting with the first chapter of Genesis, God first had an idea and then actively "saw" it fulfilled. Remember, at each stage he had a concept and then saw that it was good. We, too, have to complement our ideas with seeing them in order for them to come into being. Just having an idea isn't enough. We have to complement it with the energy of seeing it happening. That seeing is what faith is. When we say that someone has faith, it means they have seen and been convinced that the harmony they seek will come about, and it does to the degree that they see it.

Faith is the seed we plant in consciousness. The Scripture says *"Behold, I have given you every herb bearing seed, which is upon the face of all the earth, and every tree, in the which is the fruit of a tree yielding seed…"*[6] Those seeds, like the mustard seed, symbolize seed-thoughts. *"In the beginning was the Word* (the seed)*, and the Word was made flesh,"*[7] means that the word is a seed that is planted in consciousness, and then by being "seen" becomes flesh. That is faith in action. When our seed-thoughts are conceived of and then seen as reality, they complement each other and become activated faith. Faith that succeeds is not something that happens from outside. It is the result of our seeding our own thoughts in consciousness, and then faithfully energizing them by seeing them into being.

In Genesis, it says that while we are still at the earth level, the level of personal sense, we have a time to plant our seeds and a time to harvest the results. But, through Spirit, the planting and harvesting can be instantaneous, as Jesus said, "*Say not ye, There are yet four months, and then cometh harvest? behold, I say unto you; Lift up your eyes* (your seeing), *and look on the fields; for they are white already to harvest.*"[8] When we need something and can see it into being, miraculously the harvest will appear.

Whether you know it or not, you are having faith all day long, because you are constantly planting thought-seeds and seeing them in your mind's eye. That is why I say that misguided faith can produce negative results as well as positive ones. It depends on what you have faith in, what you seed ("see" with the addition of a "d").

We plant the seed and then we wait. However, waiting is not static. Waiting is not silent resignation. It is active service. In the same way that we are waited on in a restaurant or a store, we must wait on God, wait on the principles of faith to be active as our consciousness. We must see it, serve it, love it, honor it, and actively co-create with the divine process of imagination. "*But they that wait upon the Lord shall renew their strength; they shall mount up with wings as eagles; they shall run, and not be weary; and they shall walk, and not faint.*"[9]

You have been given an insurance policy, a spiritual law for faith; a law that will assure you that faith will create your highest good. That law is, "*seek* (see) *ye first the kingdom of God.*"[10] Plant that spiritual seed, see it, and your faith-full seeing will create it in form. Make sure that the seed you are planting is spiritual, is constituted of love and divinity. Have faith that God's will is being done, not will be, or should be, but see it as being done. *"Let not your heart be troubled: ye believe in God, believe also in me* (in your inner self)."[11] Plant yourself in God. *Then you will have gone beyond faith, because you will "be" faith.*

Beyond Reason—Chaos

*W*hen I was in New York City for a visit, I made a dinner date with a young female avant-garde violinist I had known for some years. On the day of our engagement, she called to inquire if I could change the evening. When I asked her why, she said she had to go to a concert that she felt I would not enjoy, as the music would be loud and discordant. I told her that I wanted to go because I wanted to experience the consciousness, and I wanted to see who was there and what they got from it. When the evening arrived, we went down into lower So-Ho into a refashioned warehouse building in which an eclectic group of eighty or so, mostly young people, assembled, mutually sharing a somewhat religious, though abject, devotion to the proceedings. Without fanfare, two male "artists" came onto the makeshift stage, and without introduction, began to perform. One plucked, struck, fingered, and massaged various electronic instruments, while the other scratched, beat upon, and wiggled records on several turntables—often two or three at a time.

The audience listened with rapt attention for more than an unbroken hour. At first, I could only hear an amalgamation of mostly chaotic sounds, and I wondered just why this meant so much to those who had paid to hear. Not wanting to waste the experience, little by little I found myself becoming interested and involved. First, I found out that in order to understand what was going on, I had to stay in the "now." By that I mean I could not hang onto a past thought, nor could I project into what was going to happen in the future. I could only take the sound for what it was at that moment, and then let it go.

Second, the music was so spontaneous that I felt privileged to be listening to it, knowing that there was no way it could ever be reproduced. It was purely a once-in-a-lifetime experience. Third, it became obvious that the two musicians were communicating with each other at a level of, rather than of logic. Whereas jazz musicians often consciously play off of what they hear from each other, these two were unconsciously sharing a mutual inspiration at what might be called a level of spirit rather than of an intellectual assumption. There was definitely a symbiotic merging of the sounds each was producing.

Finally, without human intention, a kind of rhythm or beat emerged from the chaos that was divinely intentional and purposeful. There was a kind of order in the chaos that allowed me to feel secure in abandoning myself to it.

Currently, Stephen Hawking, the most prominent physicist on the horizon, has been stating that the universe was created out of chaos—a claim that has threatened traditional religionists. They feel threatened because something within human nature does not want to let go of reason. Reason requires a logical explanation for creation, for God, and for religion, but in the final analysis, the Spirit, the Spirit of creation, is experiential and not logical.

It takes a leap of faith to experience God. It will take a leap of faith to live at this time—a time at which we have to come to terms with chaos. Reason and logic cannot make that happen. We have to sense an order behind the chaos of life that is beyond reason, and when we do, perhaps for the first time, we will be able to experience that it is all God.

I doubt that the young people who attended that concert consciously knew what it was in them that drew them to an appreciation of the experience. Yet I feel that at some level they were recognizing that creation comes out of chaos, out of the void, and out of our need to come to terms with it, even to feed on it. My reward for being open to the experience was that it somehow showed me where our spiritual evolution is headed.

As I said earlier, I believe that the Lord God who told Adam and Eve that they should not eat of the Tree of Good and Evil was a deceitful scoundrel. The only way anyone can go beyond good and evil and "be as the Gods" is to go right through both of them and out the other side. That is why I rejoice in knowing that this is the time when we go through chaos and beyond—into ascension consciousness. We arrive at ascension consciousness when we sense an order in the chaos, an order that reason cannot discern, but that faith can. Chaos comes from a Greek word meaning "empty space." As such, chaos is neither good nor bad. Like good and evil, it is something one goes through in order to get to the other side. Chaos is the womb of life out of which comes a reborn universe or a re-born self. It is similar to the nature of error—a nothingness.

In reacting to chaos, once more it is not what but how. Those who view life only from the objective viewpoint, those who have not recognized the nature of God, have given the word a negative and fearful spin. In doing so, they create for themselves exactly what they imagine. Like faith, chaos is the substance of things hoped for, the evidence of things not yet seen. Chaos is a state of mind. Remember that our lives are exactly what we make of them via the images we allow and entertain. Either we start seeing chaos subjectively as an introduction to new freedoms and greater love, thereby creating a glorious future, or we carry the objective viewpoint of the past on our backs and remain stuck in the void.

As human beings, we live in the time continuum, and until we ascend we have to deal with time, which is to say, we have to deal with chaos, because chaos is a creature of time; otherwise we wouldn't recognize it. But we can pray. We can enter our inner closet and stop the clock for a long enough time to heal and to put chaos into perspective. Contemplating the twenty-third Psalm does the trick for me. Whereas the Lord's Prayer may be a prayer of protection in anticipation of chaos, the Twenty-Third Psalm addresses chaos and deals with it. Paraphrased:

> *The Lord "is now" my Shepherd, so even in chaos*
> *I will not want for anything. I have been created*
> *to lie down in green pastures, even in the face of*
> *chaos. In the midst of chaos, I am led to a stillness.*

*When chaos has affected me, the Spirit restores
my soul. Even in chaos, it leads me in the right
direction because God is the only power. Lo, though
I walk through the valley of chaos, I will fear no evil
because I can lean on the spirit, and it keeps me in
line. It prepares a table before me in the presence of
fear and doubt. My cup of life runneth over. Surely
goodness and mercy shall follow me for the rest of
my days, and I will live forever in the house of Spirit,
where there is no chaos.*

Beyond Infinity—Nothingness

*W*e hear mystics talk of entering the silence. It is not that the silence is a thoughtless state where the mind is obliterated. It is a state where the mind is consciously aware of a presence—a sense of Spirit or God—and yet there are no thoughts that define it. The silence is a conscious experience of "*no-thing-ness.*"

It is impossible to have a fear or a worry in the world without projecting yourself out of the "now" into the past or future. Try it. By the same token, it is impossible to have a worry or concern without some "thing" being involved. If you are depressed, it is over something—some thing. If you have anxiety, it is because of something. If you get angry, it is because someone has done something.

We know that the universe was created out of the void. Genesis 1 tells us that out of the void came the nights and days, the earth and the waters. The void is a "no-thing-ness" As such, it is a zero. Zero is another word for the silence because zero is the absence of any thing. In one, two, or three there is something that is being defined in order for there to be a one, two, or a three, but zero is mental silence. When we pray, our goal is to enter the silence, the silence of God or creation. When we contemplate the I—the I AM—we may still have a sense of ourselves "and" something, but when we contemplate the void, when we think of all that zero stands for, we can come closer to entering the silence that is beyond specific thought. Again, try it.

Contemplating the infinite nature of Omnipresence, Omniscience, and Omnipotence can also help you arrive at a state of no-thing-ness. That is because being infinite, infinity is beyond any one thing. If you experience the infinite nature of God or yourself, you enter a silence that transcends all things, a soul silence where it is all God.

Beyond Atonement

*D*oes the word "atonement" send a shudder through you? Does it bring up a sense of guilt? If so, it is one of those words that needs to be sanitized in order for our Judeo-Christian myth to be freed from the distortions that have made it unpalatable, if not unlivable.

Once more, the key depends on whether one begins with an objective approach or a subjective approach. Atonement is a most vital part of the Old Testament and of the Jewish religion, but atonement has mainly been conceived of objectively, as a kind of penance. It is part of the Jewish custom to practice a day of atonement, a day when one withdraws and spends the day contemplating one's sins of the past in order to be atoned. In ancient days, the Day of Atonement was accompanied by a blood sacrifice. It was the one day of the year when the high priest entered the Holy of Holies. Of all the different robes the Rabbis would wear, this was the day they put on their final garment, a one-piece seamless white garment.

Symbolically, there is no more important day for you than the one when you enter your Holy of Holies and come face to face with the I AM of your self. At that moment, you experience your atonement, but your atonement means what the word says— "at-one-ment." In that state of mind, you are clothed with a seamless, pure, radiant consciousness of a high priest. Yet many Christian churches, and particularly metaphysical ones, have eliminated the ritual of atonement from their celebrations. When atonement is not actively celebrated, they may be depriving themselves of an experience that is, like reconciliation, the Gospel truth, the "good news."

We can rejoice at the prospect of realizing our "at-one-ment" if we really look at the true meaning of the word, shout it from the housetops, and hold it in our hearts. Instead of atonement being a day of sackcloth and ashes, we should celebrate it as a day of great joy and Self-appreciation. Rather than atonement meaning anything connected with sin, it should be thought of as a time when we acknowledge that sin is not a power, and that we do not have to fall short of the mark because we are always at one with God.

From beginning to end, Jesus' message was that it is all God, all one, and that when we realize we are that one, we are empowered; we are free; we have life eternal, and we will have overcome all limitation—all through at-one-ment. Instead of the Day of Atonement being a once-a-year event, as it is practiced in the Jewish faith, every day should be a day of atonement. We should walk around every day experiencing our oneness with God. Every meditation and prayer should be seen as a time of atonement. And, hopefully, we will eventually go beyond atonement, because we will be so atoned that it would be redundant to think of it one way or another. We will hear the tone of atonement, and it will be the sound that tells us it is all God.

Beyond Prayer

*W*e spend our lives rattling around in our bodies looking for a way out. We distinguish between our souls and our bodies because we sense that there is something about us that does not have to be trapped in the physical, that is free to go beyond a personal sense of self. Prayer is our attempt to find an escape-hatch. Through prayer, we are reaching out to some presence or power that will free us from human limitations. Hopefully, through prayer, we can identify with the Omnipresence and Omnipotence that personal sense denies us. We honor saints without realizing that what we have appreciated in them is their realization that they are more than finite bodies, and that realization is what has given them influences beyond personality. Those saints may have found their escape hatch through prayer; however, having done so, they have gone beyond praying into direct communication with powers beyond human limitation; so if we pray, maybe we can, too.

One of the greatest helps I find when I begin to meditate or pray is the realization that I do not know how to pray. Certainly, I know a number of techniques that are designed to take me into the experience of meditation or prayer, but none of them can guarantee the adventure of prayer because prayer is not a mental exercise. It is an experiential encounter with Higher or Divine Consciousness.

When divinity is experienced, one goes beyond what we think of as prayer into a different dimension of life, a level called illumination. It is called that, because where there was darkness the light of reality now shines. Though we cannot make the light shine, we can try to eliminate anything that blocks the light from shining. The light is within every living being just waiting for the grime to be removed from the window pane so that it can shine through.

In place of talking about, thinking about, or contemplating spiritual principles, many spiritually aimed philosophies today try to instill in people a sense of "being" or "beingness." Most have borrowed this concept from Oriental teachings, such as those found in certain Buddhist approaches or from such Sufis as Osho, previously known as Rajnishe, who wrote that "*Sufism is not thinking about existence, it is being existence.*"[12] When I talk about "being" existence, rather than thinking of one's self as the thing that exists, it is my attempt to get people to see themselves subjectively rather than objectively. However, it is nearly impossible for a human being to think at all without being objective, and often when subjective words are used, those words are interpreted with a kind of refined objectivity. Unless one can double think and fulfill the two commandments by being aware of one's self objectively, and simultaneously being aware of what one's presence symbolizes spiritually, prayer is no more than a mental exercise. When the two are "real-istically" integrated, "beingness" is experienced.

Until one has gone beyond prayer, one most likely thinks of prayer as something one does. When we think or say prayers, we are indulging in an objective approach. To go beyond praying is to *"be" prayer*. In order to do that, *you have to transcend conscious thought by merging with the process*. You have to see yourself as "being prayed" rather than as praying. Both thought-filled prayer and experiential prayer have value, and either, when exclusive of the other, may find itself unsuccessful. Unless conscious seeds of faith accompany the experience, there is no direction, and unless thoughtful prayer is spiritually experienced, it is a futile endeavor.

Many have been led up the garden path by having been told that they should "pray without ceasing." If they see prayer as an objective act, then to pray without ceasing would mean they would have to be thinking of prayers all day long. Many in and out of monasteries have tried this by either countless repetitions of mantra-like prayers or by hours upon hours of sitting, kneeling, or bending in prayer. Others have believed that there is the possibility of being so selfless as to be able to live at a permanently impersonal level of Higher consciousness, but they have failed, because totally transcending the personal while still in a body is impossible. Jesus didn't.

In the new paradigm, at which time we go beyond old concepts of prayer, both the act of praying and the experience of spirit fit together in a perhaps surprising way, a way that takes us beyond prayer. For instance, some people believe that a mystic is someone whose thoughts are constantly on God; however, a modern mystic is one who has reconciled life into a oneness where it is all God. He or she may only pray or meditate for a relatively short period every morning, and not at all throughout the day or night unless something calls on him or her to return to a conscious realization of oneness. In other words, modern mystics have a time when they consciously meditate, when they clean the slate, tune in to the Spirit, and receive guidance. However, for the rest of the day, they go about the business of living or working without consciously thinking of God or "beingness" because they are actually being it. That is, they do until or unless something comes up that signals them to return to their center, to stop whatever they are doing, and remake contact.

It is like this. In the morning by praying you turn on a kind of spiritual Muzak. You consciously listen to the music until you are in tune with it, but after a while you go to work, and before long you are no longer aware that Muzak is playing at all. You are not conscious of the music in the background—until it stops. Once it stops you immediately sense that something is different, something is amiss. If you recognize that feeling, it becomes your signal to drop whatever you are doing and go meditate to get the music going again. On those days when I cannot hear the music, I go on about my business, but I remind myself not to try to discipline anyone or make any important decisions until I once more hear it.

If you start your day centered and in conscious contact with your Christ, your higher consciousness, your day follows suit in that spirit. As everyone is affected by what is taking place in the collective consciousness, you must listen to the signal, then when the music stops, through prayer or meditation you can once more place yourself under the umbrella of your Higher Consciousness.

If you spend too much time praying, it becomes similar to Shakespeare's advice, "Methinks the lady doth protest too much." Too much time spent praying is a denial of faith, rather than an affirmation. Remember, your unconscious knows your intent. To try to force contact only widens the gap. After a while, a lengthy prayer becomes a mental activity rather than a spiritual one. After a reasonable time of quiet, if you still believe you will miss out unless you keep on praying, to stop praying is an affirmation of faith. You can always try again every once in a while and eventually the music will start again. Many short prayers are always more affective than single long ones that tend to get mental.

A child does not keep asking its mother if she loves him or her. To do so would show that one doubts that one is loved at all. On the other hand, to give one's mother a hug and be enriched by her love for a moment each day is enough to send one off for the day secure and ready to face life.

There is a golden key that unlocks the mystery of prayer. Complicated theologies, superstitious rituals, and elaborate metaphysics can lead you further away from the mystery, until you finally realize that there is no wrong way and no right way to pray. All roads lead equally to Rome if, at the center of your heart and soul, the one magical element that transcends all others is pure—*your intent.*

The intellect with all its often inhibiting shortcomings and confusions is set aside if at a level beyond thought or theory your intent is to evoke the Spirit of the divine in and as your life. No matter what church you do or do not go to, no matter how well you know the Bible, no matter how much time you spend praying, no matter if you feel you have never experienced God, if your intent is pure and heartfelt, you can put aside everything that has gone before and the miracle will ultimately happen.

God is not mocked. Despite the jungle of words and thoughts, your unconscious soul knows the purity of your love and desire. Your intent is the altar upon which the Sacrament rests. It is how you take communion with your Holy Self. It is the magical key that opens the door to prayer. Honor it. Keep it pure and it will pray you.

Beyond Church

*C*hurch, as we have known it, is undergoing a rebirth—or extinction. For a great number of people, the old form has had its day. Here, too, it is not a matter of either/or. We will always have what will be called "Church," and it is most likely that people will dress up on Sunday and go to a particular building called a Church. However, we will have gone beyond what we have objectively thought of as church in the past. Instead of thinking of church as a particular organization, a particular theology, or any other objective symbol, church will be what Jesus intended it to be when he said, "*upon this rock* (on this state of consciousness) *I will build my church.*"[14] Church will happen whenever and wherever two or more are gathered together in the Christ consciousness, even if there are no walls to define it.

This closing of the gap between the objective and subjective understanding of church isn't taking place in terms of organization alone. For individuals, it means the coming together of idea and experience, of the Word and the Spirit. Neither the new person or the new Church will be seen as an effect, as a body or a material edifice, but, rather, as a state of consciousness wherein the Spirit of truth takes precedence over the letter of truth. We will realize that at any time or place where the Christ consciousness is being expressed, a church service is underway. The church service will be identified by Spirit, not by place or time, bricks and mortar, theology, or title.

In other words, our old third-dimensional time and space definition of church was a physical one built on exclusive membership, exclusive authority, exclusive theologies, exclusive place, and exclusive participation. That approach to church will no longer dominate the so-called spiritual scene. Church will be where the message, the person, the race, the sex, the man of earth, or the man of God within each individual, will be united inclusively by growing together, experiencing together, and sharing together.

The New Church is the truly Christ Church. When Jesus asked his disciples, "*Whom do men say that I the son of man am,*" he was asking, "Whom do materially minded people say that I am?" The disciples' first response was based on personality, "*Some say that thou art John the Batist: from Elias* (or Elijah); *and others Jeremias, or one of the Prophets,*" a human identity—an exclusive identity. Then he asked, "*Whom say ye that I am,*" and Peter answered "*Thou art the Christ, the Son of the living God,*"—as we all are.

Then Jesus recognized Peter's state of consciousness by saying, "*Flesh and blood* (personal sense did not tell you that).... *thou art Peter, and upon this rock* (this subjective state of consciousness) *I will build my church.*"[15]   His statement shows us that the real church is not a building but a state of consciousness. What state of consciousness? *It is the inclusive state of consciousness where we are not only all One, but where we are all priests as well.*

Twelve-Step groups are churches, consciousness-raising retreats are churches, picnics where people gather together to joyously share an experience of oneness and the presence of God are churches. Church may or may not take place in a building. It may have a mailing list and a schedule by which we can be informed of times and activities, but it will not be set apart from our daily lives. It will not be an exclusive activity nor demand conformity. It will not be governed by laws. That is to say, it won't have set rituals or routines to which everyone will have to conform. It will be an intuitive association of souls. When we live in that consciousness, we will be living in our Churches.

By all means, we should go to the Church we presently attend, support our Church, build the Church, and be the Church. Then we can help transform our present Churches into the New Church where those of our spiritual family can grow and share our spiritual revival. The New Church—like heaven—will be recognized as a state of consciousness and not a place. It will be understood as the presence of the all-inclusive Christ that includes saint and sinner alike. It will be composed of those who agree with Jesus' instruction to "*go ye into all the world,*"[16] inclusively· It is the consciousness that there is only one, and this One includes us all. It is a church whose goal is for everyone to receive illumination.

The New Church is present wherever and whenever the Spirit of Love is present, wherever and whenever practicing the presence of God is taking place. And whenever anyone is wearing the robe of the Christ Spirit, that person is the priest, and that person's heart is the altar where Communion is served.

There is no more perfect description of the New Church

than the one Joel Goldsmith included at the beginning of all his books:

> *Illumination dissolves all material ties and binds*
> *men together with the golden chains of spiritual*
> *understanding; it acknowledges only the leadership*
> *of the Christ; it has no ritual or rule but the divine,*
> *impersonal universal Love; no other worship than*
> *the inner Flame that is ever lit at the shrine of Spirit.*
> *This union is the free state of spiritual brotherhood.*
> *The only restraint is the discipline of Soul, therefore*
> *we know liberty without license; we are a united*
> *universe without physical limits; a divine service*
> *to God without ceremony or creed. The illumined*
> *walk without fear—by Grace.*[17]

Beyond God—the Thirteenth Step

As I go beyond old concepts, I realize that the most frightening, important, and necessary one to go beyond is my old concept, or rather all concepts, of God that I have continued to rehearse as a kind of spiritual insurance policy. Ever since human beings with the capacity for rational thought came into being, consciousness has been climbing a stairway of ever-evolving concepts of God. Step by step, fragmentation has risen toward union, and an evermore perfected awareness of oneness has been evolving. If you analyze them, each one of the twelve steps upon which Alcoholics Anonymous bases its program equates with a stage of spiritual evolution that leads to an awareness of the presence of an all-inclusive being or beingness. You might say that consciousness has been on its own Twelve-Step program. The evolution of consciousness aims at giving us the ability to comprehend union with God, but, nevertheless, as long as one conceives of ones' self as having an identity other than being one with God, a subtle addiction to duality still remains and a thirteenth step is needed.

The Eleventh Step in AA, which is arrived at after making contact with God, asks that we do His will and that we have the power to carry it out. The Twelfth Step acknowledges having received awakening and it asks that we dedicate ourselves to living by that experience. Finally, after the twelve steps have been taken, disturbing as it may seem, we find there is another step to take—a Thirteenth Step—*a step beyond being an instrument for God or of doing God's will.* As long as we think in terms of doing God's will, as though it is or could be other than our own wills, there are still "two," something that needs to be united with something else. As long as we think of achieving union with God, we have yet to see that right now we are already God appearing as us. *Right this minute, we are all that God is.* When we experience that, we will have taken the Thirteenth Step.

The Thirteenth Step is the step beyond deity. Ancient Yogis or sages in both India and the West have tried to propose this totally absolute step, but because evolution itself had not progressed to the place that it is now, that step could not be explained or lived by the majority. In the past, it was thought that taking the Thirteenth Step meant rejecting the world and one's humanity, that taking the step beyond concepts meant transcending all action, and that unity and multiplicity were in conflict. Our evolved ability to simultaneously think from two different viewpoints or dimensions now makes it possible for us to be aware of and live in both the visible world of personal sense and the invisible world of Spirit without being caught between two worlds and without denying individuality or contradicting our absolute oneness. The Thirteenth Step does away with the limited, abstract, and remote concepts we have assumed God to be, or at least takes us beyond the limits of anything we have been able to conceive of as God.

As long as God remains only a thinkable concept to you, you are still in the past. Until you know what it means to experience the Spirit beyond words and thoughts, the Thirteenth Step cannot be taken. Each previous concept of God leading up to your experiencing union with God brings you closer to a sense of One being. Finally, you come to the Thirteenth Step, a step beyond being a channel for God or beyond hearing God's words, as though God is other than your own self. That step is taken when the concept of God "and" is replaced by the realization that everything including your own self is God appearing "as." This final step allows you to be active in the world without duality because you realize everything is God appearing individually.

Does going beyond God "and" mean that there is no God to call on? Certainly not. If God is the Infinite Source within you, when you call on God you are calling on your own Higher Consciousness, and that is as necessary and mysterious as it ever was. That kind of prayer is the only way you can go beyond past concepts.

Let me repeat — *there is no way you can possibly go beyond words and thoughts unless you have become consciously aware that it is all God.*

Beyond Jesus

> *...He that believeth on me, the works that I do shall he do also; and greater works than these shall he do; because I go unto my Father. And whatsoever he shall ask as my name, that will I do, that the Father may be glorified in the Son. If ye shall ask any thing in my name, I will do it.* John 14:12

*I*f we have the strength to look in the spiritual mirror, we will see just how controlled we still are by an objective approach to life. Just ask your self if you are ready to go beyond Jesus. Does even having the thought of going beyond Jesus seem blasphemous? Are you so deeply conditioned to believe that you are less than all that God is that it frightens you to even think of putting yourself equal to or beyond Jesus? Then ask yourself what Jesus meant when he said, *"He that believeth on me, the works that I do shall he do also; and greater works than these shall he do."*[17]

When you think that "works" means the healings he performed, his conjuring up loaves and fishes, or his walking on water, you are still confusing objective results with the spirit or consciousness that brought those experiences about. Subjectively, works symbolize levels of consciousness. So ask yourself, could Jesus have meant "greater levels of consciousness shall you arrive at," meaning a greater "expansion" of consciousness? Perhaps he meant that spiritual evolution would take us further along, that we would develop expanded intuition.

There are two things that keep us from going beyond where Jesus was. Unless we go beyond those two things, we will be among the walking dead—those people who are frozen at the level of material existence. First, we must stop seeing Jesus as a person who was born and who died. We must arrive where Paul was when he said, *"though we have known Christ after the flesh, yet now henceforth know we him no more."*[18]

If we still see Jesus as an object that came into being 2000 years ago, then we probably still see ourselves as people who just came into being these last few years. But if we see that Jesus was the human name we use to identify how the Christ appeared as spiritual consciousness 2000 years ago, we too will be able to add the Christ to our given names at those times when we are in that Christ consciousness. When that happens, we will have gone beyond Jesus—not in quality but in time. Because Jesus introduced Christ consciousness, which has now permeated the collective consciousness, we have gone beyond where he left it. When Jesus made the statement that greater works shall you do, he was speaking to himself —the "himself" that is you.

Second, there is no way you can do greater works unless you are able to love yourself completely—completely enough to believe you are not only potentially as good as Jesus, but that you are the same as the Christ. Is that blasphemy? Yes, it is if you see the Christ story only objectively , if you are trying to love a personality called Jesus rather than the name he gave us, which is "I." Yes, it is blasphemy when you confuse your personality with your Higher Consciousness. In order to go beyond Jesus, total self-love is necessary, and total love means total acceptance of yourself. It means the end of thinking you will be more lovable after you have improved, no more needing to become, no more needing to prove anything. It does require the capacity to see what is called your humanity, your Jesus self, as the perfect tool for your ever expanding evolution, so that greater and greater levels of consciousness will result from your having existed on earth. Jesus knew what he was saying when he said, that we would do greater works.

Personally, Jesus knew and had experienced the full truth. Jesus did his best to convey the truth that God and man are One and the same, but none of his disciples was quite evolved enough to take the Thirteenth Step and go beyond conceiving of God as something outside of themselves. I understand their dilemma, because I face the same problem with myself. Most of the time I am aware that God is that life force within me, but *at those times that I think of God rather than feel it, a sense of separation insinuates itself. As long as there is the slightest belief that God is in any way other than or apart from myself, I have not gone beyond where Jesus left his followers.* If I do not recognize that the capacity to provide, show the way, or heal exists for me as it did for Jesus, then I am denying his truth. As long as God is a concept rather than an experience, I have not gone beyond where Jesus left us. That is to say, I have not yet gone beyond the limitations of my personal sense of self as often as I would like to; however, I do more often now than I used to, because I more often consciously open myself to Myself and the Thirteenth Step.

Now, those are frightening and potentially egotistical statements. What am I feeling when I make them? Is it possible for me to see myself as God or Jesus while I simultaneously know that God is more than I am? Yes, it is when I am aware of what it means to simultaneously be an observer and the observed. It means I have to double think, at which time I am simultaneously aware of two different concepts of myself, one as man of earth and one as man of God. In order to do that, I must know the nature of error, the nature of the mistaken identity that we call personal sense or egotism, and I must know the nature of my spiritual being as the I AM—as the way, the truth, and the life. I must simultaneously be aware of two Jesus's and two me's, the non-absolute and the absolute, my objective self and my subjective presence.

When a student graduates, he is not greater or more advanced than the teacher, but he goes out into the world beyond the teacher. When I say there is a stage beyond Jesus that we must go to, I am talking about our need to show our love for Jesus by making his ministry a success. Unless we go beyond the point where we were when we were being taught, our teachers have failed in what they hoped to do. To go beyond Jesus is to go beyond seeking a God outside of ourselves, beyond believing some God will help, or even beyond believing that we need God. It is to consciously be God's presence. It is to know that it is all God, just as Jesus did.

Beyond Your Self

Some people say they have guides "from the other side." Some feel God talks to them. Some say they channel the Christ. They can be right or they can be wrong, depending on how they actually see it. As long as someone believes that their inner guides, their "voices," or the messages they receive intuitively, are from someone or some source other than from their own higher Selves, a duality is entertained and omniscience is not their heritage. We say that God is all knowing, all knowledge, and that we are one with God. If so, then everything we hear or the inner voices that speak to us come from our own Selves, our union with Omniscience. That One may appear to us as other entities, guides from another dimension, or even angels, but as there is only one infinite Self, in whatever form they appear, they are projections of our own Oneness.

I'll admit that it helps to see our guidance as though it is coming from another level than our finite sense of self, and it helps to consciously ask for and seek help from unknown or unconscious entities as long as we realize that those entities are part of our own consciousness. In seeking guidance, we are rightly trying to go beyond our limited sense of self. That is fine as long as we know that the limited self we are going beyond is our assumed limitation, and the source we are appealing to is none other than our own infinite God Self, for it is all God.

Beyond Purse or Scrip

*Y*ou can read the Scripture and make a good case for needing to give away everything you have, leaving the security of your job, and going out into the world with no more than the shirt on your back. Of course, that is an objective interpretation of those Scriptures. As all objective observations are only important if they illustrate a subjective principle, it would be a spiritual mistake to give power to money, jobs, the accumulation of possessions, or anything else by believing it is necessary to give them all away.

It would be a pity for everyone to believe that owning and enjoying material possessions would preclude living a spiritual life. Basic to the Christian message is the belief that God is the only power. Certainly then, the problem isn't in possessing riches but in one's dependence on them. To give away all of one's money out of the fear of not being able to find God gives riches a power greater than the Spirit. To believe that you should go out without purse or scrip is judging those effects as though they are evil and other than God's presence. I'll admit that if you cannot have possessions without your depending on them for your good, then perhaps you should let them go in order to prove to yourself that you have that within yourself that will fulfill all your needs, and to prove that you actually live by Grace, not by possessions. But, in the end, the way to prove the powerlessness of possessions is for you to have them and not be affected by them one way or the other. Perhaps you would then be free to use those possessions in order to make the world a better place to live in. The answer is—possess but don't be possessed by.

To go beyond purse or scrip means to go through life without depending on anything other than that which is within yourself. Whenever you look to a person, a place, or a thing, including money in the bank, for your good, you are a materialist. If so, then perhaps you do need to lose everything in order to find out that you have been putting your trust in princes and principalities. However, that is a pretty inept way to go about it. You won't have to lose everything if you learn to look within yourself for the Spirit to provide for you. Though your good may not come "from" another person or circumstance, it may come "through" another person or circumstance. Where it comes from is not for you to judge, but to appreciate. *There is no need for you to strip yourselves of the blessings your consciousness has drawn to you, but there is a need for you to recognize the source—God, your Higher Consciousness.*

The paradox is that when you release your dependency on things they flow in to you. At those times when my supply has seemed limited, in order to get the flow going, I have usually gone out and bought something. I can't tell that to most people because they might not understand that that technique succeeds only if it is done in the right spirit. I do it in order not to affirm the law of lack, and by doing so I break that law. Most of those I have known who have inherited a great deal of money somehow feel guilty for their bounty and often become over-cautious about it. What they have to realize is that it has been their consciousness to inherit money, and if they can see themselves as stewards of their money, they need not be in bondage to it.

Until one has found the presence of Spirit and a life lived by Grace, it is a good thing to be aware of and suspicious of the trap that possessions can impose. The ultimate and final freedom is to be able to have abundance and see it as the fruits of the Spirit. That way one does not depend on material things but rather on the spirit that created them to begin with. That is what it means to go beyond purse and scrip.

Beyond Morality

*M*orality, as we know it, is based on laws that pertain to specific human objective acts. Therefore, one is not judged in terms of the quality of Spirit in which one has performed an act but rather on the act itself. In saying this, I am not putting down the existence of moral laws. We need them. Moral laws are necessary guidelines for those who have yet to learn or consciously experience the Spirit of Love, and who are therefore unable to judge a situation in terms of that which is the loving thing to do.

Moral laws came about because in most cases those who go against the laws set forth for human conduct have done so in a spirit of lust, dishonesty, betrayal, self-indulgence, or deceit. They have done so because they are under the law of self-centeredness, rather than a Christlike realization that we are each other. They have not experienced what it is to live by Grace. Admittedly, to live Grace-fully, which is to live by the Spirit of Love, is subtle and difficult to follow as long as one still conceives of life in terms of good and evil, rather than in terms of the quality and presence of the Spirit that underlies everything. Human beings have been conditioned by lifetimes of living by law, and for them to completely rely on Grace or Spirit is a totally new way to live, a way to live that cannot be understood until they have experienced the Christ of themselves. Once that happens to us, we become able to monitor our Spirit without ceasing. It then becomes easier and easier because we have gone beyond the law of morality into the Spirit of Grace.

In *The Ultimate Revolution*, I tried to establish some guidelines for living that were not based on good and evil. I proposed a new kind of morality, a morality based on Spirit, a morality that would at first shock those who do not trust themselves to live beyond commonly accepted man-made moral laws. I suggested that it is not so much what we do, as the spirit in which we do it and the spirit that results from our actions. The morality of Spirit has nothing to do with observing the human scene one way or the other. It has nothing to do with anything outside of the individual. It does have to do with one's ability to listen to the language of Spirit. We can more or less do anything we want, as long as it does not violate the Spirit of Love.

It works this way: *Every thought or action carries a quality of spirit; so at any moment we can silence the thinking mind and feel or listen to the spirit we are entertaining or which will result from our actions, and then we can see if we are being spiritually immoral.* If the spirit of the act is un-loving we are spiritually immoral, and vice versa.

This approach has nothing to do with any of the rules that belong to the old morality we have been brought up with. It has to do with being aware of the spirit that is present or will be present in what we think or do as we proceed. This spiritual morality may surprise you in many ways, because you will see that some of the things you have done in the past, though logically justifiable, produced the wrong spirit in you and others. You may have been immoral Spirit-wise in surprising ways. For instance, in the past we have thought that working long hours was a virtue, that it meant we were conscientious, but the spirit of anxiety that produces a work-a-holic is a violation because it exhausts us and depletes the energy and time we need in order to fulfill our love for others.

If you can increase and maintain the Spirit of Love, if you can continue to feel the Spirit of the presence of God, then you are spiritually moral. If you take on something that will bring you down because you have been told you "should" do it, or if you allow some negative spirit to engender excessive concern or regret, then you are being spiritually immoral.

By and large, the moral laws established by society fit most situations, but when the Spirit of Love becomes your guideline and by your acts you are adding Love to life, there is no need for you to measure yourself against a man-made set of rules. When Spirit dictates your actions, you have gone beyond morality.

Beyond Death

*W*hat is beyond death? Nothing. No "thing" is permanent in its present form; therefore, there is nothing, as is, that goes beyond what we call death. If you believe that death exists and that it will end your or anyone else's existence, you have a "mummy" consciousness. Either you are the reincarnation of an ancient Egyptian or you currently think like one, and that is that you believe life depends on perpetuating material form. If you believe in death it shows several revealing facts about you. First, that you are still under the first law of human nature, which says that survival is purely a physical matter. Second, that you look at life solely from an objective standpoint. Third, you do not believe that Jesus' crucifixion and resurrection symbolized that life is eternal; therefore, there is no death.

Earlier, when I talked of the two ways of looking at the Communion service, the importance wasn't in which of the two viewpoints you take, but whether you understand the scientific fact of transmutation and its spiritual relevance. You do not kill a piece of wood when you burn it. You transmute it. You send it into the hereafter. After it transmutes into gases, it continues in another form. It resurrects into a less dense and, perhaps, more Spirit-like form.

What a futile existence our lives would be if we could not transmute, if we could not evolve, and if the word did not become flesh! It is no accident that we feel creepy when we see a mummy in a museum. We shudder because we feel "there but by the Grace of God go I." Death is feared because it says life ends, but we actually fear death for another reason. We fear not being able to change. Life would become unbearable if change were not possible. In fact, whereas in the past change was something we adjusted to, today we, and particularly our young, feed on change.

Until we end the fear of death, we cannot go beyond death into eternal life. If you want to live forever, I can tell you how to do it: Stop believing you were born. You did not just come into being "X" years ago, and you will not cease to be in "Y" years. At the core of your being you feel the truth of that. That is also why I have always felt that the only reason for celebrating our birthdays is to show our mothers our appreciation for their having brought us into this incarnation, not to celebrate the calendar.

Birthdays, like special relationships, tend to place one under the laws that say at this birthday you begin to lose your eyesight, at this birthday you are no longer able to perform as you were ten years ago, or at this birthday you will most likely die. To go beyond birthdays is to go beyond believing you were born at the time that you assumed the physical body you currently inhabit. To go beyond death is to realize you are the consciousness that is expressing itself as your body, rather than that you are the body, and as such you are life eternal.

We go beyond death by realizing that the concept of being born-again is a misnomer. How can we be born again if we have never died? We do not die, because we are consciousness and consciousness never dies. It has always amazed me that those who call themselves Christians believe that it is possible to kill anyone. A form may be laid to rest, but the Spirit, the soul, the Christ of everyone, including unborn children, is never apart from its eternality.

In both the Old Testament and the New, there are examples in the Bible of many people who believed in reincarnation. Whether they were referring to reincarnation subjectively, as the reappearance of different states of consciousness, or objectively, in terms of personality, I do not know. However, I do know that whether those, past or present, who believe in reincarnation know it or not, they show that they believe in life beyond death, because they are affirming continuity.

Scripture explains the transformation process that takes us beyond death:

> Behold, I shew you a mystery; We shall not all sleep
> (die), *but we shall all be changed. In a moment,*
> *in the twinkling of an eye, at the last trump: for*

the trumpet shall sound, and the dead shall be raised incorruptible, and we shall be changed. For this corruptible (concept of self) *must put on incorruption* (truth of being), *and this mortal* (belief in death) *must put on immortality. So when this corruptible shall have put on incorruption, and this mortal shall have put on immortality, then shall be brought to pass the saying that is written, Death is swallowed up in victory,...*

and we will have gone beyond it.

Beyond Love

I doubt that the lyricist who wrote, "love makes the world go round," consciously knew that he was talking about spiritual energy. Jesus knew. That is why he told us in the two commandments that we had to actively express our love both for the world of God and for the world of effect in order for us to be free. Then, how can we believe that it is either possible or desirable to go beyond love? It is, if we still believe there is an opposite to love.

God is Love, and God is the only cause, the only presence, and the only being. That means that Love is the only cause, the only presence, and the only being—but how many of us believe that? When we see man's inhumanity to man, when we see disasters that destroy the lives of thousands, when our own lives seem empty or lonely, we would have to be insane to believe that there is only Love in the world? Well, that is exactly what we have to be, because to material sense, it is insanity to believe God or Love is the only power. To go beyond believing that Love can be present or absent, that we can love or withhold love is a necessary requirement in order for us to ever become aware that it is all God. The reason we were told we were not to eat of the Tree of Good and Evil was because only when we eat of it and see that both good and evil are illusions, are we able to go beyond believing that love is good and that its absence is bad.

Every step on our way to ascension consciousness leads us to finally going beyond "having" love to "being Love." It is impossible to be "Love" as long as God, Love, or Omnipotence are just words, but when, despite appearances, there is no question as to God's allness, we have gone beyond love being just a concept. Then everything that is becomes a synonym for Love. When we become so filled with Love that we can live in this world and not react in any way that implies God is either absent or in a contest with evil, we will have gone beyond loving into being Love.

How can such a mind-boggling idea as going beyond love be of any value to you or me as thinking persons who exist at the human level? In a time-rushed world, we can no more take the time to constantly think ourselves through a maze of theology or positive thinking than we can constantly monitor all our unconscious bodily functions. It is much more important for you and me to step right into the void, where our rational minds cannot enter, where we consciously go beyond our limited concepts of love. Then, by going beyond our concepts of love, we will have gone beyond trying to achieve love *into being it.* If we can take that leap in one jump, we will see that time itself is the illusion that has kept us from going beyond loving into being the very presence of Love—where it is all God.

Beyond Free Fall

s human beings, going beyond faith, church, law, Jesus, God, and time means that it leaves us nothing to hang on to; so where are we? We are about to jump off the cliff. We may have free will, but at this point in our evolution we do not have free choice. We will either jump off the cliff into a life lived by faith in ourselves just as we are, or we will be pushed off the cliff. One way or the other, as the Scripture says, "*We shall not all sleep, but we shall all be changed.*"[20]

To jump of the cliff means to let go of all the mental and physical things or people that we have been holding on to. We have to let go of all our old concepts, all our pet theories, all our mind stuff, as well as all of those co-dependent personal relationship we are anchored to. In order for us to move into a conscious realization that two parallel worlds exist—the world of spiritual beingness and the world of material sense—we have to jump off the cliff. That doesn't mean we won't continue to have the loved ones and loved things we currently cherish, but we will have let go of dependence on them.

On our way up to this point, it was important for us to program our internal computers by concentrating on principles—the nature of error, the nature of prayer, the nature of God, and for us to believe that through the letter of truth we could have some kind of control over our lives. The time has now come to go further— to jump off the cliff and go beyond the letter of truth, beyond past concepts, beyond teachers, beyond religion, and, most of all, beyond believing we have to have intellectual control of our lives. Realizing that the time to jump off the cliff is here may help some people understand why so many things no longer work in their lives as they once did. It may help them understand why their once powerful prayers are no longer effective, why redoubling their efforts or trying new ways no longer work, or why nagging or serious physical problems continue to hang on. If so, it could be that those difficulties are signals telling them that the old ways no longer work, because it is time to abandon them by jumping off the cliff in order to arrive at ascension consciousness.

There is not anyone who does not have at least a little anxiety in anticipating this leap. Totally letting go in order to live completely by inner Grace is a shocking experience. What everyone is experiencing today is future shock — spiritual future shock. Over twenty years ago, Alvin Toffler and his wife wrote the book, *Future Shock.* They proposed that because of the impact of our fantastic technological inventions, humankind has now shut down its iris of awareness to the point where most people are looking at life through a pinhole, because we are unable to face the all-inclusive changes that are taking place. Well, in parallel, our spiritual future shock is even more earth-shaking. Unable to face the fact that the "Christ way" subordinates personal sense to spiritual power, we have closed down our spiritual irises. In doing so, we have slowed up our personal transformation and cut ourselves off from Pentecostal experiences. That does not mean that we have to eliminate being aware of our humanity, but rather that we have to jump off the cliff and live by Grace.

Everything I have written in this chapter up until now has been leading up to what happens to us after we have jumped off the cliff and how to appreciate it. Having jumped or having been pushed off, we now find ourselves in a state of FREE FALL. Many of us probably have been in it for some time now without knowing it. In fact, the world is now in free fall as well. All of those who feel they have lost control of their lives, those who recognize but can no longer either comprehend or keep up with the changes that are taking place, are in free fall. Those who feel as though they are being lifted right out of their old identities are in free fall. Those who feel that what they have wished for all their lives is right around the corner are most likely in a state of free fall.

Free fall is like sky diving. To the degree that one still exists under the first law of human nature, the prospect of jumping out of the plane is terrifying. There is nothing left to hang on to. As for all of our lives we have sought security—security in money, in relationships, in knowledge, in truth, and in health—we are now asked to translate ourselves into a totally different dimension, similar to something out of a kind of spiritual twilight zone. All the dependencies we have had in the past were right for their time and for the stages of evolution we were in, because they got us to this altitude of consciousness where we are now able to jump. However, now we have to experience a new way of living. We need a new set of guidelines for how to live in free fall.

The rest of our lives will be involved in not only learning how to live in free fall without any mental or physical insurance to back us up, but also how to rejoice at the prospect of limitless living, at which time we will understand why Jesus said "ye are Gods." The paradox is— by letting go of all the things we thought we wanted in our parallel human existence, they will now come about for us. They will come about because we have learned how to consciously enter the parallel dimension of *"My Kingdom"* which, in turn, transforms its counterpart—*"this world."*

The reason we have not heretofore understood these parallel worlds, or what it means to live in them, is because we have kept trying to see spiritual truths in personal or objective terms. When I say it is time to jump off the cliff, I am really saying, "You have done your homework; so no longer mentally concentrate on trying to improve, change, elaborate on, or trying to further penetrate into what you have thought you needed to do in order to become a master. Now abandon yourself to the Spirit you are." You will never get there by believing you will arrive though learning more, by deserving more, or by trying to more perfectly live what you have previously been working on. Let it all go. Due to your past studies and efforts, what was needed has already been computed in your unconscious. Trust that; jump off the cliff, and free fall!

There is no either/or to anchor to in free fall. In free fall you love both conditionally and unconditionally. What you are falling into when you enter free fall is to fall in love—in the truest sense of the word. You have not heard people say they walked into love, bumped into love, or ran into love. No, they always say they "fell" in love. They had no control over it. In free fall, love is not something you achieve. It is Pentecostal. It surrounds you. It achieves you. To free fall is to fall into the consciousness of Love.

Remember, no one sky dives without a parachute. All the Scriptures you have studied, all those truths you have learned, and those past proofs of the power of Spirit you have witnessed in your life constitute parachutes. However, your parachute is not something apart from your Self; it is an extension of your Self. So, you do have some control, but it is not control in a worldly sense. Your control is your faith and your free will to remember. If, as a sky diver, you panic and tighten up into a ball you will spin helplessly, but if you have faith in yourself and open yourself to the experience and you spread out your ever-loving arms, though you have nothing to hang on to, you can direct the fall and the trip will be a joy.

Please hear me. Because *"My Kingdom" is a different dimension than this world, there is no need to reject or judge this world because the world is our jumping off place, our school.* Without it we would never have reached convocation. Thank God that this world is a parallel universe to which we can return not only for a refresher course when we need it, but also where we can rejoin our human/spiritual friends for a class reunion and share our experience with those who are still bewildered. From now on our classes, studies, and meditations will consist of responding to the Spirit, not in trying to gain more knowledge to hang on to.

For instance, listening to tapes may hint at an experience, but the kinds of experiences which transform your being cannot be captured in either words or pictures. Seminars, classes, and such will no longer be the result of hanging on to the words of a speaker; instead, they will be an intuitive group experiences. The messages will come out of the collective divine consciousness of the group.

Skydivers who jump in groups join hands to achieve a collective experience that one who jumps alone cannot imagine. That is just another way of saying, *"For where two or three are gathered together in my name, there am I* (your spiritual identity) *in the midst of them."*[22] That "I" comes when two or three or more not so much fall as ascend, ascend into a free state of conscious awareness, and it lifts the collective presence into a Pentecostal experience. In this new day, the quintessential reason for going to an intensive, retreat, or Church will not be to receive from a teacher but to co-create the Pentecostal experience where two or more are gathered in the realization that it is all God.

Chapter 11

INCLUSIVE HEALING

*W*atch out what you ask for! You may get it in sur-prising ways, as I have found out and will explain. For many months I asked for an additional understanding of healing. I said, an 'additional" rather than a "greater" understanding, because, as part of the current shift in consciousness, our awareness of healing is now ready to be lifted beyond the narrow confines of human judgment or bodily function into a realized power that touches every aspect of our lives. In asking for a deeper understanding of healing, it wasn't that I hadn't achieved the consciousness of or successfully practiced the "spiritual" healing principles that I had been taught at the feet of spiritual healing masters, or that I hadn't participated in a number of physical transformations for others that had escaped rational explanation as well.

What I am talking about now is not a refutation of what I had learned and experienced in spiritual healings, but rather it is the result of a persistent feeling that kept coming to me. I felt that a heightened understanding of healing was emerging, one that will go beyond either the objective level of medical healing or of healings due to the presence of spiritual consciousness. This level will go right to the heart of healing and make it a present, consistent, and predictable way of life.

I call this next level "ascension-consciousness healing." By his resurrection, Jesus demonstrated that it is possible to realize a pure non-physical dimension beyond time and space. Yet even after the resurrection, by his saying, "*touch me not; for I am not yet ascended*,"[1] he implied that his healing was not yet complete. Soon after making that statement, he achieved the final step into pure ascension consciousness beyond all conceptualization. It is said that healing is a matter of revealing—revealing the truth beyond concepts. Concepts are what clothe us with human identity, so by being healed of concepts at the ascension, Jesus did not have to appear at the physical level any longer and was then completely healed.

Though we have not figured out scientific explanations for spiritual healings, many so-called miracles do indeed take place. Physical growths actually disappear without any obvious therapy, and commonly accepted fatal diseases vanish without medical aid, because someone has spiritually pierced the cloud of unknowing. So when I claim that all healing is spiritual, I am not denying the priority that Jesus gave us when he said that the first and great commandment was the love of God—realizing God as the only power. It is paramount that to the best of one's ability one faces every situation in life by first and foremost consciously opening one's self to one's higher Christ consciousness. Having done so, however, the resultant healing may then appear in a number of different ways, some obvious and explainable, some not.Perhaps the following parable explains why all healings are of God better than I can. There was a man sitting on the roof of his water-surrounded home in a flood when someone came by in a boat and offered him a way to safety. The man turned it down saying that God would save him. Later, when the water almost covered the roof, a helicopter came by ready to take him to safety, but he waved it off, saying, "God will save me." Finally the house was washed away and the man drowned. When he got to the Pearly Gates he asked God, "Why did you let me drown?" to which the Lord replied, "Who do you think sent the boat and the helicopter?"

On one hand, your guidance may remind you that Daniel saw the stone cut out of the mountain without human hands, letting you know that nothing humanly needs to be done. It may also tell you to call on the enlightened consciousness of a friend or practitioner for spiritual help as an avenue to healing.

On the other hand, your guidance may direct you to seek the aid of a God-provided medical practitioner. By judging a human resolution of a problem as being less spiritual, inferior, or less divine, you would be denying the very Omnipotence and Omniscience you may claim to believe in. Any either/or approach is purely third-dimensional, purely mental, purely a result of one's believing in good and evil—out of which the entire human misconception of existence has been created. It is all God.

Second, if you believe that you have failed when you have not manifested harmony at the material level, you are denying your own inherent divinity. Instead, realize that all error is impersonal—that all error in thinking or performance is due to your being temporarily under the influence of the collective ignorance. In that way, you will not take on guilt, which is a worse sickness than any physical illness. Your having felt guilty is what probably caused the sickness to begin with.

After all, Jesus temporarily stumbled and fell and finally found himself on a cross with physical nails piercing his physical hands. At that moment, he appeared to be manifesting the ultimate physical failure. His ultimate triumph, the resurrection, wasn't intended to show that there was only one way to heal the situation. Rather, it was to reveal that we are not just bodies and that we can live by Spirit and overcome all physical limitation in every aspect of life—not just in extreme cases. Jesus did not turn his back on his physician friend, Dr. Luke, nor demand that he stop practicing. He even advocated the laying of physical hands on people. Perhaps today, the hands that are laid on are physicians' hands with scalpels in them.

In healing blindness, Jesus' spittle became a kind of medicine. The story of the Good Samaritan's using wine and oil to heal could be interpreted as a medicinal remedy. Nowhere did Jesus exclude any form of healing, but he often spoke of including everyone in the healing process.

The founders of our metaphysical traditions, such as those who became Christian Scientists, thought they had to reject all material means, because at that time, they were reinventing spiritual healing, and they were trying to swing the pendulum back from a purely material approach into an acceptance of spiritual healing. In turning to medical science for help today, one still has to watch out that one does not cut one's self off from or be tempted to discount the possibility of a hands-off spiritual healing. Healing via pure Spirit should always be our first choice, and to the best of our ability, we should try and contact an inner understanding before deciding on an outer action. We should always *leave space for the miracle.* When that has been done, the condition will then have either disappeared or we will have received instruction from our Higher Consciousness relevant to the so-called human steps we should take.

Now for the clincher. I wrote most of what I have just been saying in a 1995 letter to my mailing list. Spiritual healing was in my consciousness because for several weeks before I wrote the letter, I had received several times the number of calls I ordinarily had from people wanting help, and, by and large, most received the help they had asked for. I attribute those successes to be the result of my callers' own faith. As Jesus often said, "*thy faith hath made thee whole.*"[2] Secondly, I wrote about healing because, for a long time, I had felt that a new spiritual paradigm was demanding a revived or more in-depth and inclusive interpretation of healing, one that did not eliminate medical healings but included them. Thirdly, and most importantly, I was writing what I thought about healing, because I had just found out that I had malignant prostate cancer and would be undergoing major surgery in three days.

Before Thoughts

*I*n my newsletter I wrote my "before-thoughts," thoughts I had before going to the hospital, which I will now share verbatim. A bit later on I will quote my "after-thoughts," the thoughts I had on my return home from the hospital. Because I want to accurately portray the state of mind I was in before going to the hospital, I will quote the rest of my newsletter as I wrote it in advance of and after surgery:

Now, let us look at the implications of what happened to me when I found out I had cancer and my reasons for sharing it with you. A few weeks ago, I was meditating and it came to me out of the blue that I should go take the PSA blood test for prostate cancer that I had read about. I had absolutely no symptoms whatsoever to prompt my investigation, nothing that would ordinarily make me believe that I needed to have such a test. I felt perfectly healthy and full of abundant energy, but I follow my listening, and my inner guidance told me to have the test; so I did. When the results were in, my HMO immediately sent me to a urologist. I was put through a series of further tests. Finally biopsies were taken revealing an advanced state of malignant cancer. In fact, the physician told me that most likely the cancer had spread, and, if not I was fortunate to have come in when I did, because if I were not operated on as soon as possible it would certainly spread.

At that point I received my first gift. I laughed when the doctor told me the news because he had such a serious demeanor, and I did not feel a twinge of fear or anxiety. The experience was a gift, because we do not know if we have faith until it is tested, and the greatest reward is to find that we do.

I do believe that the diagnostic abilities of modern medical science are a divine blessing that we should honor and respect. However, listening to the still small voice is paramount when it comes to how we decide on the prognosis—what to do about what has been diagnosed. Diagnosis reveals but does not judge. Prognosis involves judgment. That is where divine guidance and listening is needed, because each of us is unique, and it is up to us and our guidance to decide what to do and how much medication is right for us after we have been diagnosed. So after I was diagnosed, I returned to my home, and, as usual, meditated until I felt a release. Before I did any thinking about the situation one way or the other, I tuned within to my higher consciousness.

My guidance reminded me to use my whole self, and that included my intelligence; so, for a second opinion, I tracked down a physician who is considered to be the top authority in San Antonio. Two days later, I went to see him feeling that because of the spiritual work that was being done, I wouldn't be surprised if the cancer had gone away. It hadn't. The physician examined me and told me that when one is my calendar-age, medical practitioners feel it is too late to do anything about a condition such as mine. As you may imagine, I told him "age is a fiction; so get on with it." He outlined the different approaches. I went home, weighed them and their various side effects, which in most cases, such as the use of radiation, or chemotherapy, drastically affects the whole body and one's life style. I feel most comfortable with the less comprehensive approach of surgery; so that is the approach I have decided to take.

I know that I may sound like Pollyanna, but though I don't relish the fact that I have this thing growing in my body (not in me, in my body) I have absolutely no fear, none. That is partly because I do walk my talk in knowing that I am not just a body. I have the body, but it doesn't have me for I am life eternal. Though I am a combination of the physical, the mental, and the spiritual, I will keep this physical body in the best shape I can, just as I do my automobile, but when it has served its purpose, I will let it go and get a new model. Also, after I found out that I have a problem, when I meditate my inner voice says, loud and clear, 'You aren't going anywhere until you finish what you came here to do and that hasn't happened yet.

I also feel that because consciousness expresses itself in form, if I were to continue to visualize that a malignancy remains in my body, I might give it power and reality; so I have decided that the best thing for me to do is to get rid of it in the most expedient manner possible, and not try to prove anything one way or the other.

It also comes to me that though I have personally experienced many remarkable hands-off healings in the past, this time I would like to go through this one medically in order to see how the Spirit works at that dimension. I also want to help others who have been studying metaphysics overcome their feelings of guilt that so many have had when they get sick or ask for medical help. If I were to meet this particular situation without medical help, then all those who hear me tell of it in the future or read about it in my books would feel that they were failures when they found themselves having to turn to medical science. That's why I am letting everyone know what I am experiencing.

While I'm on the subject of guilt, I want to jump up on a soapbox and talk about one of my pet peeves—misguided mystics. Misguided mystics are those who deceive others in the name of God. They are those who are not authentic because they do not share their humanity as well as their divinity. They imply that they are so spiritual that they are above and beyond human emotions or difficulties. Anyone who sets himself or herself up as a spiritual healer, teacher, guru, author, or priest, and then hides his or her illnesses and weaknesses stabs their followers in the back. Anyone who projects the image of perpetual serenity, perfect peace, and the absence of all human cares, as though they are beyond temptation, lays a guilt trip on all who believe in them. The devil's most potent weapon is guilt. If love frees one of guilt, then any teaching or any person who suggests that they have completely transcended human conditions while still on the earth is the devil's advocate. There is no doubt that spiritual consciousness can heal, and it breaks the law—break the law of limitation. One can, indeed, overcome many of the limitations imposed by personal sense, but not completely while still in a body. Jesus didn't until he attained full ascension consciousness, at which time he left the human scene.

All growth takes place because our need to cope with human conditions pushes us into it. Human conditions—our shadow side—are the fuel, the energy, and the catalyst, for initiating creation. So, I now consider my experience to be an initiation. I feel it has come about because I have something to learn that will initiate a new level of consciousness in me, and that it will take me from one level to another. I have faith that it will. I feel that if it is my time to leave the earth plane, one way or another, nothing will stop it. If not, nothing will make it happen.

The only way I can lose is if I waste the experience. Objectively "waste not, want not," has to do with material things, but in this case, it is subjective, and it relates to my love of God. If I waste this experience through either fearing or ignoring what it can tell me, I will find myself wanting, but if, rather than being used by the experience, I use it to reveal and realize divinity, I will break the law of limitation and become freedom itself.

For example, I have already learned more about the meaning of fear through this experience. Though, as I said, I had no sense of fear of the illness when I was told of the condition, nevertheless one day I found myself full of anxiety and a sense of fear. I was confused until finally in meditation it broke and I found out what the fear was really about. It was a good fear. Remember, in omnipresence and inclusiveness, everything has its place, even fear. I didn't fear for my body. I was fearing that I would not learn what the experience has to tell me, that I will not see the hand of God in it, that I will not grow through the experience, that I will not walk my talk. My fear was a kind of spiritual growing pain, not the ordinary garden-variety fear but rather Spirit or Higher Consciousness trying to break through the finite. It was saying, 'waste not want not.

There is a consciousness within me of which my human thought is not fully aware. This consciousness beats my heart, digests my food, mends my bones, generates and replaces the cells of my body and performs countless other acts. Though I am not aware of it, this supremely intelligent consciousness is my own consciousness. It isn't someone else's consciousness, it is not outside of myself, and it is not a divinity that is other than my own being. It is my own individual consciousness of the divine process of creation recreating me.

Healing prayer is no more or less than a kind of appeal to my own divine consciousness. It is the recognition of the existence of the creative consciousness that I AM. Its aim is to remove any mental doubt or limitation that could get in the way of its fulfilling itself—not by my outlining how that is to be done, but by my having faith in God appearing "as." This consciousness can, and often does, result in an instant healing, but Spirit is just as much at work whether my healing comes from the surgeon's knife as from my prayers.

Thus in preparation for surgery and in recognition of the power inherent in the healing consciousness that I am, I gave myself this prayer:

The divine creative consciousness which has given birth to me in the beginning, which has nurtured, grown, and healed me through all these years, I honor and respect thee as being my own divine presence. Thou art the God consciousness of my forefathers, my saints, and my teachers. Thou art the presence I have found within myself at the sanctuary of my being. I turn to you now to erase any doubts or fears that may come to me in moments when I am not aware of your presence. I release all judgment in the acknowledgment of the healing and regenerating process that is taking place through my own higher divine consciousness.

I feel this, my Christ consciousness, flooding my whole being, running through my veins, healing discords, replacing used up and ailing cells, refreshing both my body and my spirit. I feel Christ consciousness stilling my limited sense of self. I feel it telling me that I have a body, but that this body is only a part of me, that the consciousness I am aware

*of at this moment is my true all encompassing
spiritual body and Self.*

*Hear the words which say, Walter, I have
come that you might have life and have it more
abundantly. This I is the consciousness of creation
in which there is no death. I never destroy; I
replace. I replace disease with harmony, lack with
completeness, and anxiety with joy. Amen*

After Thoughts

The following are my afterthoughts, which I included
in the newsletter I sent out after I returned home following the
surgery:

It's been ten days since the operation, and
after four days in the hospital, I am home. Has the
experience been wasted? No, thank God. I have a
great deal still to digest and will be sharing what I
am finding for some time to come, but experience
confirms speculation and initiates an ever-greater
awareness of how all the pieces fit together.

First, though the surgeons made a rather large
incision from the front because of the possibility
that the malignancy had spread, the operation
went so well that they didn't feel it was necessary
to put me into intensive care as planned. The lab
results showed that though fully developed, the
cancer had not spread outside the prostate and
I am completely free of any further signs. The
physicians reaffirmed that it had been caught just
in time. Within a day they were openly impressed
with my rapid recovery—and then came my first
lesson.

Feeling puffed up by my speedy recovery, I
caught another dis-ease, the two H's—Hubris and

Hypocrisy. Without a doubt, Spirit had guided my quick recovery, but it wasn't Walter's ability to make it happen that did it, as though Walter's superior knowledge had power over the material universe. If that were true, then despite all my talk I would have been right back at the level of seeing things in terms of either/or, spiritual or material. By indulging in hubris over my rapid recovery, I was doing the very thing I complained about misguided mystics doing. I was claiming power over the material universe, thus making others who would have slower recoveries than mine feel they were failures when their illnesses were not met as quickly. To be sure that I would learn my lesson, by the second day I came down with a nice little case of pneumonia with fever up to 102 degrees.

The next thing I realized, at a greater depth than ever before, was that no one can do it alone, and the reason why they can't. When physical pain, fever, or such dominates one's consciousness, one had better have those of realized consciousness to reach out to in order to bring the power of Spirit to bear, because at that moment one can't do it for one's own self. Though I contacted a couple of individuals beforehand and didn't have time to notify everyone personally, the presence of the entire circle of my spiritual family, and particularly those who I had come to know personally, were a very real presence with me. I found that all I had to do was to reach out in my consciousness to you, my spiritual family, my support group, and I received all that consciousness represents. Each of us can touch that presence at any moment, no matter how serious or innocuous our problem is, and we can know "...*if I make my bed in hell, behold, thou art there.*"[3] That I is the Christ, the spiritual family. It is a great comfort just to know that the spiritual family exists.

The most significant and mind-shattering thing that happened to me through this experience, and the most difficult to write about in a few words, happened the fourth night in the hospital. I love you and the wholeness of myself enough that, though the experience was very personal and multi-dimensional, I'll try to share what happened.

I haven't taken any sleeping pills in many years, partly because I have long ago learned how to meditate myself to sleep, and partly because I don't like taking anything that affects my consciousness in the way that drugs can. I do believe that there are some painkillers that do not have that kind of adverse effect, and if one has need of them, they should seek guidance in that area, but I've stayed away from sleeping pills. However, on this night my fever was high, and having to sleep on my back all the time made sleeping more difficult, so I decided to take a pill when the nurse offered me one.

Around three in the morning I woke up with the most horrible nightmare you could imagine. All I remember is the demon-filled black horror of that hell-like moment, and that I woke up thrashing around in the bed trying to escape. When I pushed the button that raised my head and my feet, gas pains became devastating, but when I lay back, bile came up into my throat and choked me. I was in a prison of physical, mental, and spiritual agony. I couldn't even begin to meditate; so I decided that the only solution was to get up and try walking around a bit. I struggled out of the bed, took hold of that thing on wheels that I was attached to, pulled it along with me, and got as far as the door. The fever, the pain, the weakness, and the drugged feeling from the pill were overwhelming. I panicked. I didn't know what to do. I couldn't move forward and I didn't even think I could get back to the bed to ring for a nurse. In desperation, without thinking I literally put out my hand and heard myself say, "JESUS, HELP ME." What happened was so powerful, personal, and instant that I choke-up even now when I talk of it. A wave flowed over me. It was though a light was turned on in a tunnel of gloom. The pain and anguish melted away. I felt myself straighten up; felt this hand in mine; walked the hall in peace; returned to my bed; the fever broke, and I slept soundly the rest of the night.

Why "Jesus?" Why not, "the Christ," why not "Higher Consciousness," why not "Divine Mind?" They are all the same. It's all God. Yes, but God is multi-dimensional, and when you can only comprehend or get help from the personal level, you may need a personal Jesus or some other personal symbol to identify with. I may not have realized it at the time, but because of my Judeo/Christian background, at the subconscious level, the name, "Jesus," symbolized for me all that the Christ stands for.

When I was at the door that night full of pain and confusion, fancy subjective ideas, abstract impersonal concepts, being aware of the I AM, and all the theories about metaphysics or Spirit, though true, were out of my reach. I was locked totally in a personal physical level and the only thing I could possibly identify with had to be something personal—Jesus. Certainly, Jesus, the Christ, the anointed one, God, and the other synonyms for "beingness," are all the same, but locked in that personal level, the only thing that could get through to me was an objective example of how the Spirit manifested in the flesh. At my subconscious level, calling on that name activated all that the name stands for—help in time of need, freedom, healing, compassion, love.

Why that particular name? Why not Tom, Bill, or Joe? For those of us who were brought up in the West, there is power in the name of Jesus. Rupert Sheldrake uses the word "morphogenetic," by which he means "the evolution of form," to explain this phenomena. Though a word is a form or effect, through the years it builds up a kind of energy, power, or what the Hindus would call darshan. That is why in the beginning is *"the Word"*, then *"the Word"* is made flesh and dwells among us as power. So many millions of people have identified with the name of Jesus over the years, each in his or her own way; so many have called on the Christ Spirit that just calling on it has a power that has evolved morphogeneticlly through the centuries. The name has come to be a kind of spiritual shorthand, and calling on it brings forth the power of all that is associated with the name.

On the other hand, I believe that those who blindly call on the name of Jesus for everything he or she wants or needs, without realizing that Jesus is not just the name of a particular person, are short-changing themselves. It is what the name symbolizes—the Christ, the anointed consciousness—that gives the name its power. Unless one is consciously aware of what is behind the name, one cuts oneself off from realizing that the thing the name stands for is also within himself or herself and not just in one man.

Though calling on Jesus has the power of centuries behind it, to some degree we can reach out in spirit to any of those with whom we have studied or from whom we have received healing and also lift our consciousness into the Oneness with them that we are. They too re-present the family of God.

Anyway, the morning after my Jesus experience I awakened in such an improved state that the doctor released me and I returned home. Just a few days later I gave someone a walking tour of the ranch. I don't want you to think that my talking of the speed of my recovery contradicts what I said earlier about laying guilt trips on people who don't have speedy recoveries? No. All healing, slow or fast, is spiritual. I'm saying that there is a new way of looking at healing that lifts it beyond what we have thought healing to be.

To my great surprise this medical experience was not only not wasted, but the most important thing that I learned from it seemed to come from out of left field—I learned about Love. It was really a love experience. I had always thought of healing in terms of results rather than cause, but no longer. *A healing represents a change in consciousness that is brought about by Love, not a getting rid of symptoms. I realized that healing is the removing of any concept whatsoever that stands between me and God in any and all circumstances. Whether medically or spiritually, healing is revealing. It is a matter of revealing the divine nature of a person or situation. Healing is the awareness of the presence of Love. When we become aware of the presence of Love, a healing is revealed. In turn, healing is love expressing itself as the perfection of body, as the perfection of relationships, as supply, and as freedom from fear. All healing, no matter how it comes about, is Love (God) manifesting itself. Healing and Love are the same word.*

Whenever you reach out to another person for spiritual healing, you are really reaching out to Love, for God is Love. The Spirit of healing and the Spirit of Love are the same. Whenever Love is present, healing is present. What we must do now is divorce ourselves from thinking of healing in terms of results and we can do that by always thinking of healing as Love in action. Love always, in all ways, heals. It is not just in physical healings alone but in the healing of emotional problems, in healing lack, in healing relationship confusions, love is the power that heals. That means, as I said in The Gospel of Relativity, to Love is to "know." To know the true identity of another person or the truth of a situation heals it. So whenever the need for getting rid of anything that seems to stand in the way of God appears, you have to know the truth—Love heals. Do not seek a solution to a problem — seek Love.

Teilhard de Chardin said that Love is the only energy capable of totalizing the world. As total means whole, and as whole is the Greek word for "heal," love is the energy that heals the world. We need not worry about or even think about healing. When we start loving, wholeness will swallow up whatever is lacking, be it physical, mental, emotional, or soulful.

To "*render unto Caesar the things that are Caesar's*"[4] means that when a spiritual healing has not taken place, it is all right to turn the physical over to the physical just as it is to render unto the Spirit its own coin, Love. Pure and simple, *God is Love and Love is an expression of faith—faith in the*

healing Spirit operating within as Love, faith in the
Spirit of Love in others, faith in one's own higher
Christ being. Surrender to that faith and watch the
miracles appear in whatever form and whenever
needed.

Remember, though love is not a faucet that
you can turn on and off, there is something you
can do that brings love presence into being. You
can be forgiving. You can give up the belief that
there is anything other than Love present, and at
work. You can let go of any judgment you have
for another or for life itself in the knowledge that
Grace is Love in action.

My fear of wasting my visit to the hospital
certainly went unfounded. It turned out to be one
of the most valuable experiences of my life, a kind
of initiation through which I was born again. From
now on, I will never think of any form of healing
without seeing it as Love in action. Whenever
anyone asks for healing, I will know they are asking
for Love. From now on, whenever it appears that
a healing is necessary, I will see that Love is what
is necessary. Whenever a healing has taken place,
I will know love has been revealed.

End of letter.

$\mathscr{C}$hapter 12

AFTER THE TALK

Rejoice in the Lord (your anointing) *alway: and again I say, Rejoice. Let your moderation be known unto all men. The Lord* (your higher consciousness) *is at hand. Be careful for nothing; but in every thing by prayer and supplication with thanksgiving let your requests be made known unto God. And the peace of God, which passeth all understanding, shall keep your hearts and minds through Christ Jesus. Finally, brethren, whatsoever things are true, whatsoever things are honest, whatsoever things are just, whatsoever things are pure, whatsoever things are lovely, whatsoever things are of good report; if there be any virtue, and if there be any praise, think on these things. Those things, which ye have both learned, and received, and heard, and seen in me, DO: and the God of peace shall be with you…I know both how to be abased, and I know how to abound: every where and in all things I am instructed both to be full and to be hungry, both to abound and to suffer need. I can DO all things through Christ, which strengtheneth me.* Philippians 4:4-13

*A*fter the talk is the walk—the doing. We are energy—spiritual energy individually expressing itself—and now we must and can consciously live who we are. The twenty-first century is the century when action becomes more important than theory, when our very existence depends on our combining our "being-ness" with our "doing-ness."

I find that I can pick up my Bible and once more go over Scriptures that I have rehearsed countless times in the past, and suddenly a couple of words I have never been aware of before will pop out that change the whole meaning the Scripture had for me in the past. When least expected, a couple of previously ignored words can be catalysts, miraculously propelling me into a different level of consciousness. I came across two such words just last year that revolutionized my understanding of prayer, one of which was most likely the reason Jesus got crucified.

To explain, I have often quoted the Scripture in Matthew and Mark, where Jesus, being told that his mother and brother were waiting without, answers, "*...whosoever shall do the will of my Father, which is in heaven, the same is my brother, and sister, and mother.*"[1] Previously I interpreted that statement to mean that his family were those who believed as he did, and I left it at that. But I ran across that same incident in the Gospel of Luke, and this time I saw that he answered, "*My mother and my brethren are those which hear the word of God, and do It.*"[2]

I never saw the "hear" and "do it" part before; so I looked up the same reference as quoted in Matthew and Mark. I was surprised to see that though I had missed it before, there ,too, He had said that we had to "do" in order to be in his family. Praying alone is not enough. We also have to do. Though I had missed it before, those two words now made me aware that faith and belief alone, are not enough. There is a condition: We have to "do" the word as well as "hear" it. Just praying, just talking, just appreciating, is not enough. We are not in the family of Christ consciousness until and unless we act, unless we release energy into the world. We may be full of spiritual energy, but until we consciously open a way out for its expression, we are self-indulgent with a small "s." As the Poet Browning said, "Truth is within. We must open out a way for the imprisoned splendor to escape."[3] We must consciously open out that way.

What I hadn't seen before was the double thread nature of the Scripture as quoted in Luke. By saying that we had to both hear (God) and do (to our neighbor), Jesus was underlining the complementary nature of the two commandments that are necessary in order for all the law to be fulfilled. Hearing is pointless without the doing, and doing is useless unless one has heard. Hearing programs the computer. It sets up *"the Word"*, but then *"the Word"* must be acted upon in order for it to become flesh. So doing is the complement of hearing, and vice versa. *We must both hear the word and do it in order to be included in the spiritual family. Once we have "heard" the word—that we are made in the image of God—we must realize there is nothing, no one, and no God or Jesus outside of ourselves that will do for us what we have to do. No one else can do it for us.* No excuses. We must do it, or it won't be done.

This is a new day where the hearing and the doing are combined. In the past, the Traditionalists or Fundamentalists "did." They built hospitals, schools, and social institutions, but instead of listening to "hear" their own inner guidance for instructions, they were told what to do and how to do it to by the church. In the past, the Gnostics or metaphysicians "heard," but they were so preoccupied with their own with-in-ness and with living by Grace that they didn't "do" for others. When our two selves come together we can listen and then do. We can follow the priority Jesus gave us and seek first to "hear" and then "do."

We may not see it at the moment, but the realization that we can and must do the doing is the greatest gift we have ever been given. It is truly a gift, because as long as we feel that there is a God or some force outside of ourselves that does the doing, we are not free agents, nor are we honoring our divine heritage. Until we realize that we completely control our own lives by a combination of our own hearing and doing, we are helpless victims of circumstance and of forces beyond our control. However, when we finally face up to the fact that our lives are completely the result of our own consciousness, we are free to make of them what we will. Believing that God will do it for us often means that we don't love ourselves enough to accept that we are all that God is within our own being and therefore able to do the doing. By realizing our oneness with Omniscience, there isn't a problem that can't be solved, no overwhelming obstacle or hopeless situation that can't be overturned. We can resolve all complexity by demanding our heritage as God's representatives. Sometimes our doing is our demanding.

After Jesus announced who his spiritual family was, he repeated the principle in another way: He said, " *For whosoever hath* (does), *to him shall be given and he shall have more abundance: but whosoever hath not* (does not), *from him shall be taken away even that he hath.*"[4] This is another Scripture that is most often interpreted objectively, as though Jesus were talking about receiving and giving material things. Subjectively, it relates to hearing and doing: Those who "hear" and "do" have, and those who are not doing will soon use up the little they seem to have because without doing, what they have had in the past will not be renewed.

Consciousness alone does not do anything. Consciousness tells us what to do. Then consciousness has to be acted upon. Sometimes it tells us not to take any physical action, and at those times our "not doing" becomes what we must consciously do. Other times it tells us to stand up and be counted, and that becomes the thing we should do.

The objects we have accumulated in life are the result of either our, or someone else's, having spent creative energy doing something creative. All material things represent the "Word" that has been energized through doing in ways that make it become flesh. Nothing is created without someone's hearing or envisioning and then doing. Envisioning is a powerful act of doing, but completion always involves an outer doing as well as an inner one in order to manifest creation. In other words, faith, which is "seeing," has to be acted upon in order for it to really be faith. Everything we do represents degrees and expressions of energy. Doing can be an example of mental or meditative energy/action as well as a physical one, but the substance of what one has conjured up must be consciously energized—not just thought. On the other hand, doing without first hearing is fruitless.

Some people think that entering the "silence" is a passive state. It isn't. True silence is unconditioned energy in its most alive state, and it inevitably results in outer movement. There are those who have accumulated an abundance of material things, and there are those who have accumulated an abundance of other people whose lives they have affected. Both represent individuals who have manifested the energy that was needed in order to project into form what they have envisioned . Those who have little are those who have neither heard nor done. They most likely are among those who are waiting for God, chance, or the lottery to supply them, not realizing that they themselves in their divine state are the only God that does anything. Just as *"the Word"* becomes flesh, the flesh represents *"the Word"* expressed through doing.

What Jesus tried so hard to say was that there is no accident or chance in life. He demonstrated the fact that there isn't any God outside of our own infinite consciousness that heals us or performs any unrelated act for us. Our own hearing and doing return to us as material substance, as loving relationships, as respect, as healing, and as fulfillment in all ways. Those who receive respect from others, who leave behind a trail of healings, who evidence abundance and exemplify rewarding riches of Spirit and joy, show that they are givers. They "hear" and then "do" the will of their creator Self. Because our giving—not our taking—creates our getting, unless those who do not hear and do start doing, they will soon have nothing to show for themselves at all.

In the simplest terms, you may not have a penny in your purse, but you can pick a wild flower by the road and give it to a stranger, and that flower will grow into a bouquet, and the bouquet into a garden. However, it is your doing that makes it happen. There aren't any nouns anyway. There are only verbs. If I take two rocks and put a board across them and say that it is my table, I do so because the board is being a table. Thus table is a verb. There are no nouns because everything is being what it is. Every word implies an action. Everything is not just "being," it is "doing" itself. We are not fully being unless we are doing. Doing may appear to be passive, but if one is consciously knowing the truth of God, one is doing God's work. We are consciousness and consciousness is always expressing itself.

As everything always returns to self-love or the lack of it, those who fear doing often fear being. They fear being able to do, or they fear that they will do things incorrectly. Both show that they lack self-love. They do not accept that they are one with the Christ, are the Christ, and do not honor Jesus' words when he said: "*He that believeth on me, the works that I do shall he do also; and greater works than these shall he do.*"[5] He didn't say they should just let him do it, or that they should just go and meditate. We also have to do.

When getting help from a practitioner no longer seems to work, when previously successful prayers to God no longer produce results for you as they once did, it is most likely because you have now evolved past the becoming stage to the doing stage. Now only your own doing will bring results. Students still receive outside help, but once they have graduated, they are on their own.

Instead of Jesus saying that our faith is what makes us whole, he could as easily have said, "Your doing hath made you whole." Doing is not just doing. It is being the doing. Until you are being or doing what you have been created to do, you are sinning, you are falling short of your purpose. We look at an automobile and call it an automobile, but unless it is functioning as an automobile, it is not an automobile: it symbolizes the possibility of transportation, but isn't being it.

Faith, as I said, is not what someone has. Faith is what

someone does. Faith, too, is not a noun. Faith is a verb. Faith has to be an act of conviction to legitimately be called faith. As Paul said, the action of *"Faith is* (becomes) *the substance of things hoped for, the evidence of things not seen."*[6] Thinking is static, but faith is active. It does something in that it tells us something to do. Those who believe they have faith, but do not do the things they have faith in, fail because there is no such thing as having faith in any "thing." Things are results. Having faith in something, even in a religion or a God, is putting faith in results rather than cause. Unless we "do" God, we have no faith "in" God.

We actively create our entire worlds by having faith and then living our faith. Unfortunately, one can have faith in destructive and inharmonious activities as well as creative ones. We can have faith in lack, limitations, or illness, and in turn, we will create exactly what we have actively envisioned. We don't "have" an illness; we "do" an illness, and when we know that, we can stop doing illness and start doing health!

The sky is not the limit. The consciousness of our ability to do is. The sky is whatever we "do" it to be. I know that sounds as though I should take a course in grammar. However, this is my attempt to make it clear that the material world, the world of form, is an illusion as such. It exists, but only as energy actively expressing itself as form. The world is being. The world is doing. The world is actively spiritual. The world is constantly active or it would cease to appear, and that is the same for all of us. If we want to change the form, all the praying in the world won't help unless—unless we are living the prayer we are praying.

Self Prayer

When ignorance is eliminated, there isn't anything left but God—no place where God is not, no beingness other than God. Prayer, then, is the final part of the Trinity of God, Word, and Spirit, because prayer is the "doing" that causes us to experience our humanity as our divinity, and it makes of them One. Subjectively, your prayer is not defined by your words or your thoughts, but rather by a communion experience, at which time you realize your completeness. Objectively, prayer is thought to be something you do. Subjectively, prayer is an experience you are. In other words, subjectively, prayer is fulfilled when you experience your beingness or doingness as God's beingness or doingness. It demands the end of the contradiction inherent in dualistic thought. Unfortunately, we all continue to be influenced by old conditioning where there is God "and" us, which goes against everything Jesus taught us. But when you see yourself as he saw himself, your words will match your doing and you will no longer pray to a God that is outside of yourself, but rather to that within yourself that is God. If the Twenty-first Century is to be the time for hearing *"the Word"* and doing it, your prayers must be "inten-tional" prayers whose intent in no way contradicts Omnipresence and Omnipotence and, for that matter, Omniscience. Any prayer that suggests there is a place and time where God is not, that there is some inaccessible truth that is beyond your own connection with infinite knowledge, or that there is a power other than your own Higher Consciousness, that prayer is a sacrilege. In this computer age, prayer might more accurately be described as networking with and activating a program within yourself that reconciles, brings into focus, and communicates your inherent capacity for being Omniscience, Omnipresence, and Omnipotence.

Once you have experienced the realization of your own divinity, prayer becomes a conversation between your personal sense of self and your spiritual reality. Thus prayer becomes something entirely different than traditionally understood. It becomes free of contradiction. Prayer is no longer an appeal to something outside of yourself. When you realize, as Jesus did, that you are your Divine Consciousness and that there isn't anything in your being other than God, then when you pray, you are praying to yourself—to the truth of your own being. That kind of prayer shows that you know who you are.

Jesus knew who he was. Though he was aware of his humanity, he didn't see himself as becoming. He was there. If you have received illumination or if you are close to doing it, you will no longer think in terms of becoming something you are not already being. Until you love yourself enough to stop trying to become and realize, "That which I have been seeking, I already am," you are not ready for the ultimate understanding and experience of Self-prayer. As long as you talk of being created in the image of God and you still think in terms of becoming, you are in a state of denial and contradiction, and you are not ready for Self-prayer. By continuing to think that if you go to one more class, learn one more truth, study one more teaching, or pray to God one more time for the purpose of becoming something you are not, you are still in Self-denial. If you go to church, seminars, or retreats in order to share yourself, that is another matter, but to go to them in order to become something you are not already being separates you from being.

When you were still in that Pharisee state of consciousness—before you had experienced a taste of the Christ—self-denial was appropriate, because you still saw yourself as a personality. In that ego state, praying to your self or calling yourself God would have been rank heresy, but I'm not talking to a Pharisee. I doubt that your consciousness has led you to read this book if you have not at some time or another experienced the presence of God appearing in and as your being. It may have been when you were walking alone in the woods, when you were listening to a chant, our when you felt as though you were inspired from within. If you have once heard *"the Word"* you must now do it *"lest a worse thing come unto thee."*[7] As this is the century in which the Spirit demands that we hear and do, the ultimate doing is to pray the Self prayer—to pray to the Oneness that you are.

Because the consciousness that Jesus brought into being has matured, we can understand ourselves now as uncompromisingly as Jesus did himself. We can be the living prayer he was, and we can realize the mind of Jesus—the mind that allowed him to pray the Self prayer without confusing his humanity with his divinity. Even today, if you tell people that you are praying to your Self, they will crucify you, because they have not attained the consciousness that allows them to see who you really are and what that means. Have compassion for them, but don't become the occasion for their stumbling. They are not to be blamed for being unable to look at life spiritually, nor should you expect them to understand. They are just not yet conscious beings. So keep it secret, but when you sit down to pray, impersonally contemplate the nature of God, until step-by-step you end any contradiction in yourself and you see that God, being all, is your Self. Praying, then, is your way of becoming aware of your Self, of "I am." It is important for you to realize, the reason you want to pray or meditate to begin with is because at the moment you are caught up in a third-dimensional or personal limited sense of yourself, and you wish to once more realize and experience your divine self. With that in mind, enter your closet with the intent of becoming quiet in order to pray to your God/Self. Do it without confusing personal sense with the experience of your own divinity. Whether you realize it or not, any time your intent is for your outer self to experience your inner Self, you are praying. All other kinds of prayer are contradictions of oneness and denials of omnipresence, omniscience, and omnipotence.

Think of yourself as a microcosm of the macrocosm, which is to say an individual replica of the whole universe, complete in yourself. See yourself as a closed circuit, in which everything you can think of, conceive of, or imagine is included. That, of course, means that you need not look outside of yourself for anything. In fact, when you do start thinking that there is a power or presence apart from yourself, you have lost sight of who you really are.

In this paradigm, God is a part of or included in your own being, or God is present "as" your own Self-complete being. Whereas in the past you prayed to God as though God was someone outside listening to your prayers, now you realize that your personal sense of self is praying to that part of you that is your divine self. You are praying in order to be reminded of who you are.

When early Christians, particularly in the Eastern Church, prayed the Jesus Prayer—"Jesus Christ, son of God, have mercy on me a sinner"—they were obviously not conceiving of themselves as self-contained. To you, that prayer translates into, "Higher Consciousness, the presence of God, fill my being with your spirit." Thus your intent is to open yourself to your own God consciousness, without conceiving of it as being other than yourself, and when you do that, you are not allowing yourself to contradict the belief that God is Omnipresence, Omniscience, or Omnipotence. In other words, your intent is to experience your completeness, and you are calling on your own higher being to become your conscious awareness. This is the only prayer that is not, in part, blasphemy.

When you accept your completeness as a microcosm of universal perfection and you pray the self-prayer, all the different aspects of spiritual consciousness melt down into one thing— faith. When insecurity or doubt enters your consciousness, when you feel incomplete, when anxiety rears its head, you have but to come back to home base: Have faith in your Self (with a capital S). To have faith in yourself is to once more believe that you are self-complete, that you have that within and as your Self that will draw from itself all that you have sought from God.

When you hear that you need to die daily, that in order to come close to God you must mortify yourself, understand it to mean that you must die to any sense of duality that we may still have. You must die to seeing yourselves as an egotistical being with a life apart from Self-completeness. You must die to any thought that your life is anything other than all that God is. Thereby, you love God and you will know that it is all God.

Personally, I don't pray at all unless my personal sense of self feels it needs to get in contact with my Divine Self. The rest of the time I feel the presence with me as a divine echo. I do spend time every morning consciously being, consciously listening, and consciously "doing" prayer in the form of contemplation, and by writing what I hear within. When needed and if I feel any anxiety, I stop whatever I am doing, sit down, and actually pray to my own potential. I don't pray to "get" anything but to "be" something; not "to" anything but "as" something. Sometimes I don't need to think at all, but can simply feel my way toward my own spiritual existence, to that something that is the truth of my beingness.

Because I start out in personal sense, sometimes I need something personal to get me started. I need to read some inspiring book or the Bible. When I feel the Inner Self-stirring, I put the book down and try to enter into that feeling. I know I am not praying to anything outside of myself; so I find words that have the power to lead me to the experience of myself. Sometimes I repeat my version of the Unity prayer: "There is but one power and one presence appearing in my life and in the universe," or in Jesus' words, "*I and my Father are one.*"[8]   When I begin to feel the presence in those words, I may return to the most powerful prayer ever revealed: *I AM THAT I AM.*[9] As my prayer gets simpler, it becomes just I AM, and finally the word "I" alone. I am the presence I feel. I am the one who is and the one who is feeling my presence: I, I, I.

As long as I think of myself in physical terms, I cannot pray the Self prayer because my physical being is limited, but when I realize that I am consciousness appearing as form, my prayer is no longer limited because my consciousness is infinite and not restricted to a body. Then I can imagine my consciousness being all that I have always thought God to be. From my infinite omniscience comes *"the Word"* —whatever word Walter needs to hear. In prayer, Walter opens himself to his own active yet still small voice, which can speak most loudly. When Walter says "I," "I am that I am," he is opening himself to the divinity he is, at which time God is his being, being "I." He asks nothing from this "I" but to experience it, because it is God. When that happens, Walter is both into and has become prayer, for *"the Word"* has become his flesh. There is nothing to ask for because God is all that "I" is. Being prayer there is nothing outside of the Self. *"the Word"* is the Self, and the action that follows is prayer in action. Hearing the word is doing the word, at which time Walter is not "in" the family of Christ: he has become the family.

In your prayer of self-realization, you are actually loving both your humanity and your divinity. You are loving your humanity for being the temple in which your divinity resides, and for its help in finding your Self. You are saying to the self who needs to pray that you want to experience your divinity, and in that moment the two you's become One. Prayer to your Divine Self is your way of being honest with and about your Self.

One day, I heard my Self repeat the Lord's Prayer formula in terms of oneness with God:

My creative source, which is all-knowing spiritual reality, wholly be thy recognition. Let this awareness of myself be experienced at the personal level, as it is when I am aware that it is all God. Provide for my wholeness each day the vision of who I am. Release my consciousness when it has not been able to see that I am one with God as I release others who have been unable to know who they are. Lead us not into the temptation of accepting an identity apart from our divinity and deliver us from contradiction and dishonesty. For the kingdom of love, the power of love, and the glory of the love, is the I AM of all beings.

Don't Lose the Magic

At this point there is something we have to watch out for. No matter how dedicated we are in our quest to understand the meaning of God, we are in danger of throwing the baby away with the bath water. If, in our quest to realize we are God's presence, we get too metaphysical, we can intellectualize, analyze, and dissect the mystery right out of our lives. In our hunger for truth there is no more important spiritual or significant breakthrough than the realization that our God is indeed not outside of ourselves. Nevertheless, when we stop seeing God as a mysterious power beyond human comprehension, a God which is capable of transforming the world, we may be in danger of strangling the magic right out of our experience. Instead of an awareness of divine intervention and freedom, we may dry up in a morass of personal responsibility and end up with a bad case of existential anxiety.

Your Spirit self cannot be intellectualized. It can only be experienced. You may mentally conceive of the possibility of your being a self-complete expression of God, but thinking it does not take you very far. By the Grace of God, experiencing your "Godness" can and sometimes does happen. That's the mystery, and when it does happen to you it always feels miraculous, glorious, radiant, and magical, but the more you mentally dissect the phenomena, the more difficult it becomes for you to experience it.

I may sound as though I am contradicting myself when I say that we still have to reach out to something that is actually within ourselves, but to the degree that we are aware of a self that can of itself do nothing, the mystery still exists. There, again, the only answer that allows us to have our cake and eat it too—to be objective about our humanity and yet keep the mystery alive—is to double think. If I can experience the silence that is beyond words and thoughts, it becomes possible for me to recognize those times when I am feeling personal and in need of the healing magic of Spirit. I can reach out to God apart—apart from the ego self I am mired down in. I can remind myself that the supernatural does indeed exist. Though that supra-natural Higher Self is my own being, nevertheless when I pray I can call on it with the same awe and wonder as I used to call on God before I heard that God was my own being.

If you still have the same reverence for the mystery that you had when you put your foot on the path, you can contemplate the truth without cutting yourself off from the childlike faith that has healed you so many times in the past. You can call on it, and though you may make your bed in hell, the miracle of life can break through the shell of loneliness and you can regain the magic.

Mystics are called mystics because they evoke the mystery—the miracle. To that part of you that is of the earth, it is a miracle that *"in my flesh shall I see God."*[10] It is a miracle that by faith you can move mountains. It is a miracle that love can heal all your wounds. It is a miracle that "I" will go before you and make the crooked places straight. It is a miracle that by your contemplating Jesus' words, "*I am the way, and the truth, and the life*"[11] all limitations go away and the spirit fills your being. It is a miracle that you can open your soul and become aware that the Kingdom of Heaven is here and now. It is a miracle that you can have it all.

Imagine if someone were to bring you a mysterious ancient box, and they told you it contained the most precious jewel that had ever been discovered, that with this mysterious jewel you could buy everything you ever wanted, including perfect health, loving companionship, and worldly fame. If they did, you would give everything you have to possess that box. Finding that box is no different than the quest for the Ark of the Covenant that was made by the hero of the movie, *Raiders of the Lost Ark*. Within the Holy of Holies was or is the secret of life, God, the I that I am. Without a doubt, if personal sense sees this precious jewel it will be burned up, because the ark contains all energy and infinite potential. It will cease to exist as anything other than God expressing itself, because when the light shines darkness ceases to exist. That is the mystery, and if we lose that we have nothing.

Well, everyone has that mysterious box at the center of his or her being. It is mysterious because it isn't visible to the human eye, but nevertheless, it is within each of us. First, we have to realize that the mystery exists. Second, though we may not know how to open the box, we must be in awe of its content. We must treasure it. Third, we must realize that this most precious jewel is our rightful inheritance. Fourth, we must be prepared to die to our fears and to personal concerns, because when we are able to look at the contents of that mysterious place within ourselves where God exists, we will experience the magic and behold that life is full of infinite possibility.

Until you are able to look into the box, just holding it, just knowing what is in it, just knowing it contains the mystery, just preparing for the grand opening, is enough to make your life a wonder and joy a reality. If you cannot open the box at this point, keep reminding yourself of what is in it and what the future will bring. Prepare yourself, and when you least expect it, without thinking one day you will lift the lid and you will behold the glory you are.

The Circle of Christ

*W*hen you have successfully prayed, you will have experienced the Trinity. You will have realized that you are the observer, the observed, and the observing; the teacher, the student and the teaching; the parent, the child, and the parenting; and life will become an all-inclusive circle. You will be fully, wholly, and completely in life, in the world, and in love with your life, while at the same time there will be that part of you that is enjoying itself being the process. The end of the twentieth century marks the day of homecoming, the completion of a circle, a return to your roots, to square one, to acceptance, to where you —like the prodigal son—began and where you will return to "...*the glory which I had with thee before the world was.*"12

A circle is a significant symbol. It represents the feminine principle, the womb from which all life comes and to which all life returns. Circles are important because they are all-inclusive and infinite. If any element or experience in life is eliminated, any part left out, one's ultimate freedom is short-circuited. The Circle of Christ that is transforming the world, is the invisible interconnected union of all those who join hands around the world to share what the Christ consciousness stands for. They are those who became aware that separation is an illusion because there is but one consciousness and one presence, be it appearing as Hindus, Buddhists, Moslems, Jews, Christians, or all of the above. This circle is the fabric of your life experience, which includes every step, forward or backward, that has led you to become aware of your true self as the Self.

Once you have jumped off the cliff and surrendered to the experience of free-fall, life becomes a moving feast in which the changing picture is an amazing, ever intriguing adventure—sometimes exhilarating, sometimes ordinary—but always accompanied by a sense of divine purpose. You will wake up to the fact that you now have a multi-dimensional sense of who you are that is beyond just being a body or a personality.

Looking down on your life, which we all do at times, you may feel that your life is a failure because you seem to have been going round and round over the same old ground, over and over, with little progress. However, if you are able to stand aside and view your life with spiritual detachment from an impersonal perspective, you will see that the circle is really a "spiral," an ever-ascending evolution.

Every repetitive experience has lifted you a bit higher, a bit closer to God. Yes, you have gone round the same trials, the same relational experiences, and the same lessons, but each time you have risen higher in consciousness. Because I know this is the same for me, I am willing to go around the circle again, with all its tribulations and its rewards. I am willing, because I know that eventually the spiral will reach ascension consciousness and I will be, as the Hindus say, "off the wheel." I will not cease to exist, but I will be free from the laws of distress and limitation, knowing I am God appearing as that which is in the world. So will you.

When you return to your roots, to the source from which you came, you will see that all your ventures, all your experiences, all your relationships, all that the Scripture calls "this world" has been necessary segments of the circle. Without each segment the circle would not have been complete, would not be a circle. When, by gratitude, you honor the circle, you will become free as never before to see that It is all God and all in divine order. You can now become aware that those shadow experiences you have encountered in your journey around the circle were not there to hurt you, but rather to propel you forward. From those experiences you will have learned that when you embraced the shadows, you were able to heal them by seeing that they were only shadows and not real, not the goblins you thought they were at the time. This realization gives you the freedom to dive into life anew, taking chances you once would have feared. You will no longer be afraid of letting go of any person or thing to which you have become attached because you will realize that everything is included in the circle of life. Therefore, you will never be without any part, any person, or anything in your life that is necessary for your joy and well-being.

Having completed a cycle, you can stand aside and finally erase time by realizing that you have always been one with God because "*That which hath been is now; and that which is to be hath already been.*"[13] You will get rid of the past and release it once you realize that everything that has happened to you in the past has had a divine purpose. In that way you cease thinking that some of your experiences were good and others bad, some representing your perfection and others, not. If you can see how the past and all of its conditions, both good and bad, were necessary to bring you around the circle to your spiritual fulfillment, the past ceases to exist except as a part of now. As for the future, when you realize that you are now able to think of the future without either anxiety or desire, you can stop the mind from leaping out of now into a mentally created illusion.

Once you get rid of thinking in terms of the past or the future, you will be in the "now" where God is all of the circle of Christ. When you rise above trying to get rid of anything, you will experience Omnipresence where there are no false appearances; Omniscience where there are no lost or unavailable ideas; and where there is only one life living itself. When you cease trying to get rid of illusion, illusion ceases to exist, and you will behold that right where you have thought good and bad existed is the perfect all-inclusive, circle of life, the perfect evolution of being – atonement.

As you continue around the circle, you may think you have changed, but the eternal Self that you are has never changed. What did change is how you saw yourself. Despite appearances, the process is an unchangeable perfection. When your viewpoint seems to contradict that truth, you can change your judgment by realizing what you are seeing is only a segment of the circle and not the whole circle. The seeming miracle is that when you change your viewpoint, your reality seems to change, and the perfection you actually are appears as greater supply, greater healing, greater harmony, and an abundance of love in your life.

There is one final way you can know whether the circle is complete, whether you have returned home or not—*if your innocence has returned.* When you have regained your innocence, the innocence you sacrificed when you began to accumulate concepts—objective concepts or subjective concepts, concepts of conduct, of morality, of psychology and of religion—an awareness of the purity of your being returns. Most of all, you regain the innocence you originally had in your infancy when you were at home in and fascinated by your body.

The minute all of us set foot on a formal religious path, we were in danger of being mis-taught because we were told that our bodies were sinful. When we were labeled sinners, we began to become alienated from our bodies. Instead of being in command of our bodies, we were commanded by them. However, in order to become conscious, perhaps we had to first go through a sense of separation from our bodies in order to gain perspective and be able to observe them. In the process, we began to blame our bodies and try to put a distance between ourselves and our bodies. We denied our bodies both power and existence, claiming they were purely carnal. We denied our bodies, mentally as well as physically and even sexually, until we were completely alienated from our bodies. The result was, and is, that all our fears, all our animosities, and all our shortcomings took form in our bodies as dis-eases. Spiritually we became alienated from our bodies but, by the same token, spiritually we can return to and love our bodies when we come full circle and regain the innocence we had before we accepted duality.

Your body is how your soul appears as form. It is possible that you have had to mentally separate yourself from your sense of body so that you could consciously experience your soul, but having done so, you must return full circle to your body. By seeing your body as your "soul-body," the gap is closed and your innocence returns. When you once more honor your body, you will be fully honoring the Spirit. You honor the Spirit of your body when Paul's statement, *"Your body is the temple of the Holy Ghost,"*[14] becomes a constant and conscious reality to you. After that, you no longer defile your body by act or thought. At last, you can be consciously aware that what you have thought of as your bodily limitations, be they age or physical conditions, are ideas-expressed and, as such, are no different than ideas. You can realign the body with perfect idea as it is intended to be, and the circle is closed. You are home, back to your innocence that existed before judgment or sin entered the picture.

For the last time, do not listen to my words. Listen to what I am saying. I am saying that these coming years will bring a well-earned sense of an ongoing ascension, an ascending evolution of the spiral that will lift you into a greater experience of love than you ever had before– love for yourself, your body, and for others. This sense of returning to your roots, to your innocence, will enable you to love everything, everybody, and every experience with a more profound awareness of God than you have been able to embrace ever before. You will be able to look back and see that because every level of being you have touched in this lifetime has made this possible, there is nothing for you to regret.

If you can sense the divine continuity of the circle of life you will be able to love fully the whole of life because you will be able to see it as a whole. You won't just speculate on your being one with God or as God's oneness, because you will see that every person and experience in your life has been a necessary part of the circle. You will see that at this very moment every other person is in his or her right place, right religion, and right level of development as a part of the evolution of our collective Soul. You won't have to forgive or forget, because you will be so aware that it's all God that there will be nothing to forgive and no regrets.

The one who had the vision to say, " *And I, if I be lifted up from the earth, will draw all men unto me,*"[15] is now rejoicing. He is rejoicing because you are approaching ascension and he knows that as everyone is included in the One Self that is his Self, until the whole Self rises, including you, his life will not be completely fulfilled.

I am not saying that when you and I experience ascension everyone on earth will consciously do the same at the same time, because the majority has not become aware of that which is drawing together the Circle of Christ. However, look at it this way, the collective soul is like a rocket that is taking off for outer space. At blastoff, the rocket first seems as though it isn't moving at all, then it slowly picks up speed. Soon the speed increases geometrically until before you know it, the space ship breaks through the sound barrier—the limitations of human thought. Once the thought barrier has been pierced by the collective consciousness, the linear sense of life becomes a many-faceted cluster. Life is no longer something we all experience. It becomes something we all are. We are no longer bodies experiencing God; we will become God experiencing bodies.

Before I went full circle all the way around the world, I made visits to a number of foreign places, but the world was always "out there," and I was only scratching the surface. Once I went all the way around the world, it was as though I had swallowed the world. It was now a complete unit inside of my consciousness. After that, I no longer lived in the world; the world lived in me. By the same token, once you see your life as a never-ending circle, you are no longer on the circle but instead you include the circle.

Once you finally realize that the person you thought you were individually was really the vehicle within which you traveled around the circle, it becomes possible for you to allow the world to be without fear or anxiety, and you will still participate fully in the world. You will still have your ego and your confrontations, but you will now see them as segments of the circle, and they won't affect you in any meaningful way. The segments change, but you remain the same—a spiritual being simultaneously observing and participating in the human drama.

Feed My Sheep

*A*s disciples of the Christ consciousness—off the wheel but appearing as the wheel—life now has a different purpose. We now receive a commission—the final instructions Jesus gave to his disciples before his ascension. Jesus was sharing his last meal with his disciples, a meal symbolizing the last spiritual food he fed them. As today, the word "love" was being bantered around; so Jesus asked Peter if he loved him in order to see if to Peter love meant action as well as emotion. Peter, of course, answered that he loved Jesus. Then Jesus:

> *..saith unto him 'Feed my lambs.* (As though he had not heard Peter's answer) Jesus *"saith to him a second time, Simon, son of Jonas, lovest thou me?"* Peter again responded, *"Yea, Lord; thou knowest that I love thee,"* and once more Jesus said, *"Feed my sheep."* Again, for the third time, Jesus repeated, *"Simon son of Jonas, lovest thou me?"* Peter was getting pretty upset by this time, probably because he felt Jesus doubted him or that he was missing something. In anguish he repeated, *"Lord, thou knowest all things; thou knowest that I love thee,"* and once more Jesus said, then *"Feed my sheep."*[16]

Words without actions mean nothing. The time has now come when, if we want to be included in the Christ family, that we must take action by feeding our neighbors, many of whom are starving for what we so abundantly have—both spiritually and materially. Actions complement words. The sheep and the shepherd are one. When we feed ourselves with Spirit, we are also feeding the collective Self as well. The passages I just quoted are only half-truths unless the complementary verse that followed Jesus' instruction to feed his sheep is included. Right after Jesus told Peter to feed his sheep, he told him how and why he now could. "...*When thou wast young, thou girdeth thyself, and walkedst whither thou wouldest: but when thou shalt be old, thou shall stretch forth thy hands, and another shall gird thee, and carry thee whither thou wouldest not.*"[17] When you were a beginner in your spiritual evolution, you were full of self-created or self-accepted concepts, and you thought and acted as you would according to your own belief in good and bad, but now you have matured spiritually. You have gone around the circle. You have jumped off the cliff into a life lived by Spirit. In spiritual free fall, you must now stretch forth your listening mind, and your Christ consciousness will girt you, will take over your awareness, and will lead you mentally and physically where you would not have chosen to go before. And you will go happily.

When you truly return to your roots—to the unconditioned spiritual identity with which you were born, you will continue to act, you will continue to be involved, but you will now leave the responsibility for the results to God. Your life, or what you had mistakenly thought were your human responsibilities, will disappear. There will no longer be anyone you have to protect, have to defend, have to change or implore—not your family, not even yourself. You will have a life, but that life will be "girt about" with a sense of the Christ. Your life now will be dedicated to feeding your sheep—your neighbor's wholeness, and your own one-ness.

Your consciousness of love is what will feed your sheep; so in your oneness you will be both the one who feeds and the fed. You will not avoid the dark; you will not run away from difficulty; but you will shine the light of Spirit on it, knowing that no matter how confrontational you have had to become, the ultimate responsibility is not yours but is that within by which you are "girt about."

To the outside, your life will seem ordinary and natural. Those of the world will not see any difference in you because they do not have the eyes to see, but your sheep will know you. You will still partake of the usual pleasures and usual concerns, but now there will be a difference: you stumble but do not fall. You live effortlessly because you welcome each experience—each segment of the circle—knowing that you are not just one segment but rather you are the whole circle.

You will not feed your sheep with words alone. You will feed your sheep by feeding yourselves with Spirit because that is what Love is, and that is what you have to give. You feed your sheep every time you know that God is the only power. You feed your sheep every time you know God is the only presence, and you feed your sheep when you know that you and everyone else is the Omnipresence, God. You take responsibility for one thing—the robe of Spirit you now wear.

The Robe

*W*hen you were young, you were responsible for your personal life. You went to those places where self-satisfaction seemed possible. You went to the teachers you thought could help you. You practiced the disciplines that you thought would give you power over life. Those were all necessary steps leading around the full circle so that you could become a spiritual elder and wear the robe. Now that you have stretched out your hand, you are robed by your higher consciousness. Those who wear the robe have the responsibility to feed their sheep, and that means to eliminate anything that gets in the way of your or their being able to live in that Spirit.

Just because you have returned to the starting point, and will now be girt about by the Christ, does not mean that it will not take you some time to get used to the robe, to let go of old human habits and sometimes judgmental thoughts. There will be a time of transition in which you will have to learn what it means to be responsible for the robe.

The first responsibility (response-ability) in living the law of true spiritual realization is to remember that you are never dealing with anything apart from your Self, apart from your own consciousness. What you are dealing with is your own relationship to yourself and the robe of healing Spirit you have been given to wear.

The Robe lives in you as your higher calling, and you live in the robe when you are aware of its presence as your consciousness. In honoring it, you honor yourself. The Robe is ascension consciousness. It is the I THAT I AM. Wrap the robe around you. It will protect you. It will comfort you. It will lead you in the paths of righteousness for its sake. It is the air you breathe, the life you live, the love you love, and it is all God.

Being confident of this very thing, that he which hath begun a good work in you will perform it until the day of Jesus Christ.

Philippians 1:6

Endnotes

Introduction

1. Teilhard de Chardin, *The Divine Milieu*, (Harper & Row, 1960)
2. Matthew 22:40
3. Joel Goldsmith, *The Infinite Way*, (De Vorss & Co.,1947)

Part One

Chapter 1

1. Matthew 7:9
2. John 4:21-23
3. Matthew 7:9
4. John 14:12
5. John 17:21-23
6. *Gospel According to Thomas*, edited by Raghavan Iyer, (Concord Grove Press, 1983)
7. Ibid.
8. Ibid.
9. Ibid.
10. Ibid.
11. *Matthew Fox, Breakthrough, Meister Eckhart's Creation Spirituality in New Translation*, (Image Books, Doubleday, 1980)
12. Ibid.
13. Ibid.
14 Ibid.
15. Romans 7:14-15
16. John 5:30
17. John 10:30
18. John 14:9
19. Matthew 17:1-2

Chapter 2

1. Pierre Teilhard de Chardin, *Christianity and Evolution*, (Harcourt Brace & Co., 1974)
2. Ibid.
3. John 1:1

4. John 20:17
5. Rabbi David A. Cooper, *God Is A Verb*, (Riverhead Books, 1997)
6. Pierre Teilhard de Chardin, *Hymn of the Universe*, (Harper & Row, 1961)
7. John 6:57
8. Philippians 2:5
9. Carl Jung, *Basic Writings of Carl. G. Jung*, (Modern Library, 1959)
10. I Corinthians 2:18
11. John 1:1
12. Peter Russell, *The Global Brain Awakens*, (Global Brain Inc. 1995)
13. Ken Wilber, *Spectrum of Consciousness*, (Quset Book, 1977)
14. Exodus 21:24
15. John 17:22-23
16. II Corinthians 5:18
17. II Corinthians 5:19
18. John 3:16-17
19. Luke 23:34
20. John 6:15
21. John 6:26
22. John 6:28
23. John 6:53
24. John 6:65-66

CHAPTER 3

1. John 7:24
2. Rabbi David A. Cooper, *God Is A Verb*, (Riverhead Books, 1997)
3. Genesis 1:1,3,4
4. John 1:1
5. Romans 11:36
6. John 17:21-23
7. Pierre Teilhard de Chardin, *Christianity and Evolution*, (Harcourt Brace & Co., 1974)
8. I John 1:15
9. John 4:23
10. John 4:24
11. I John 4:1-3, 6-8

12. Revelation 1:10
13. Revelation 2:17
14. Revelation 4:1-2
15. Galatians 6:7-8
16. II Corinthians 3:14-18
17. John 18:36
18. John 16:13
19. John 4:23
20. John 17:18-23
21. Exodus 3:14
22. John 17:6
23. Luke 4:14-21
24. Isaiah 61:1
25. John 10:30
26. Philippians 4:13
27. Matthew 28:19-20
26. Ibid.

CHAPTER 4

1. Matthew 13:45-46

PART TWO

Chapter 5

1. John 18:36
2. Matthew 5:45
3. Matthew 25:40
4. Mark 16:15
5. Luke 23:34
6. II Corinthians 12:9
7. Luke 15:31
8. John 15:4
9. Matthew 16:19
10. Galatians 6:7
11. Matthew 12:48
12. Mark 3:35
13. John 13:35
14. I Thessalonians 3:12

Chapter 6

1. John 1:1
2. John 20:17
3. Lama Govinda, *Creative Meditation*,(Theosophical Society, 1958)
4. John 1:1
5. Matthew 7:1
6. Matthew 9:22
7. Mary Baker Eddy, *Science and Health with Keys to the Scriptures*, (First Church Christ Scientists, 1875)
8. John 7:24

Chapter 7

1. Rabbi David A. Cooper, *God Is A Verb*, (Riverhead Books, 1997)
2. II Corinthians 14:9-11
3. James 1:22
4. *Noetic Sciences Review*, Winter 1996
5. Matthew 22:36-39
6. Matthew 6:31-37
7. Luke 10:38-42
8. Matthew 7:16

Chapter 8

1. John 10:18-20
2. John 5:30
3. John 10:30
4. John 14:9
5. John 8:15
6. John 8:16
7. John 8:18
8. John 8:58
9. Romans 7:15
10. John 10:30
11. Philippians 4:13
12. Psalm 139:8
13. Isaiah 45:2
14. John 16:33

PART THREE

Chapter 9

1. John 2:19
2. Philippians 2:5
3. John 15:13
4. Acts 12:4
5. Acts 12:7
6. Acts 12:10
7. Luke 12:31
8. Matthew 18:20
9. II Corinthians 5:11
10. II Corinthians 5:14
11. II Corinthians 5:15
12. II Corinthians 5:16
13. II Corinthians 5:17
14. II Corinthians 5:18
15. II Corinthians 5:19
16. II Corinthians 5:20
17. John 12:32
18. Matthew 6:33

Chapter 10

1. John 8:32
2. Luke 17:4
3. Matthew 17:20
4. Ibid.
5. Hebrews 11:1
6. Genesis 1:29
7. John 1:1
8. John 4:35
9. Isaiah 40:31
10. Matthew 6:33
11. John 14:1
12. OSHO, *The Mustard Seed*, (The Rebel Publishing House, 1975)
13. John 12:32
14. Matthew 16:18

15. Matthew 1614-18
16. Mark 16:15
17. Goldsmith, *Spiritual Illuminaton in The Infinite Way,*
18. II Corinthians 5:16
19. I Corinthians 15:51-54
20. I Corinthians 15:51
21. John 10:34
22. Matthew 18:20

Chapter 11

1. John 20:17
2. Matthew 9:22
3. Psalm 91:7
4. Matthew 22:21

Chapter 12

1. Matthew 12:50
2. Luke 8:21
3. Robert Browning, Paracelsus
4. Matthew 13:12
5. John 14:12
6. Hebrews 11:1
7. John 5:14
8. John 10:30
9. Exodus 3:14
10. Job 19:26
11. John 14:6
12. John 17:5
13. Ecclesiastes 3:15
14. I Corinthians 6:19
15. John 12:32
16. John 21:15-17
17. John 21:18

For personal correspondence with Mr. Starcke, information relative to his books and tapes, newsletter, schedule of lectures and seminars, or to order copies of the STUDY GUIDE for IT's ALL GOD write:

Eron Howell
GUADALUPE PRESS
P.O.Box 865
Boerne, Texas 78006
or e-mail:
wstarcke@walterstarcke.com
www.walterstarcke.com